Edge of Catastrophe

Edge of Catastrophe

Erich Fromm, Fascism, and the Holocaust

ROGER FRIE

OXFORD
UNIVERSITY PRESS

Oxford University Press is a department of the University of Oxford.
It furthers the University's objective of excellence in research, scholarship,
and education by publishing worldwide. Oxford is a registered trademark of
Oxford University Press in the United Kingdom and in certain other countries.

Published in the United States of America by Oxford University Press
198 Madison Avenue, New York, NY 10016, United States of America.

© Oxford University Press 2024

All rights reserved. No part of this publication may be reproduced, stored in a retrieval system,
or transmitted, in any form or by any means, without the prior permission in writing of Oxford
University Press, or as expressly permitted by law, by license, or under terms agreed with the
appropriate reprographics rights organization. Inquiries concerning reproduction outside the scope of the
above should be sent to the Rights Department, Oxford University Press, at the address above.

You must not circulate this work in any other form,
and you must impose this same condition on any acquirer.

CIP data is on file at the Library of Congress

ISBN 9780197748770

DOI: 10.1093/9780197748800.001.0001

Printed by Integrated Books International, United States of America

Contents

List of Figures   vii
Acknowledgments   ix

    Introduction   1
1. The Holocaust Correspondence   19
2. How Is This Possible?   55
3. Yearning to Submit   75
4. Confronting Genocide   105
5. Cultivating Love and Hope   149

Notes   165
References   183
Index   193

List of Figures

Figure 1.1.	Gertrud Brandt and Georg Brandt, 1932, Poznań/Posen	26
Figure 1.2.	Sophie Engländer and David Engländer, 1934, Berlin	43
Figure 2.1.	Käthe Kollwitz, *The Parents*, 1923	56
Figure 2.2.	Käthe Kollwitz, *In Memoriam Karl Liebknecht*, 1920	63
Figure 3.1.	Erich Fromm in the Mid-1930s	81
Figure 3.2.	Book Cover to the First Edition of *Escape From Freedom*, 1941	89
Figure 4.1.	Henny Gurland, 1945	112
Figure 4.2.	Erich Fromm, 1945	114
Figure 4.3.	Heinz Brandt Being Greeted by His Family After His Release From East German Prison, 1964	125
Figure 5.1.	Erich Fromm, 1970	159

Acknowledgments

This book developed over many years and with the help of a great many people. During the course of my research and writing, I have been privileged to learn from colleagues and friends who kindly shared their expertise and gave graciously of their time. No one has been more central to this project than Rainer Funk, Erich Fromm's last personal assistant, literary executor of the Fromm Estate, and Director of the Erich Fromm Archive and Institute in Tübingen, Germany. He tirelessly answered my many questions and pointed me in new directions. I owe thanks to Sonja Gojman de Millan, who was Fromm's student in Mexico City, for sharing her memories with me, and to Edgar Levenson, who kindly recounted his interactions with Fromm at the William Alanson White Institute of Psychiatry, Psychoanalysis and Psychology in New York. The inspiration for this project undoubtedly stemmed from my friendship with Philip Cushman, who tragically died during the final stage of writing. Phil's remarkable ability to combine the cultural history of psychotherapy with social analysis and political activism has been an important source in my own growth as a scholar and psychotherapist.

This book, like Fromm's own background and writing, is inherently cross-disciplinary. It is at once a work of history, focused on the Nazi past and the Holocaust; an examination of the traumatic psychological legacy of that period; an exploration of the German Jewish refugee experience; an elaboration of psychoanalytic ideas; a set of reflections on the nature of personal and cultural memory; and a discussion of the state of our individual and collective psychologies in light of the social and political crises we face today. These themes are all refracted through the life and work of Erich Fromm, one of the best known, yet arguably least understood, 20th-century public intellectuals.

In line with the book's interdisciplinary reach, I have been privileged to interact with and draw on the work of fellow historians, psychoanalysts, psychologists, sociologists, and political scientists. I would like to thank above all the following people, who kindly shared their scholarly and personal knowledge, read parts of the manuscript at various stages of its development, or provided the support that was necessary to complete this project (in alphabetical order): Seth Aronson, Ofra Bloch, Dan Burston, Lynn Chancer, Aleksandar Dimitrijević, Ana Altaras Dimitrijević, Mark Freeman, Chris

Friedrichs, David Goodman, Aner Govrin, Sue Grand, Atina Grossmann, Susannah Heschel, Gail Hornstein, Chris Jaenicke, Marion Kaplan, Thomas Kohut, Phil Langer, Neil McLaughlin, Richard Menkis, Peter Rudnytsky, Jill Salberg, Pascal Sauvayre, Hanna Schissler, Catherine Silver, Catherine Soussloff, and Jeff Sugarman.

A visiting professorship at Kyoto University, Japan, in 2022 provided me with the opportunity to undertake a good deal of the writing. I benefited from interactions with Japanese colleagues and friends and was invited to present different aspects of my work at various universities and institutes. I especially want to thank the following people for their generosity (in alphabetical order): Soh Agatsuma, Emi Ibi, Tayoka Imai, Naoto Kawabata, Ken Okano, Ayumi Osagawa, Yashushi Sugihara, Koichi Togashi, and Kyoko Toyohara.

Over the course of my research, I have had the privilege of presenting aspects of this book at venues in Canada, Germany, Israel, Japan, and the United States. The impact of reading and hearing the Holocaust letters in Fromm's family has led to many rich and important conversations on the nature of trauma, memory, and responsibility. I specifically want to acknowledge the presentation I made in Berlin, Germany, where I was invited by Rainer Funk and Thomas Kühn to give the annual Erich Fromm Lecture. My lecture coincided with the commemoration of the November Pogrom (Kristallnacht). Presenting the letters of Fromm's family members in the city in which they lived, and not far from where they were deported, was a moving experience. The depth of historical trauma and the obligation to remember are still very present despite the passage of time. We simply cannot afford to ignore history's impact as we face the renewed threat of fascism in our present age.

I am fortunate to be able to publish this book with Oxford University Press. As a publisher, Oxford continues to support the kind of cross-disciplinary thinking and writing that informs this project, as well as my earlier book, *Not in My Family: German Memory and Responsibility After the Holocaust* (2017). I want to express my special thanks to my editor, Hayley Singer, for her support and encouragement, and to my editorial readers for their helpful suggestions.

Finally, I wish to express my deep and continuing gratitude to my family: Emily, Elena, and Andreas. Words are not sufficient to describe the meaningful support that they have shown me as I once again confronted the painful depths of the history of Nazi Germany and the Holocaust.

Introduction

In 2018, 80 years after the November Pogrom of 1938, I was invited to give a Kristallnacht Memorial Lecture in the city of Pittsburgh. I had been asked to speak as a result of my work on German memory and the Holocaust. I felt honored to accept the invitation but also experienced trepidation. What might it mean for me, a grandson of the German generation of perpetrators and enablers, to speak on such an important and meaningful occasion? Two weeks before my lecture, the unthinkable happened: 11 Jewish worshipers were brutally murdered at Pittsburgh's Tree of Life Synagogue, close to where I would talk. Nothing I had seen or done up to that point could possibly have prepared me to address members of a community that had just experienced the worst act of antisemitic violence in the history of the United States.

I had spoken to audiences about the obligations of German memory in the aftermath of the Holocaust. I had talked about the emotional dynamics within German families that sought to keep the Holocaust at bay. I had explored the limits of Germany's memory culture and argued for the need to engage with a felt sense of history's traumas. Until that point, however, I had always believed, or perhaps naively hoped, that the dark shadows of Germany's Nazi history might remain consigned to the past.

After the massacre in Pittsburgh, it became impossible to avoid the upsurge of Nazism in the present. In the years that followed, there were more attacks on Jewish communities across North America, and racial violence against Black, Indigenous, and people of color was widespread. In many Western nations, incidents of antisemitism and racism increased exponentially. In Germany, racially motivated riots in the city of Chemnitz in 2018, and an attack on a synagogue in Halle in 2019, broke through Germany's culture of remembrance, leading many to wonder what, if anything, had been learned from the past. The violent threat posed by the extreme right seemed to be everywhere in evidence.

It is easy to feel powerless in the presence of such racial hatreds. But as I have also learned, we cannot stay silent, lest we become complicit in the evil we abhor. We need to come together and speak out against injustice. The audience that attended the Kristallnacht Memorial lecture in Pittsburgh had gathered to demonstrate their solidarity with the Jewish community and stand up against racial hatred and the murderous violence that claimed so many lives. As I looked out at those in attendance, I couldn't help but wonder what would have happened if more Germans of my grandparent's generation had spoken out against the growing Nazi threat before Hitler and his followers took full control. What if they had banded together and protested the racial discrimination against their Jewish neighbors, rather than looking away, supporting, or even participating in the hateful actions?

In view of the social and political crises we face today, these questions take on additional meaning. The need to address the racial hatreds in our midst has rarely been more pressing. We must redouble our efforts to educate people about the causes of racial violence and genocide and, above all, address the contemporary reality of antisemitism and racism. But what, we wonder, might this process involve? As a historian and psychologist, I seek to understand how we are shaped by the traumatic histories we inherit. The stories of our lives are embedded in the history and culture of our families and communities. The question that concerns me is how the violent and traumatic past is intertwined with the hateful present. Indeed, as psychoanalysis reminds us, the effects of traumatic histories don't disappear; they keep showing up, reminding us of their presence.

Psychoanalysis has been called a traumatized profession because so many of its early members were directly and indirectly effected by the rise of the Nazis and the Holocaust. Jewish psychoanalysts were forced to flee Europe in the face of racial oppression. Once they arrived in North America, they often revealed little about what they had endured. Our understanding of the effects of the genocide and its perpetration emerged slowly over many decades. The process of addressing historical trauma, be it in the psychoanalytic profession or in society as a whole, was only possible with an acknowledgment that we are fundamentally social beings who are shaped by the culture, politics, and the time in which we live.

The intertwining of self and society was central to the work of German Jewish psychoanalyst Erich Fromm. Over the course of his long and multifaceted career, Fromm explored how we are consciously and unconsciously determined by social forces. Fromm's life reflects the dislocations wrought by the 20th century's two world wars and the Holocaust. Born in Frankfurt in 1900, Fromm grew up in a Jewish Orthodox middle-class family and was influenced by the intellectual milieu of the Weimar Republic. Fromm fled Nazi Germany and found refuge in the United States in 1934. He moved to Mexico in 1950, where he spent more than two decades, and then returned to Europe, where he lived in retirement in Switzerland until his death in 1980.

Fromm trained as a sociologist and psychoanalyst in Germany and was an early member of Frankfurt's Institute for Social Research. Following the war, he became a recognized social critic and developed a global readership that numbered in the many millions. Given Fromm's persona as a public intellectual, it is easy to overlook that he was first and foremost a clinician. In fact, Fromm's psychoanalytic practice was perhaps the one constant in a career that spanned different intellectual disciplines, countries, cultures, and languages. During a time when most practicing psychoanalysts felt that the individual mind and the therapeutic setting should be the sole focus of their attention, Fromm consistently addressed the reality of social and political inequities. He believed that helping the patient live a more satisfying life and building a more just society went hand in hand.

In the United States, Fromm became known as a purveyor of hope whose writings offered humanity a way forward. He commanded large audiences and wrote about a host of topics, from the quest for solidarity and nature of love to the dangers of the cold war and the need for nuclear disarmament. His most recognized book, *The Art of Loving* (1956), was an international bestseller that sold more than 25 million copies and fed the perception of Fromm as a popular psychologist. But underlying this image was a more complex reality: a thinker and a clinician who kept returning to the threats posed by authoritarianism, racial hatred, and destructiveness, ever wary of the cruelty that humans were capable of.

In October 1979, only a few months before he died of a heart attack, Swiss television aired an interview with Fromm. The interviewer asked whether Fromm thought humanity had changed as a result of the atrocities committed in the Holocaust. Fromm's answer was as brief as it was disquieting:

> From a social perspective, I do not see that we have changed so much for the better, that under certain historical circumstances, what happened forty years ago could not also happen again. It would require that human beings had themselves significantly changed and become more alive, engaged and courageous, but unfortunately that is not something we can say. (Fromm, 1979).[1]

Fromm's statement is bracing. Given the level of racial hatred we see today, and the mass violence and genocides that have occurred since the Holocaust, what he says still rings true. Unspoken in the 1979 interview is the extent to which Fromm's own life was shaped by Nazi Germany and the Holocaust. After Nazism forced him to leave Germany, Fromm witnessed the perpetration of the genocide from afar. Fromm's family members, friends, and colleagues were murdered in the catastrophe. Yet the Holocaust history in Fromm's family, and its impact on his life and work, has remained virtually unknown.[2] Given Fromm's status as a public intellectual of global renown who is recognized for his analyses of fascism and destructiveness, and his insights on human solidarity and love, this omission is striking.

This book is the first to explore the history of the Holocaust in Fromm's family, and the impact of Nazi Germany and the genocide on the trajectory of Fromm's life and work. The experiences of Fromm's family members are disclosed in a series of unpublished letters that were written from the late 1930s up until the day they were deported and sent to their deaths. The letters I will share in this book document the sorrow, suffering, and terror that was endured by a single German Jewish family, a catastrophe that was repeated over and over, seemingly countless times. As the Holocaust was unfolding, Fromm made ever-more-determined attempts to rescue his relatives. He was one of the only members of his extended family who had reached safety abroad. Fromm had an established position and income and was seen as the hope for obtaining a visa and freedom. Despite his best efforts, however, aunts, uncles, and cousins who remained in Germany were all killed.

The correspondence in Fromm's family is important for a number of reasons. Reading the letters breaks through the abstraction and historical distance with which we often encounter the Holocaust. The letters challenge us to view the atrocities not from afar, but from the perspective of the victims.[3] They describe the effects of discrimination and hatred and foster an understanding of the suffering endured. Up until now, Holocaust survivors have courageously shared their stories. But with their passing, the written documentation we have from the period takes on an added importance. This is especially true in light of the rise in Holocaust denialism and antisemitism. The letters also help us, as readers, to consider what it means to be implicated in societies that practice systemic racism, segregation, and violence. And they stand as a warning and a reminder to be vigilant, lest the social and political conditions that gave rise to National Socialism and state-sanctioned genocide be once again allowed to flourish.

Beyond their intrinsic value, the letters deepen our understanding of Fromm and his work. When readers encounter the Holocaust correspondence, they enter into Fromm's "subjective world" and are able to gain insight into how Fromm was affected by the plight of his relatives. Witnessing the depth of trauma in Fromm's family enables us to consider the ways in which these tragedies could have shaped Fromm. Although Fromm never talked openly about the murder of his family members, neither did he ever forget what happened. He retained copies of the letters among his most cherished possessions throughout the remainder of his life. Long after the Holocaust took place, the memory of his family members remained a meaningful presence in his life.

The correspondence also sheds light on Fromm's complicated relationship with the country of his birth and his struggle to reconcile his early life in Germany with knowledge of the catastrophe. Growing up in Germany, Fromm experienced the demise of the Weimar Republic and the rise of the Nazis. After Hitler was elected to power in 1933, Fromm knew that his life was in danger. Had he remained in Germany, his fate as a Jewish and Marxist psychoanalyst would have been sealed. Yet were it not for the Nazis, Fromm would likely never have left the country, culture, or language in which he grew up. Indeed, when the decade of the 1930s began, Fromm was at the beginning of a very promising career that combined academic research with clinical practice. He had just been appointed director of social psychology and psychoanalysis at the Institute for Social Research and was one of the cofounders of a new psychoanalytic institute in Frankfurt. Though the danger posed by Hitler and the Nazis was real, few would have dared to think that only a few years later they would ascend to power.

After Fromm arrived in New York, he was consumed with trying to find ways to rescue those who were left behind. Being so far from Germany did little to assuage the anxiety and worry provoked by the Nazi regime's antisemitic policies. Writing provided Fromm with a means to respond to the political and personal upheavals of the time. Over the course of the 1930s, as the likelihood of war and the Nazi terror increased, there was an urgency in Fromm's writing that was unusual for an academic. It was as though Fromm recognized the need to address the present moment, rather than sit back and observe, waiting to see how events in Germany might develop. In 1941, Fromm published *Escape From Freedom*, which was his response to the threat of fascism in Europe.[4] The book spoke to a broad readership eager for an explanation of why so many Germans had turned to National Socialism and enthusiastically supported Hitler.

When the war ended and the scale of the atrocities was revealed, Fromm turned his focus on Germany's highly ambivalent struggle to address its Nazi past. Over the course of the following decades, Fromm returned again and again to examine the destructive social and political forces that gave rise to National Socialism, which he defined as an extreme form of fascism. The themes of authoritarianism, racial narcissism, and destructiveness held his attention. Fromm sought to explain why human beings engage in malignant aggression. His express aim was to guard against the "socio-political" conditions that could give rise to "another Hitler."[5] Thus, while Fromm was able to leave Nazi Germany, we might say that "the question of Germany" never really left him.

It is surely no coincidence that Fromm's writing career is bookended by two works—*Escape From Freedom* (1941) and *The Anatomy of Human Destructiveness* (1973)—that deal directly with the origins and consequences of the Nazi regime. Not only are these books the most deeply researched of Fromm's writings; they are also arguably some of his most personal works. The themes of these books emerged out of Fromm's experience as a German Jewish refugee who lived in the shadow of genocide. And in a strange twist of fate, Fromm's last book, *To Have or To Be* (1976), found its most fervent audience in the very nation that was responsible for the Holocaust. A new generation of West Germans looked to Fromm as they sought to address the crimes of their parents and build a more humane society. The attention Fromm received from younger Germans in the final years of his life must have been satisfying, but the tragic irony couldn't have escaped him.

Encountering Fromm

In the late 1930s, as Fromm was developing the arguments that would find expression in *Escape From Freedom*, he could hardly know the trajectory his career would take. *Escape From Freedom* was published just before the United States declared war on Germany and Japan. It became internationally recognized and established Fromm's expertise in the public sphere. From that point onward, Fromm had the liberty of writing on topics of his own choosing. The clarity of his writing meant he could reach a wide readership eager for answers to the social and political challenges of the day. By the

1950s, Fromm had become a respected and sought-after public intellectual. In English-speaking countries, and particularly in the United States, Fromm reached the height of his popularity during the 1960s. In Europe, Mexico, and South America he remained popular well into the 1980s. After the fall of the Iron Curtain, Fromm's books reached large audiences in Eastern Europe and Russia. In China and other East Asian countries, his works continue to be studied today.[6]

Given the scope and diversity of Fromm's writings, readers have come to know him from many different perspectives. These pathways shape which of Fromm's books are read, how they are understood, and what ideas are applied to the reader's own situation in life. For example, Fromm may be known as an early member of the Institute for Social Research, a critic of fascism, a peace activist, a radical humanist, an unrepentant socialist, a social psychologist, or a popular theorist of love. All of these accounts are correct, yet if taken on their own, they provide only a narrow and perhaps one-sided view. Above all, we find that Fromm's role as a pioneering psychoanalyst is frequently neglected.[7]

Over the course of my career, I have approached Fromm in equal measure as a historian and social philosopher, and as a psychologist and psychoanalyst. I bring each of these perspectives to bear in the chapters that follow. But my reading of Fromm is also and inevitably of a more personal nature and relates to my own German family history. I don't think I can responsibly write about the Holocaust, or translate and discuss the letters of Fromm's family members, without acknowledging my location at the intersection of history and culture. I am a third-generation German, a grandson of the German generation of perpetrators and enablers.[8] I believe that our response to the Holocaust is often related to who we are, to where we stand in relation to the traumatic history of the Nazi past. My inherited family history undoubtedly shapes the approach I take in this book, which is also why it is important to disclose what that history is.

My parents were born in the midst of the Third Reich and joined a large number of young Germans who emigrated to North America in the postwar decades. I grew up with two languages and two cultures and had a sense of both belonging to and being separate from Germany's history and culture. My knowledge of the past was shaped by what was talked about in the context of my family and community. I learned about Germany's responsibility for the Holocaust from my parents at an early age. It was important to them that my sister and I know about the heinous crimes committed and understand the obligation to remember. But there was much that remained unsaid.

My grandparents played an important role in my early life, and I knew that they had all lived through the war. One of my German grandfathers was a soldier in the Wehrmacht and was killed on the Russian front early on. The other worked as a civilian in the armaments industry until late in the war when he joined the Luftwaffe and became involved in the V2 rocket program. What was not discussed was whether and to what extent my grandparents were supporters of the Nazi regime. The dynamic in my family followed a familiar pattern in many postwar West German families, where some aspects of the past were acknowledged and others remained out of bounds. During regular childhood visits to Germany, the past was spoken about chiefly in terms of the "suffering" experienced by my family members during and after the war. What was missing was any acknowledgment of responsibility or talk of my grandparent's own participation in the Third Reich. It was as though this topic had been cordoned off. As children we sensed that certain subjects were off limits, and it was difficult to know how to formulate questions since there was no oral narrative of this history on which to draw.

Given my family background, the fact that I chose to study history and politics as an undergraduate is perhaps not surprising. At the University of London, I was mentored by the historian Frank Snowden Jr. In our tutorials, we explored the reasons for the growth of fascism, and our discussions often reached beyond standard history texts. With Snowden's encouragement I wrote my long vacation essay (similar to the American senior thesis) on Fromm's *Escape From Freedom*. I was interested in Fromm's interdisciplinary approach, particularly the way he combined insights from history, sociology, social psychology, and psychoanalysis. But above all, I wanted to know more about Germans of my grandparents' generation and why they had supported Hitler. Of course, the fact that it was the 1980s and I was living in Thatcherite Britain also played a role. I was active in left-wing student politics and found Fromm's Marxist perspective to be especially appealing.[9]

When my vacation essay on Fromm was finally returned, it was full of red marks and scribbles. The examiner, it turned out, was a specialist in the history of elections and had used German electoral data from the early 1930s to deconstruct Fromm's arguments. But perhaps tellingly, the examiner made no mention of Fromm's analysis of the psychology of Nazism. Nor did Fromm's trenchant account of authoritarianism get a response. It seemed as though Fromm's interdisciplinary insights had fallen on deaf ears. I am sharing this anecdote because it illustrates the challenge that Fromm's work has often faced in academic circles.

When I subsequently went up to Cambridge University to pursue graduate study, I was supervised by the sociologist Anthony Giddens. In our first meeting, he asked me what books I had recently read, and I mentioned Fromm's *Escape From Freedom*. His response, as I remember it, was why would I want to read something so "woolly"? Giddens's viewpoint is not unusual and needs to be understood in the academic context in which it was made. After Fromm left the Institute for Social Research (later known as the Frankfurt School of Critical Theory), he began writing for a general, educated public and became less interested in the dictates of academic discourse. Over time, Fromm developed a penchant for using binaries to explain complex issues, and he often preferred broad statements over detailed conceptual analyses. This turned out to be an obstacle for dialogue with professionals who felt, rightly or wrongly, that Fromm's work lacked the necessary rigor. Yet the ready dismissal of Fromm overlooks an important fact. Fromm believed that social change begins in society at large, not in the academy. If writing for a wider audience in pursuit of that goal meant losing the favor of some colleagues, then it was a step he was more than willing to take. And indeed, Fromm found great success precisely because he was able to speak clearly and persuasively. It is likewise my hope that this book may reflect Fromm's better impulses and reach the scholar and the general reader alike. The issues are simply too important to be discussed only in an academic setting.

At Cambridge, Giddens redirected my attention, but I continued to search for ways to integrate my interests and reached out to the historian and noted Freud scholar Peter Gay. At the time, I was unfamiliar of the politics of psychoanalysis and had not considered the implications of Fromm's critique of Freud. In fact, it was Fromm's belief that Freud neglected the social sphere that led to his departure from the Institute for Social Research and his later expulsion from the International Psychoanalytic Association. Fortunately, Gay seemed unperturbed and became an important interlocutor for me. It wasn't until much later that I discovered that Gay had himself been engrossed in Fromm's work when he was a young academic. Above all, Gay recognized Fromm as a fellow German Jewish refugee who sought to understand the nature of the human condition. As Gay writes,

> I was under the influence of Erich Fromm, a psychoanalyst and Socialist who was exploring prospects of fundamental social reforms open to

individuals and even societies once they submitted themselves to the analytic discipline and learned how to apply their new knowledge to humane left-wing politics. To me, at least then, the happy collaboration of Freud and Marx seemed the most desirable way of dealing with the human condition. Here were two Europeans, one of whom (Marx) was of course only too well-known, and the other (Freud) was really quite a stranger to me. Here was a small personal instance of how refugees were making their impact on the United States. (Gay, 2008, p. 122)

According to Gay, after he discovered the work of Freud, he "learned, fairly soon, that Fromm's optimism was really alien to Freud." The defining difference, for Gay, came down to whether Freud was right in asserting that aggression was one of the givens of human nature, or whether, as Fromm believed, aggression was the result of specific social and political conditions and thus open to change. Gay sided with Freud, undertook psychoanalytic training, and wrote what many still consider to be the definitive biography of Freud (Gay, 1998). I followed Gay's lead and became a psychoanalyst, though the path I chose was mapped out by Fromm.

What made Fromm stand out as a psychoanalyst was his emphasis on understanding human suffering through the lens of society. As a profession, psychoanalysis has often failed to account for the role of society, culture, and history in the shaping of all human experience. This is also why the profession, which was populated by Jewish refugees after the war, struggled to acknowledge the presence of historical trauma in its own ranks.[10] When I decided to train as a psychoanalyst, I looked for an approach that was sensitive to the social and cultural contexts in human experience. I chose the William Alanson White Institute of Psychiatry, Psychoanalysis, and Psychology in New York, which was cofounded by Fromm. After arriving at the Institute, I was surprised to find that although Fromm's name figured prominently in the Institute's history, his works were only sparsely read. Once Fromm left New York for Mexico, his influence at the Institute began to wane, and the psychoanalytic approach he helped to establish focused less on the role of society than on the interpersonal dynamic between the patient and analyst. However, as Fromm liked to remind his psychoanalytic colleagues, therapeutic practice "cannot be divorced from philosophy and ethics nor from sociology and economics" (Fromm, 1947, p. ix).

In the course of building my therapeutic practice, I came to appreciate how society, culture, and history flow through us as human beings (Frie,

2018). Over time, I worked with many patients who were descendants of Holocaust survivors or the victims of other forms of racial and systemic violence. This made me sensitive to the effects of historical trauma, which can remain long after the violence first takes place. It also made me curious about what it meant to inherit a perpetrator past. Hearing my patients talk about the traumas their families endured at the hands of Germans, or other perpetrator groups, made me realize that there was much in my own family history that remained unknown.

After glimpsing an unfamiliar photograph of my grandfather in uniform on a trip to Germany, I began a long and difficult confrontation with the unspoken Nazi past in my family. This personal process of inquiry eventually led to the publication of my book *Not in My Family: German Memory and Responsibility After the Holocaust* (Frie, 2017). What became clear to me in writing that book and in speaking with audiences about the legacies of perpetration is that in order to respond to history's traumas we need to enter into dialogue with the voices that have shaped our understanding. Being engaged in this kind of personal and historical inquiry is never easy. Asking potentially difficult and painful questions is about taking a stand.

As I emphasize throughout this book, the genocide was not simply the work of sadistic perpetrators, but the result of everyday individuals, families, and communities who willingly, even enthusiastically, submitted. Fromm referred to this as the "yearning for submission" (Fromm, 1941, p. 8). My family members belonged to the vast majority of Germans whose participation in the policies of the Nazi regime enabled the perpetrators to carry out their heinous crimes. Their complicity haunts me and stands as a warning, lest we remain silent in the face of the right-wing extremism we see today.

In view of my German family background, I want to explain my approach to examining the difficult and often painful subject matter of this book. I feel a particular need to be sensitive about making interpretations in regard to what a German Jewish refugee or émigré may or may not have felt or thought in the face Nazi aggression and the Holocaust.[11] My stance also reflects my own practice as a psychoanalyst. There are different approaches to interpretation within the profession. Many psychoanalysts offer interpretations based on the belief that they can discern meaning in the minds of their patients. In contrast, other psychoanalysts, such as myself, believe that meaning and understanding are always created in dialogue between the analyst and the patient. In the same sense, my aim in this book is to invite the reader to engage with me in an empathic dialogue with the circumstances of Fromm's life and the topics that he chose to write about, and thus to reach an understanding about what Fromm may have been experiencing.[12] If this explanation seems at little too abstract, let me simply add one more point before returning to the contexts of Fromm's life.

My discussion rests on the exploration of three main sources: the unpublished Holocaust correspondence in Fromm's family; Fromm's life experiences as revealed in unpublished letters and German biographical sources; and Fromm's published and unpublished writings. As such, my study draws chiefly on primary sources and archival materials. The Holocaust correspondence is housed at the Erich Fromm Papers in the New York Public Library and at the Erich Fromm Archive in Tübingen, Germany. In addition to the family correspondence, I draw on Fromm's letters to Horkheimer and associated members of the Institute for Social Research. Taken together, this documentation provides an important account of the world in which Fromm lived and enables us to to consider how he was impacted by Nazi Germany and the Holocaust.

There are undoubtedly different ways I could have written about the subject matter of this book. The path I take reflects my position at the intersection of history and culture and my particular interests as a historian and psychoanalyst. While historians may understandably seek to keep their own lives separate from their scholarship with the aim of remaining impartial, psychoanalysts increasingly accept that any understanding they achieve is through the lens of their own subjective and cultural experience. Rather than assume that I can maintain some kind of neutral stance, I have chosen to bring my German family history to bear in this book. Some readers may look askance at my approach, but I believe that the nature of my family background requires me to ask what lessons can be learned. What meaning can I derive from the fact that everyday Germans like my own grandparents could become supporters of a regime driven by racial ideology and eventually genocide? And how, ultimately, might we react differently in our own lives when faced with similar circumstances? These questions are at the very center of Fromm's concerns.

While the Holocaust letters in Fromm's family shed light on the horrors of the past, they are equally a warning to us to be vigilant in the present. Fromm argued that no country is immune to the dangers of fascism and destructiveness. His analysis of the fragility of freedom and his emphasis on human solidarity in the face of right-wing authoritarian leaders remain his most vital contributions. These ideas seem, once again, to have a frightening contemporary relevance. As the historian Fritz Stern, who was himself a German Jewish refugee, pointed out, "We owe the victims of the last century's descent into an inferno of organized bestiality an enduring, awed memorial: a prudent vigilance—and the knowledge that the bacillus that killed them did not die with them" (2006, p. 11).

German Jewish Refugees

Fromm's complicated relationship with Germany and the Nazi past will form an important part of this study. In contrast to many German Jewish refugees, Fromm adapted to life in New York relatively quickly and mastered working and writing in English within a few years of his arrival. Unlike his colleagues from the Institute for Social Research, Max Horkheimer and Theodor Adorno, Fromm never seemed to have an inclination to return to Germany. This was likely a reflection of Fromm's tendency to look forward, rather than dwell on the past. He greeted life with a sense of hope, despite whatever personal traumas and tragedies he experienced. It is perhaps not surprising, therefore, that he never shared with readers his subjective experience of disappointment and loss at having to flee his native country. Yet as Peter Gay reminds us in his memoir *My German Question*,

> More than a half-century after the collapse of Hitler's Thousand Year Reich, every surviving refugee remains to some extent one of his victims. . . . My point is a simple factual one: even the most fortunate Jew who lived under Hitler has never completely shaken off that experience." (Gay, 1998, p. 21)

Fromm did not see himself as a "survivor." Nor would he have necessarily seen himself as a "victim," a term he would likely have identified with his family members who were murdered by the Nazi regime. It was presumably Fromm's reticence to place himself in this category that led Fromm's biographer, Lawrence Friedman, to proclaim,

> Because his immigration had not been particularly onerous Fromm never elected to characterize himself as a refugee from Hitler's Germany, even though his return was precluded at least until the end of Nazi rule. Even so, and despite having to leave behind many of his books and possessions,

Fromm considered his move to America his own choice rather than the result of an immediate threat to his survival. (Friedman, 2013, p. 68)

These sentences should give us pause.

Immigration under any circumstance can be difficult, even painful. But being forced to leave because of a persecutory racial ideology involves unimaginable loss. Immigration to another country may provide a sense of safety, but it is also accompanied by betrayal, grief, and trauma. A life that was once taken for granted has been forcibly ripped away. We know that Fromm spent much of the early 1930s in Switzerland in recovery from tuberculosis, and there is strong indication that he looked for opportunities to remain there after Hitler and the Nazi Party (officially the National Socialist German Workers' Party) were elected to power in 1933. When the possibility of immigrating to New York in 1934 became a reality, he grasped the opportunity and left not only his books, but his family, friends, and colleagues behind. He was lucky to gain entry. Admission to the United States was becoming increasingly difficult due to harsh immigration restrictions.[13] Looking back, it is hard to imagine that Fromm was unaffected by these turbulent changes in his life. This makes it all the more curious that the impact of Nazi Germany and the Holocaust on Fromm's life and work has received so little attention.

To be sure, there has been much valuable scholarship carried out on Fromm over the past years and I have benefited from this research. Among the major books in English are an account of Fromm as a global public sociologist (McLaughlin, 2021), an elaboration of Fromm's radical humanism (Durkin, 2014), and two intellectual biographies (Friedman, 2013 and Funk, 2019).[14] These publications speak to a renewed interest in Fromm and cover the wide scope of Fromm's interests. Taken together, however, they provide only a brief account of Fromm's family history, and there has been no attempt to contextualize the place of Nazi Germany and the Holocaust in Fromm's life and work.

A key reason for this omission is that Fromm kept details of his personal life strictly separate from his scholarship and never produced a memoir.[15] He has also been described as an exceedingly private person.[16] As a result, we don't have access to his memories of the rise of the Nazis, or what it was like for him to board a ship for New York. Nor do we know exactly how he reacted when he received news of the deportation of his family members to concentration camps. In addition, only a selection of Fromm's early letters still exist.[17] And because Fromm died in 1980, many of those who knew him are no longer alive to share their knowledge. An important exception is Rainer Funk, the executor of Fromm's literary estate and Director of the Fromm Institute and Archive in Tübingen, Germany. Funk was Fromm's last personal assistant in the 1970s, and I am fortunate to be able to draw on his memories of Fromm in this book.

While the dearth of available documentation may help to explain the lack of discussion of the Nazi past and the Holocaust in Fromm's life, there are also other factors to consider. First, Fromm was one of many European Jewish refugee psychoanalysts who did not openly discuss their own memories or the experience of their family in the Holocaust.[18] The interpersonal psychoanalyst Edgar Levenson, who participated in several of Fromm's clinical case seminars at the William Alanson White Institute, has no recollection of Fromm ever mentioning the Holocaust.[19] As Funk has acknowledged, Fromm had little to say publicly about the genocide, at least in relation to his own life. Similarly, the psychoanalyst Sonja Gojman de Millan, who trained under Fromm in Mexico City in the early 1970s, has no memory of hearing Fromm discuss the Holocaust or its effect on his family.[20] The memories that Funk and Gojman de Millan shared with me are particularly telling because both interacted with Fromm during the period when he was engaged in researching the Holocaust for his book, *The Anatomy of Human Destructiveness* (1973). I am not suggesting that Fromm's reticence to talk about his family history supports the questionable narrative of a collective silence about the Holocaust after the war. Rather, Fromm's reticence helps us to understand that a refugee's decision about whether or not to reveal their past varied from one person to the next.[21]

A second reason for the lack of discussion about this topic is that we are not accustomed to thinking about Fromm as a victim of history. Readers tend to identify Fromm with qualities such as courage and agency, and to see in his work possibilities for achieving progressive social change. The aim of this book is not to challenge these important attributes but, rather, to expand our knowledge of who Fromm was and why he chose to write about specific themes and topics, from authoritarianism, racial narcissism, and destructiveness to the human capacity for love and solidarity. This will require us to engage in a rather more somber and melancholic account of a thinker and clinician who was shaped by the legacy of historical trauma, even as he worked toward the betterment of society.

Understanding the impact of Nazi Germany and the Holocaust on Fromm's life and work is particularly important in view of the kind of social and political crises we face today. A more developed awareness of who Fromm was and why he was able to write so persuasively about difficult and essential topics can help us to take measure of his work. I believe that Fromm has much to teach us about the present moment, though a word of caution is in order. The impulse to see our present reflected in the past easily neglects the way in which our circumstances and concerns, and even the language we use, can vary with time.[22] We must be careful about imposing our current assumptions onto history, just as we cannot effortlessly transpose writings from the past into the present. The more we grasp the nuances of history, memory, and trauma, the better we will be able to grapple with these challenges.

Plan of the Book

My discussion will proceed in stages. In Chapter 1, "The Holocaust Correspondence," I document the trauma and tragedy experienced by Fromm's family members and Fromm's many unsuccessful attempts to save them. I begin with a brief biographical overview of Fromm's early life in Germany before turning to the letters themselves. I have divided the family correspondence into three parts: the first section presents the plight of Heinz Brandt, a Communist Party activist and cousin of Fromm's who was sent first to a prison and then to a concentration camp; the second section presents the correspondence of Gertrud Brandt, Heinz's mother, whose letters were written from the ghetto of Ostrow-Lubelski in southeast Poland; and the third section presents the letters of Fromm's aunt in Berlin, Sophie Engländer. The letters reveal the powerful emotions of suffering, loss, and longing experienced by Fromm's family members and give us a glimpse into what their daily lives were like up until their deportations and deaths. They also detail the tremendous strength and courage shown by Fromm's aunts and the experience of German Jewish women in the unfolding catastrophe.

The subsequent chapters build on the knowledge we gain from the letters and follow the chronology of Fromm's life. When the Nazi Party was elected to power in Germany, Fromm was 33 years old. At the end of World War II, when news of the atrocities was revealed, he was 45 years old. In order to grasp how Fromm responded, first to the rise of the Nazis, and then to the Holocaust, it is important to understand the formative events and experiences of his life. In Chapter 2, "How Is This Possible?," I examine

Fromm's life in Germany before 1933, focusing on his personal and professional development amid the social crises that shook Weimar Germany and fed Hitler's rise to power. In order to capture the emotional and psychological ramifications of this turbulent period, I draw on the German expressionist artist, Käthe Kollwitz, whose work sheds light on the terrible effects of World War I. As Fromm later revealed, World War I was "the event that determined more than anything else my development" (Fromm, 1962a, p. 5). In its aftermath, Fromm sought to grasp the social and psychological origins of violence and began to formulate his theory of compassion and solidarity. Fromm and Kollwitz both spent their careers struggling with the horrors of World War I, not daring to imagine that the cumulative deaths of that war would be surmounted by another. By the time that Hitler and the Nazi Party were elected into power, Fromm was familiar with the human proclivity for destruction and hatred, but nothing could prepare him for what was to come, or for how personally painful these tragedies would be.

In Chapter 3, "Yearning to Submit," I trace the source of Fromm's impassioned arguments against fascism in *Escape From Freedom*. With his arrival in New York in 1934, Fromm began a new chapter of his life as a German Jewish refugee. He watched from afar as the political situation in Europe deteriorated, ever conscious of the growing threat of Nazism for his family members, friends, and colleagues who remained in Germany. In 1938, Fromm traveled back to Europe for the first time. When the November Pogrom broke out, Fromm was convalescing in Switzerland from an attack of tuberculosis. In his weakened state, Fromm corresponded regularly with Horkheimer, and his letters reveal the depth of worry and doubt that Fromm felt as he sought to help his family members from the isolation of his hospital bed. When Fromm was finally well enough to return to the United States, he simultaneously engaged in a campaign to save his relatives and elaborated his arguments on the dangers of fascism, which would form the basis for *Escape From Freedom*. Writing provided Fromm with a means to respond to the spiraling events in Germany. His analysis of the psychology of Nazism remains arguably as relevant today as it was when he first wrote it.

In Chapter 4, "Confronting Genocide," I suggest that the personal dimension of the Holocaust in Fromm's life helps to explain why the question of Germany and the destructiveness of Nazism played such a formative role in his postwar writings. Shortly before the end the World War II, Fromm married Henny Gurland, a fellow German Jewish refugee. She had accompanied the philosopher Walter Benjamin on his fateful attempt to flee Nazi-occupied

France. In the years that followed, Fromm sought unsuccessfully to stem his wife's physical and emotional decline. Her tragic demise occurred against the painful backdrop of the many deaths of Fromm's family members in the genocide. Soon afterward, Fromm became involved in rescuing his cousin, Heinz Brandt, who had remarkably survived Auschwitz and was now imprisoned by the East German secret police, evoking fresh memories of the recent Nazi past.

Throughout the postwar years, the Holocaust correspondence forms the unspoken context for Fromm's impassioned stance against injustice. At the height of the civil rights movement, he spoke directly to the scourge of Jim Crow in the United States and drew parallels with the Nazi Germany's persecution of its Jewish citizens. In *The Anatomy of Human Destructiveness*, Fromm turned his sights to the Nazi leadership, Himmler and Hitler, in order to analyze the personal pathologies at the heart of the Final Solution. In his last decades, Fromm struggled to bridge his early life experiences in Germany with the reality of a postwar nation whose culture of remembrance and responsibility was just beginning to take shape. The most surprising part of this process was undoubtedly Fromm's dialogue with Albert Speer, Hitler's architect and the Nazi regime's Minister of Armaments and War Production. Reflecting on their dialogue gives us a means to consider just how complex Fromm's relationship with the country of his birth really was. Toward the end of his life, Fromm returned to the German Jewish symbiosis that he had known as a young man, reflected on the nature of antisemitism, and developed his critique of Zionism.

In Chapter 5, "Cultivating Love and Hope," I consider the meanings inherent in Fromm's elaborations on human connection and solidarity against the backdrop of war and genocide. I shed light on the powerful parallels that exist between Fromm's exploration of interpersonal love and hope and the letters that Gertrud and Sophie wrote shortly before their deaths. These ideas are expressed in Fromm's best known work, *The Art of Loving* (1956), and in his belief that love is a necessary countervailing force to cruelty and destructiveness. I also draw on Fromm's psychoanalytic writings. Although Fromm's therapeutic work is often overlooked, it the source from which much of his thinking about love and solidarity emerged. I conclude by considering the nature of our ethical obligation to others, and I ask what we can learn from Fromm and the Holocaust correspondence as we seek to respond to the social and political crises of our own age.

1
The Holocaust Correspondence

Letter writing was a lifeline that connected German Jewish refugees with family members who remained behind in Nazi Germany. The Holocaust correspondence in Fromm's family shows how the members of his family, and in particular the older women in the family, were subjected to racial persecution and terror. The letters recount the experiences of Fromm's aunts, Gertrud Brandt and Sophie Engländer, both of whom played an important role in his early life. There are approximately 100 extant handwritten letters, though the actual number would have been far larger.[1] The letters, written in German, detail the tragic history that many German Jewish families were forced to endure over the course of the Third Reich. What distinguishes this correspondence is its specific relevance to Fromm's life and work and the diversity of circumstances described by the writers. This chapter will present a selection of the letters in English for the first time, using excerpts that shed light on the plight of Fromm's family members and on Fromm's many interactions with them. Through the correspondence, we come to understand just how closely Fromm was involved in trying to help his relatives, and how, despite his best efforts, he was unable to save them.

The correspondence begins in 1938, on the eve of the Holocaust, and ends in 1943 with the writers' deportation and murder. The stories told by the letters demonstrate the challenges and uncertain futures faced by the writers. In Germany, the year 1938 was marked by an increase in anti-Jewish persecution that culminated in the organized Nazi pogrom of November 9–10. In the months that followed the November Pogrom, attempts by Jewish community members to leave Germany increased substantially, but so too did the obstacles standing in the way of reaching safety. The letters reveal the enormous challenges of securing a visa. As the situation for German Jews worsened, we witness the anxiety and urgency of the writers. By the fall of 1941, emigration from Germany was banned and wide-scale deportations to ghettos and concentration camps had begun. From that point on, leaving Germany became extremely difficult, if not impossible. In 1943, when the correspondence ceased, virtually all of Fromm's relatives who were unable to leave Germany had been killed.

Fromm's family correspondence illustrates the unfolding catastrophe of the Holocaust in a way that no secondary account ever can. The letters provide a moving picture of the rapidly worsening situation and are a kind of "contemporaneous communication" that captures daily developments in the lives of the writers and their family members.[2] Some of the letters demonstrate the depth of need and suffering that was endured; others convey a strength of spirit, love of life, and unbreakable bonds between family members. Emotions fluctuated between despondency and hopefulness. It is hard to read the correspondence knowing of the tragedy that awaits the writers or the stinging pain and sorrow that will be experienced by family members when the letters stop arriving.

I will intersperse the letters with brief historical commentary, but my hope is to let the words of Fromm's aunts speak for themselves, and thus to enable the reader to experience what they and countless other victims of the Holocaust were forced to endure. Given the personally and emotionally intimate nature of the letters, I have chosen to refer to the writers, Gertrud and Sophie, by their first names, rather than by their family names. I use the same approach when I describe Fromm's interactions with his close relatives. Before turning to the correspondence, and in order to help the reader understand the family constellation described in the letters, I will begin with a short overview of Fromm's early life in Germany.

Beginnings

Fromm was the only child of Rosa (née Krause) and Naphtali Fromm and grew up in an Orthodox Jewish, middle-class household in Frankfurt.[3] Fromm's mother stayed at home to raise her son. His father was a wine merchant who seemed to question his choice of career given the professional successes of his siblings and forefathers. Fromm described both of his parents as being very anxious individuals. His mother often felt possessive of her son and was given to depression, while his father was often distracted and obsessive in nature. Interactions with his family members seemed to provide Fromm with a balance of emotional support that he did not find at home.[4] Contact with his relatives, particularly on his mother's side, played an important role in his childhood. Fromm often traveled to Berlin with his mother.

She grew up in the city and many of her siblings lived there. Fromm described his mother as being happiest when she was around her own family. Fromm had two cousins with whom he was especially close. On his mother's side, Charlotte Hirschfeld (née Stein), the daughter of Rosa's sister Martha, was a constant companion during summer holidays and much like an older sibling to Fromm. On his father's side, Gertrud Hunziker-Fromm, the daughter of Naphtali's brother Emmanuel, was a close childhood friend and would become Fromm's lifelong confidant.[5]

Fromm grew up in a manifestly religious environment. Before he gave up Orthodox Judaism at the age of 26, his daily life was structured by religious observance. In contrast to the middle-class, liberal values for which early 20th-century Frankfurt was known, Fromm described the "medieval atmosphere" of his childhood years.[6] He was referring to the historically rooted traditions of orthodoxy. His guide was Ludwig Krause, his great uncle on his mother's side, who was a well-known Talmudic scholar and rabbi of the orthodox synagogue in the eastern German city of Posen (present-day Poznań in Poland.) On his father's side, his great-grandfather, Selig Bär Bamberger, was one of the most prominent and learned German rabbis of the mid-19th century. Fromm's grandfather, Seligmann Pinchas Fromm, was the rabbinic leader of Frankfurt's Jewish orthodox community. Given this background, it is hardly surprising that religion figured so prominently in his upbringing.

Fromm was introduced to secular society when he attended the Wöhler Gymnasium in Frankfurt.[7] Outside of school he continued to find inspiration in Jewish thinking and learning. Fromm was influenced by the Orthodox Rabbi Nehemia Anton Nobel and the liberal Rabbi Georg Salzberger, with whom Fromm was in especially close contact. Together with Salzberger, Fromm helped found the celebrated Jewish Free Learning Center (*Freies Jüdisches Lehrhaus*). The center was directed by Franz Rosenzweig, and its teachers included Fromm, Leo Baeck, Martin Buber, Siegfried Kracauer, and Gershom Scholem.[8]

In 1918, Fromm began studying law at the University of Frankfurt but soon switched to sociology. He transferred to the University of Heidelberg and received his doctorate in sociology in 1922. He was supervised by Alfred Weber (the younger brother of Max Weber), whom he later identified as a key influence on his work. Fromm's dissertation examined the social cohesion among different Jewish groups in the Diaspora. At Heidelberg, Fromm was taught psychology by Karl Jaspers and philosophy by Heinz Rickert. Between 1920 and 1925, Fromm was also inspired by the teachings of the Talmudic scholar Salmon Baruch Rabinkov, an adherent of Habad Hasidism. In addition to the religious and secular teaching he received, Fromm became interested in psychoanalysis through his relationship with Frieda Reichmann, whom he married in 1926. In 1928, Fromm moved to Berlin to complete his formal psychoanalytic training. His unique background in sociology and psychoanalysis enabled him to comment on the political events at the time and brought him to the attention of Max Horkheimer, director of the Institute for Social Research in Frankfurt. In 1930, Fromm was invited to become a member of the Institute and began his career as a German intellectual and psychoanalyst. It was not to be. The election of the Nazi Party in January 1933 inalterably changed the trajectory of his life.

The Downward Spiral

Fromm reached the safety of New York in 1934 and watched with alarm as Hitler and the Nazi regime imprisoned political opponents and consolidated their grip on power. In the years that followed, there was a seemingly endless series of tumultuous political events. Germany's hostile expansion into neighboring territories began in 1935 and culminated in the Anschluss with Austria and occupation of the Sudetenland in Czechoslovakia in 1938. A year later, on September 1, 1939, Germany invaded Poland, signaling the start of the Second World War. The regime's aggression toward its neighbors was matched by the persecution of its own citizens. From the start, anyone deemed undesirable in the Nazi worldview—Jews, Roma, Sinti, gays and lesbians, the mentally ill, and left-wing opponents of all stripes—was in peril. Marxists and psychoanalysts were high on the list of targets.

Soon after taking power, Hitler and the Nazis began implementing anti-Jewish legislation. The latent antisemitism of the 1920s turned into a persecutory racial ideology. In April 1933, there was a boycott of Jewish businesses, followed by the enactment of a series of laws that banned German Jews and political opponents from government, university, and professional positions. In 1935, the Nuremberg Laws excluded German Jews from citizenship and prohibited them from having sexual relations or marrying persons of "German or German-related blood." This was followed by a wave of legislation that sought to segregate Jews from daily life, limit their ability to earn a living, and "Aryanize," or essentially transfer ownership of businesses to non-Jewish Germans.

The Nazis' antisemitic policies culminated in the November Pogrom. On the night of November 9, 1938, and into the next day, belligerent mobs destroyed nearly 300 synagogues, destroyed thousands of Jewish-owned commercial properties and private residences, and desecrated Jewish cemeteries throughout Germany and Austria. The destruction was greatest in Berlin and Vienna, home to the largest Jewish communities, where Nazis pursued and humiliated Jewish citizens in their homes and in public. Beyond the massive destruction of property, the violence unleashed during those November days targeted Jewish male bodies, subjecting them to widespread beatings and the first mass incarceration of Jewish men in concentration camps. Some 100 men were killed that night, and hundreds more died in the coming weeks in Buchenwald, Dachau, and Sachsenhausen. After the November Pogrom, antisemitic legislation accelerated, setting the stage for the racist persecution and terror that followed. It also spelled the beginning of the end of Jewish emigration from Germany. In the fall of 1941, a policy of deportation was set in place. Years of antisemitic Nazi propaganda meant that many Germans greeted the legislated disappearance of their Jewish neighbors with a sense of disinterest, if not active support. At the infamous Wannsee Conference on January 20, 1942, Nazi leaders coordinated the deliberate and systemic murder of Europe's Jews, known as the "Final Solution of the Jewish Question." Deportations from Germany reached their height that same year.

When Fromm left for the United States, most of his family remained in Germany. At the time, many German Jews believed, or at any rate hoped, that the election of the Nazis was a momentary madness. With each passing year, opportunities for leaving Germany became more difficult, and the possibility of a return to the democratic rule of the Weimar Republic more remote. Yet until the November Pogrom of 1938, and even well after it took place, it was difficult for Germany's Jewish community to imagine that the events they were living through could possibly end in deportations, ghettos, and genocide.[9] This is an important point, since when we look back today, we inevitably examine the years of the 1930s through the lens of what we know now.

Fromm's father, Naphtali, died in December 1933 at the age of 64, having witnessed the Nazi rise to power. It is unclear whether Fromm was able to attend his father's funeral. Although Naphtali hailed from a large family, we know relatively little about what happened to his family members during the Holocaust.[10] Fromm's cousin, Gertrud, moved to Switzerland to study before 1933 and remained there once the Nazis assumed power. Despite losing her husband, Fromm's mother, Rosa, stayed in Germany because she did not want to leave her siblings behind. Fromm stayed in close contact with his mother, especially as the circumstances for German Jews worsened.

Following the November Pogrom, Rosa recognized the gravity of the situation and expressed a strong desire to leave. Fromm endeavored to secure the necessary visas, but by 1938 there were considerable obstacles. He obtained a monetary loan to pay the high fee required by the German authorities to leave the country and arranged for Rosa's travel to England. She spent the next 18 months in England along with many other refugees, so-called stateless enemy aliens. Arranging for Rosa's entry into the United States proved difficult. The policy for admitting German Jews had become harshly selective, influenced by the upsurge in American antisemitism over the course of the 1930s. After paying another hefty fee, this time to the U.S. authorities, Rosa was finally able to join her son in 1941. She spent the remainder of her life in New York and died there in 1959.

The Holocaust correspondence in Fromm's family hails chiefly from his mother's side. Rosa had six siblings and several cousins on her father's side. Rosa had grown up in Berlin, and most members of the Krause family lived in the city. In contrast to what might often be considered to be the typical assimilated urban German Jewish family story, there was considerable heterogeneity within the Fromm–Krause family constellation. Some family members identified with Orthodox Judaism and others embraced secular Judaism. Some sought to avoid notice by the Nazi authorities, and others were committed communists who openly engaged in activism against the Nazi state. Among Rosa's relatives, many members of the younger generation left for countries as far and wide as Bolivia, Brazil, Chile, Palestine, Russia, the United States, England, and Switzerland. Those who remained in Germany belonged chiefly to the older generation and faced eventual deportation.

The information we have about the Krause family is incomplete. However, we know that two of Rosa's siblings, Martin Krause (born 1877) and his wife Johanna Krause (née Weiner, born 1871) and Sophie Engländer (née Krause, born 1873) and her husband David Engländer (born 1863) were deported. None survived. A similar fate awaited Rosa's cousin, Gertrud Brandt (née Krause, born 1897); her husband, Georg Brandt (born 1875); and their youngest son, Wolfgang, who were all sent to the ghetto of Ostrow-Lubelski, near Lublin. Gertrud's three other children experienced persecution, imprisonment, and murder.[11] Rosa's cousin Therese Zehetner (née Krause, birth date unknown) and her husband Bruno Zehetner (born 1852) both died in

Frankfurt in 1940. Had they lived longer, they would also have faced deportation. Martha Stein (née Krause, birth date unknown), another of Rosa's sisters, and her husband, Bernhard Stein (birth date unknown), were able to flee Berlin for São Paolo, Brazil, with the help of their daughter Charlotte Hirschfeld.[12]

In New York, Fromm joined a growing community of German Jewish refugees, many of whom faced similar family circumstances. Almost immediately, he began to concern himself with helping those who had stayed behind. Fromm participated in a voluminous family correspondence. Letters were exchanged among multiple family members. Each tried to keep the others abreast of developments in a constant search for ways to save those left behind. Fromm came to play a central role in this process since he was one of few family members to live abroad and have an established income. Fromm helped his relatives in whatever way he could, but the draconian immigration policies and the prohibitive cost of exit visas limited what he was able to do. Letter writing was one of the few means available to sustain those in need and perhaps also a balm to assuage those who, like Fromm, escaped Germany and could only look on from afar, often beset by a feeling of powerlessness as events continued to spiral. Staying connected was essential for everyone, and as Gertrud and Sophie's letters demonstrate, the value of the communications that reached those who were left behind and imprisoned was beyond measure.

Letters of Gertrud Brandt

Gertrud Brandt's letters date from September 1938 through February 1943. Gertrud and Rosa were cousins, and Gertrud's father was Erich's first Talmud teacher. The Brandt family were members of the German Jewish community in the city of Posen (Poznań.) Posen had been the capital of the eastern Prussian province of Posen from 1848 until 1919.[13] Following the First World War it was ceded to the Second Polish Republic in the Treaty of Versailles. The German population of Posen was given a choice: take up Polish citizenship or leave for the redrawn borders of Germany. The Brandt family belonged to a minority of Germans who stayed in Posen but maintained strong cultural ties with Germany.[14]

Gertrud worked as a teacher in the city's German-speaking girls' school. Her husband, Georg, was a writer but was plagued by health problems and often unable to work (Figure 1.1). A noteworthy aspect of the Brandt family is that Gertrud financially supported her family as she took care of her husband. Over time, Gertrud became the sole income earner. The Brandts had four children: Heinz (born 1909), Richard (born 1910), Lilli (born 1912), and Wolfgang (born 1917). In 1926, Heinz Brandt and his brother moved to Berlin to finish their schooling and attend university. Lilli soon followed. Heinz studied economics and joined the Communist Party in 1931. As a communist, he was politically active in opposition to the Nazis. His brother and sister shared Heinz's political views. In 1932, they moved to the Soviet Union to escape the ascendancy of antisemitism in Berlin and continue their studies. Heinz remained in Berlin and was arrested in 1934 for disseminating a banned communist newsletter. He was convicted of treason and given a six-year prison sentence.[15]

Heinz Brandt's plight as a Jewish political prisoner forms the primary theme of the correspondence between Gertrud and Erich.[16] The record we have of their letters begins in 1938, but their correspondence very likely

Figure 1.1 Gertrud Brandt and Georg Brandt, 1932, Poznań/Posen
Courtesy of the Erich Fromm Archive, Tübingen.

began earlier. The letters detail Gertrud's and Erich's mutual attempts to secure a visa for Heinz. They also provide a glimpse into what life was like in Posen in the face of Nazi Germany's racial ideology and political belligerence. Following the Nazi invasion of Poland in September 1939, Posen's entire Jewish community was deported to a ghetto in the town of Ostrow-Lubelski, near Lublin.[17] There they lived in increasingly desperate conditions with Jews from the area in and around Ostrow-Lubelski. From 1940 onward, Gertrud's letters chronicle the indescribable suffering she and her family members, Georg and Wolfgang, endured in the ghetto.

The correspondence opens with twin letters by Georg Brandt and Gertrud Brandt. They both thank Erich for his willingness to help Heinz and reflect on the importance of family in times of need.[18]

Poznań, September 23, 1938

My dear Erich,

Your letter has delighted me exceedingly; not only, outwardly, because of the positive response to the affidavit [for Heinz], but because of its entirely warm tone amongst family. It really makes me think of the dear relationships that—just one generation before you—existed with your mother when we were young and that of course still exist today.

Your old cousin, Georg

Poznań, September 25, 1938

My dear, good Erich!

Your letter really cheered me up. I can't tell you what it means to me that someone is willing to carry this burden with me and help the boy [Heinz]...

I would like to give you the following information about our boy: Heinz Brandt, born August 16, 1909 in Posen, as a former Prussian citizen. He became a Galician citizen when Poland took over, then emigrated and was "renaturalized" in Germany. This granting of citizenship was withdrawn from all Jews who received it after 1918, leaving him stateless. That is why the entry permit for a foreign country is so important...

Thank you from the bottom of my heart, dear Erich! Thank you very much for wanting to ease our financial worries. In fact, the lack of money makes everything even more difficult—until you are completely at a loss.

Heartfelt, your Trude

Ps. I just see how disordered and restless my letter is—probably just as I am at the moment. Worry is awful.

In response to the news that Erich is going to intervene on his behalf, Heinz wrote a note to his parents from prison on October 16, 1938: *"I am overjoyed by Erich's offer to help me with my further studies. He is the best great-cousin imaginable."* Despite all the optimism Heinz and his parents may have felt, or at the very least expressed in their letters, Heinz's situation was extremely serious. As a communist, Brandt was considered an enemy of the state, and after the passing of the Nuremberg Laws in 1935, he was stripped of his citizenship and declared "stateless." There were few avenues of escape open to him.

In Gertrud's next letters, which are written in the months after the November Pogrom, the extent of her own difficulties became clear. Germany's antisemitic policies were making themselves felt in Posen. The Germans living in Posen were no longer willing to have Gertrud teach their children. Foreshadowing the cruelties and violence to come, at the end of October 1938, the Nazi regime expelled 17,000 Polish Jews, many of whom had lived in Germany for generations.[19] Most languished at the border, often without food or shelter, until the start of the war, after which their situation became even more imperiled.

Poznań, December 29, 1938

My dear Erich!

You write about the costs first, and I want to talk about them first, so that I can take this burden off my heart and then be free again.

Erich, dear, I need money. It's so awful to have to say it like that, but I can't manage by myself anymore. I urgently need a larger sum, about 500 zł. That's a lot of money. That's probably almost 100 dollars. Do you have a way to help me with this? With all the preparations, the trip to Berlin [to petition for clemency for Heinz] *cost about 200 zł; I still choke on that. . . . It's something else every day and it is so burdening...*

Georg doesn't see our situation as it is; in this I'm fighting an unsuccessful battle. He shows no trace of ill will, just an alienation from life that is very difficult for me to balance. Otherwise, I've still somehow managed to deal with a lot of worries. But for the new school year (in September) my beautiful school circle has dissolved, the German officials, most of whose children I had, no longer send me pupils. . . . This is a serious deficit for me and I can see no way to make up the loss. I've already sold everything I could sell. I was hoping to sell a beautiful old Renaissance cabinet, but there simply isn't a buyer for it. Since that also fell through, I don't know of a way out other than to talk to you about it...

Now, contrary to the first report, our newspapers have written that Cuba has already been closed and that the emigrants have been taken to a concentration camp. I don't know to what extent this report is true. It would of course be very important—and you have already also considered this—to take advantage of any open immigration quotas in order to be registered and accepted somewhere, at least until it becomes possible to immigrate to the USA. With a proof of emigration, it is already possible that this can be achieved—but of course it is not absolutely certain. But it has to be worked on in any case, otherwise we will be faced with a catastrophe at the time of [Heinz's] *release in December 1940...*

I'll copy some of his letters for you in the near future, it's just too late today—I'm a little too rushed. We have the flu here and it goes from one person to another. It was especially pronounced with the children of my friendly refugee family, who have been with us for 2 months, a lovely woman suddenly torn from her beautiful home with her children. The misery of these families is very, very great [Gertrud is presumably referring to the Jewish expellees from Germany]. *They don't know where to go. Luckily, most of them have behaved very well here, the Polish-Jewish families, by the way, much better than the German Jewish ones. They are more self-sacrificing, also less differentiated, so that they don't mind being huddled together in order to make room for a few sleeping guests...*

Your Trude

Fromm was not alone in his attempts to help Heinz and Gertrud. He was often assisted by Juliane Favez, the administrator of the Institute for Social Research in Geneva.[20] Favez came to play an important intermediary role in arranging for exit visas and communicating with Gertrud about Heinz. Over time she also became one of Gertrud's supports. A letter from Gertrud to Favez illustrates this:

Poznań, February 10, 1939

My dearly respected Mme. Favez!

Your letters always come to me as a real consolation—I can't tell you what it means to me that you stand by me in such a way and that you know how to be so kind and sympathetic and at the same time to give objective advice.... I turn to you without hesitation with my needs. Thank you so very much for that! The prospect of a visa from Uruguay [for Heinz] has of course made me extremely happy.

With heartfelt wishes,

Gertrud Brandt

Poznań, February 28, 1939

My dear, dear Erich!

Thank you so much for your faithful concern!

I already received your letter a few days ago, but I didn't know how to respond to your efforts in regard to Cuba, and in the meantime have written to Mme. Favez [above], who answered me immediately (she is very supportive). In this way I also learned that you are informed about the conditional promise from Uruguay, which I received and which I sent to support the petition for clemency...

Mme. Favez is now of the opinion that you should continue your efforts for Cuba, since we have no guarantee whatsoever for Uruguay. I wrote to her about how keen I was to save you the work and expense, but she replied that one has to have "several irons in the fire." Regarding the registration at the American Consulate, Mme. F. thinks it should be done anyway. . . . In the meantime, I have also received confirmation from the mayor of Brandenburg (as the police authority) that Heinz is "stateless." . . . How do you get a stateless passport? Miracles haven't come my way. My only concern is to hold out until the boy is helped. It's getting too difficult for me. . .

Incidentally, this time—don't be angry that I tell you this, but you wrote once that I had to let you know—the money transfer did not arrive. Maybe it's arriving late, maybe because of your departure. Or maybe you couldn't send it. I am being honest, because I really missed it. It was really hard this time because the costs were very high with expenses for Georg and because I send daily letters with return postage and the photocopies are so expensive for me. . .

With heartfelt devotion,

Your Trude

By the spring of 1939, having followed every lead in the hope of securing a visa for Heinz, Fromm seemed for the first time to have met with success. With the help of the German Emergency Committee in London, he became a guarantor for Heinz to gain entry into Britain. If Heinz could travel to England, he would join Fromm's mother, Rosa, who was already there. The relief for Gertrud is palpable, but so too is the tremendous strain she feels.

Poznań, May 22, 1939

My dear good Erich!

I've not written to you in a long time because I quite literally didn't know what would become of everything that was in the balance. Now, in fact, the possibility of a visa for Heinz in England seems to be materializing, again with your help.

In the meantime, Shanghai has been recommended to me by the Berlin Aid Association. They want a guarantor for that. I have let them know (through Heinz's friend) that we are working on another possibility for the time being. Shanghai is said to be very sad and only a last resort.

Write to me again, dear Erich, you are such a support for me.

Everything is pretty much the same for me. Only I felt a little weak and have to rest lying down for a long time. Nothing of importance, however, just a small weakness of the heart, which will resolve itself with rest. Given all these shocking experiences, it is understandable and I'll pick myself up again. I haven't heard from your mother in England yet. How is she feeling...?

Greetings from the bottom of my heart and thank you a thousand times over!

Your Trude

Poznań, August 8, 1939

My dearest, good Erich!

You've spoiled me so much with your punctual replies that I'm surprised I didn't get an answer to my last letter. I wrote to you that the petition for clemency [for Heinz] had been rejected, but that a light now beckons with the prospect of an English visa. I also asked you if you could transfer some money to London. In the meantime, I contacted the consulate in Berlin and asked that notifications in this matter be sent to me. They then informed me that they had transferred the files to Warsaw (probably because it was more convenient)...

Gertrud's letter from August 8, 1939, was delivered to Erich in New York on August 22, 1939, only one week before Germany's invasion of Poland and the outbreak of war. By the end of the summer, Fromm was finally able to secure a visa for Heinz to enter Great Britain. But it was not to be. The start of hostilities changed everything. As difficult as the situation was up until that point, it would now become much worse. In late September 1939, Favez wrote a short note in English to Fromm to express her concerns about Heinz and Gertrud. Nothing had been heard from them since before the start of the war.

Geneva, September 27, 1939

> *I am without news from your cousin Mrs. Brandt, and am somewhat unsettled. Sometime ago she gave me the exact address of her son, which I like to communicate to you (in Brandenburg). . . . I am enclosing herewith a photocopy of the British-visa granted to Mr. Brandt. The visa has been stamped "stateless." . . . As all communications between Germany and Poland were cut off till the beginning of the hostilities, he will probably be without any news from his mother and very concerned as to what has happened. . . . Where is your mother?*

After the Germans invaded and took control of Poland, they deported Posen's entire Jewish community to a ghetto in the town of Ostrow-Lubelski. Gertrud, Georg, and their youngest son, Wolfgang, were among that number. A survivor of Ostrow-Lubelski's original Jewish population, Mechl Eckhaus, later described the arrival of Posen's deportees:

> One early Saturday morning, the Germans brought a carload of Jews from Poznan to Ostrow-Lubelski. They broke our hearts with the stories of their sufferings on the journey to Ostrow-Lubelski. As the trains did not reach our town, these Jews had been made to walk the remaining ten kilometres on foot. The road was very rough and all those men, women and children who, for some reason couldn't walk, were shot by the Germans. Those who had the privilege of reaching our town were worn-out from the beatings, hardly caring what happened to them. (Eckhaus, 1987a, p. 390)

In the ghetto of Ostrow-Lubelski, Gertrud became a caregiver for the children, which meant that she was especially conscious of the suffering around her. Sickness and death were widespread as a result of a lack of food, provisions, and medical supplies. Over time the conditions in the ghetto would become increasingly dire, threatening the lives of all who were imprisoned there.

The lack of any information about Gertrud continued throughout the months ahead. Fromm was clearly worried and wrote to Favez to inquire whether there had been any news. In her reply, written in English, Favez states,

Geneva, January 26, 1940

Investigations [by the Red Cross and the Jewish World Congress] have been undertaken but a result may not be expected until 8 weeks approximately. . . . But in any case, you must count for a rather long time until a result, if at all, may be expected. There are such a lot of enquires about the unfortunate population in Poland now, that the respective services, already overcharged with work resulting from the war, only act slowly. I shall not fail to inform you via cable, if I receive any news.

On February 28, 1940, 6 months after the start of the war, Favez received a postcard from Gertrud, dated February 8. She informed Fromm immediately. Knowing that Fromm would wish to read Gertrud's words himself, Favez helpfully copied the entire postcard in Gertrud's original German:

I would be very happy to receive a sign of life from you. We are here with the Posner Group in a small town near Lublin. The winter here is difficult but beautiful. The whole town is deeply covered in snow. It's not bad for young and healthy people, but it has brought me heavy suffering; my good husband died of pneumonia. I hoped to help him and managed to get him to the hospital in Lublin, and there he sadly faced death alone. The fact that I couldn't do anything for him at the end is very tormenting. I live here with my boy in a modest rural setting and I am grateful for that. It's all the harder because we've lost all our baggage, so we don't have anything. I am very grateful to everyone who helps us in any way. Everything is important to us. Maybe you know a way. And even if you can't help me, then you would make me happy with a few lines. We feel so abandoned when our friends are silent. I haven't heard anything from the children. I don't know how my son [Heinz] is doing, but I hope finally to get an answer from Brandenburg. My boy [Wolfgang] has had a weak heart for 3 days now, there is a lack of food. The committee gives us soup and bread, but it's not enough. We lack heating, gloves, soap. We are lacking everything.

Favez goes on to tell Fromm that on February 10, 1940, she received a response to her inquiry with the Jewish World Congress and the Red Cross.

Both organizations report that they had thus far failed to receive permission "*to assist the Jewish population in Poland suffering from nazi-terror. The German authorities forbid every help.*"

Mail became less reliable as a result of the chaos wrought by war, and the fact that letters needed to cross multiple continents in order to reach their recipient. Letters could arrive out of the chronological sequence in which they were written or sent, or they went missing, thus increasing the worry of those who were waiting for news. In April 1940, Fromm wrote to Favez a second time, describing his concerns about Gertrud and his attempts to secure a visa for Heinz.[21] Fromm's letter, written in English, provides a rare glimpse into his own state of mind:

New York, April 25, 1940

Dear Mme. Favez:

I had written you a long letter at the end of February. Since I did not get an answer from you I had begun to suspect that the letter has been lost, although you may have received it in the meantime. Unfortunately, I wrote it in long hand and not having a copy of it I do not quite remember all the things I had written. Some of them will have become outdated by now by the course of events.

Since the few written lines on the printed form which you sent me, I haven't had any direct communication from Mrs. Brandt. The money I had sent her several times has been returned to me, although the German Bank returned only about 65% of the sums sent with the explanation of value differences. For the last two or three months I have been sending $16 each month through the American Express who say that that is the maximum amount one is allowed to send to one family. If you should hear anything else about this, I would appreciate it if you would let me know. I am wondering whether there is anything one could do for the boy who is in prison. His English visa I suppose cannot have any value now, since the German authorities probably would not release anybody to England. Do you think it might? Have you any idea what else one could do? There are still possibilities for a South or Central American visa, although these things change from day to day. I have heard so little from Germany in recent months that I do not know what their practice is and whether one could ask for permission to leave the country. His prison term must be *ended this summer [it would officially end in December 1940]. Do you think that his mother could make a new application from Lublin, or do you think I could write, or do you have any other idea as to what could be done. If it should be necessary to ask a lawyer, I would be glad to pay for it.*

There is nothing much I can tell you about myself which I haven't written in my last letter . . . life is always the same, working pretty much and trying not to be too overwhelmed by what is going on in the world. If we were to speak over the phone now our conversations would not be so different from what they were then, excepting that things have become still worse.

I hope you are in good health and able to enjoy some of the beauties of Geneva in spite of all. I am always very grateful indeed for all you have done for my cousin, which I shall never forget.

Yours, Erich Fromm

By mid-1940, the situation for Heinz was bleak. He was unable to use his visa for Great Britain, and without a new visa and a means to leave Germany, Heinz's life was in danger. Erich continued his seemingly inexhaustible search and now focused all his efforts on securing a visa for Shanghai. It was one the few places that European Jews were able to find refuge because of its minimal visa requirements. As a result, the demilitarized Shanghai International Settlement soon provided a safe haven for approximately 18,000 Jewish refugees, most of whom remained there until the end of the war.

Learning of Erich's efforts, Gertrud wrote from the ghetto to express her deep gratitude and to do what she could to speed things along for Heinz.

Poznań, June 6, 1940

My dear, good Erich!

How should I thank you for this great help? I really have no words for it. How happy I was to be able to tell Heinz straight away! It is a crucial help for him. I can't tell you how scared I was that this trip to Shanghai would not happen. I hope to hear from the aid association when a passage to Shanghai is possible, so that I can still petition for clemency and a possible early release.

I wrote to you some time ago regarding Heinz's visa, and gave you the addresses of Dr. Ernest Levy, Seattle, Wash. U.S.A. 5026, 22nd Ave and that of William Reichert, 727 Atlantic Ave Boston, Mass., which I am repeating to you today, so that they can help you collect the guarantee amount. Dr Ernst Levy is a cousin of Georg, who offered to help me with this.

Let me also reiterate that you shouldn't send me anything now if you make such sacrifices for Heinz. I'll find a way to help myself somehow, but the boy is unable to help himself. Until now your money transfers have arrived punctually every month and have been an enormous help to me. You can imagine what kind of support [your aunt] Sophie [Engländer] was to me. In fact, I've recovered well and Wolfgang is also feeling better. The summer is wonderful here, I enjoy every good hour gratefully and I am now provided with the most important things.

With heartfelt gratitude,

Your Trude

Taking his cue from Gertrud, Erich immediately wrote to Ernest Levy. He did not mince words when it came to describing the urgency of Heinz's situation: "*in view of the whole circumstances, it is quite possible that his life depends on having this possibility to go to Shanghai.*"[22] Erich succeeded in getting Heinz a visa for Shanghai. But the challenge was now to ensure that Heinz could leave Germany given that he was officially "stateless." The extent of the problem becomes clear in a letter that Heinz wrote from prison to Sophie in Berlin on August 28, 1940:

From my cousin Dr. Fromm, I received $160 travel money to Shanghai, and he also left the necessary $400 deposit there. So you see, financially, I'm being taken care of to the greatest possible extent. For the time being, however, there is no sea connection from here to Shanghai. Since I am stateless, I have to leave Germany immediately after my sentence

> has expired (12/8/40), so I cannot wait here until the sea route to Shanghai is possible again... I urgently need a transit visa for a neutral country neighboring Germany, from which I can continue my journey to Shanghai, or where I can stay until the sea or land route is possible there. I now urge you to do everything in your power to get me a Swedish transit visa.

When Heinz's prison term finally came to an end in December 1940, all the planning for a visa came to naught. Two policemen were waiting for Heinz at the prison exit. He was promptly arrested for a second time and taken to the main police station at Berlin's Alexanderplatz. From Berlin, Heinz was transferred to the concentration camp of Sachsenhausen. Two communists who six years earlier had been tried alongside Heinz were released. They weren't Jewish. After two years in Sachsenhausen, Heinz would be deported to Auschwitz, dashing the hopes of his family members and those who, like Fromm, had tried so desperately to help.

Letters from Ostrow-Lubelski

In early 1941, only a month after Heinz was sent to Sachsenhausen, Gertrud began a correspondence with Lisa Jacobs, a woman who lived outside New York.[23] Lisa had written to the ghetto to ask how she could be of help to those in need and her letter was given to Gertrud. This led to a correspondence between them that became an increasingly important as a source of emotional support and sustenance for Gertrud. The letters Gertrud wrote are revealing and insightful. Her reflections on the nature of human relating and love, and the fundamental importance of giving freely of oneself to others in the midst of tragedy, are deeply moving. The letters also demonstrate Fromm's continued efforts to help. I have selected a number of passages to convey their overall content.

In her first letter to Lisa, Gertrud reflects widely on her experience and the meaning of deprivation:

> *Ostrow-Lubelski, January 29, 1941*
>
> *Your questions interest me. I appreciate people who inquire deeply and try to get to the bottom of things. Of course, finding clear answers to clear*

questions is naturally difficult. Given how much a community falls apart into individual existences, and how the "common" exists only as an idea, it is a challenge for anyone who wants to report on a group of people and the effects that events have on them...

We were resettled here from Posen—more than a year ago placed in this rustic little town populated by Jewish-Polish inhabitants...

If you can get used to not expecting anything for yourself in life, really nothing, then you free yourself, at the same time, from dissatisfactions in the present as well from a fear of the future. One can learn to experience life as a "gift" so that it excludes any demand. You are happy poor, you encounter the difficulties serenely and you make every effort to help your fellow human being.

Throughout her captivity, Gertrud's thoughts shift between the needs of those she cares for in the ghetto and the needs of her far-flung children, about whose whereabouts and well-being she knows very little:

Ostrow-Lubelski, April 15, 1941

My eldest, [Heinz] of whom I wrote, is in the Oranienburg concentration camp.[24] *The camp rules, which are preprinted onto every letter, say, among other things: "Anything can be bought in the camp." So I wrote to my son immediately that he should say straight away how much money he needs. He has just answered me: "I accept your tenderness with great thanks. I have daily shopping." If my son, who is extremely recalcitrant in such matters, speaks of great gratitude, then he absolutely needs it. Because he has only ever thought not to burden me.*

There isn't any way I can actually help him, because one can't send any money from here. In any case, it simply isn't possible because I don't have anything and can only just keep my head above water. I used to get a contribution from a relative in New York [Erich Fromm], which unfortunately has not arrived the past two months. So we are both surviving only from [care] packages and the sale of our possessions. I have very dear relatives in Berlin [the Engländers] who have touchingly made every effort for my son and me, but they no longer have anything themselves. My cousin [David Engländer] *is a retired highschool teacher, which you have to take into account. They have sent my son* [Heinz] *a few marks anyway, but it's not enough. He has been managing without for many years and the last time I saw him he looked wretched.*

As time passes Gertrud's letters take on a philosophical tone, reflecting her struggle to hold on to a sense of humanity.

Ostrow-Lubelski, July 13, 1941

As important as it has become for me that you have included me in your circle of care, what really lifts me up and supports me is the fact itself: that a person draws from her own deep source and joyfully gives it to others to experience. It is this power of goodness alone that I so admire. I have no more admiration for cleverness, education, ability, if goodness is not there first, if goodness it is not completely determinative, at the center of being, and everything radiates out from it. . . . How it is possible that even with all of this so-called intelligence, civilization has not brought people even one jot further! I believe deeply in the strength of goodness and love and in its eternal and immortal power. It sustains me, when I think about it, that maybe my days will not be entirely pointless, if only a little bit [of goodness and love] *can radiate out from me to others, maybe to some child or a young woman, maybe to a young person who is engaging life and can carry forth this spark.*

Ostrow-Lubelski, September 17, 1941

I am struck with certainty that I want to pass on this love that I receive, so that this goodness can become effective as a living force. It calms me and reduces the shame I feel.

Nazi Germany and its collaborators began the systematic murder of European Jews in the summer of 1941. Throughout the latter half of 1942 and 1943, following the implementation of the Final Solution, inhabitants of ghettos in Eastern Europe began to be "liquidated." Either the mass killings took place directly, when the Jewish communities of entire towns and villages were rounded up and shot by *Einsatzgruppen*, or victims were sent to so-called killing centers.[25]

In Ostrow-Lubelski, the Nazis appear to have conducted mass killings, or *Aktionenen*, along with deportations to killing centers in May and October 1942. Bronia Waserman-Eckhaus, who like her husband Mechl Eckhaus survived the killing squads, describes what happened to the Jews of Ostrow Lubelski: "All were murdered, killed in 'Aktions' by the Nazis at the end of 1942. Mostly the innocent victims were assembled by order of the armed and powerful Nazis and their collaborators, and shot then thrown into pits around the city. Many still alive—all thrown in together and covered with soil. Some were sent to Maidanek, to the gas chambers."[26]

Gertrud's letters demonstrate that she somehow managed to survive in Ostrow-Lubelski for another year and a half, even after the deportations and mass killings described by Waserman-Eckhaus. Her final letters reflect the challenge of survival amid inhumane conditions:

Ostrow-Lubelski, End of February, 1943

The pain must not solidify and harden. I have already gone through many gates of suffering; they did not lead me into darkness. Like a blind person, when all the senses sharpen, my soul lights torches so I don't lose my way as my life darkens.

It is as though all my energy is taken away and consumed; as if the essential living force alone sustains the torches. And this need feeds new energy, that is life-sustaining. So I experience the life-saving warmth, the living proximity of other people like a blood transfusion in the midst of excessive blood loss. It cannot be compared, not a single word; it is the innermost truth. Do you feel what you have given me, how you help me with the care that benefits me, that sustains me?

It would be best for me now to be intensively active and to help as well as I can. Unfortunately, it won't be possible. The misery prevents me from confronting the need. There are hardly any who can help or are capable of helping, only those who are in need of help. How this weighs on me. The thought of finding a way through is tormenting. People say it is not possible and the conditions seem to confirm it. But I want to find a way regardless: if it is not possible, then the impossible needs to be attempted, because people are perishing of weakness. They are being lost: fathers mourned by their families, mothers mourned by their children.

And I can only modestly give of my own and share to the outermost limit. I can only really help very few. I cannot slow the giant wheel of fate. Ever since the packages have stopped arriving, the need is without end.

Ostrow-Lubelski, April 22, 1943

Every fear of change has fallen away from me. I have lived a full and rich life, and it no longer matters to me whether it now ends with a long turn around or is cut short. As long as I can be useful, I want to do it. And who can say to me that under different circumstances I can't do this just as well or even better?

Written on a plain postcard, this was Gertrud's last known communication. She adds, simply, that she has to leave Ostrow-Lubelski to make room for new arrivals. It is believed that she was deported to Treblinka and murdered there a short time later. Her son, Wolfgang, had died in the ghetto one year earlier.[27]

Letters of Sophie Engländer

The letters of Fromm's aunt, Sophie Engländer, were written from Berlin over a three-and-a-half-year period, from March 1939 until September 1942 (Figure 1.2). They were addressed to her younger daughter, Eva Krakauer (born 1901). After acquiring the necessary visas, Eva, her husband Bernhard Krakauer (born 1892), and their two children left for La Paz, Bolivia, in the spring of 1939. The Engländer's older daughter, Anna-Ruth Breslauer, had already departed for Antofagasta, Chile, with her husband Wilhelm Breslauer and their only child.

From the correspondence, we learn about the well-being and whereabouts of all the Krause family members. The letters, in this sense, become a running report of daily life amid growing uncertainty, of immigration and separation, and of rare moments of reunion among those who have already managed to escape. Rosa Fromm and her son Erich are mentioned throughout. Fromm's mother, Rosa, was a favorite sibling and a beloved aunt and is referred to with the endearment "Tante Rosinchen." Rosa and Sophie were clearly fond of one another, a sentiment that is also reflected in Sophie's attitude toward her nephew, Erich.

Figure 1.2 Sophie Engländer and David Engländer, 1934, Berlin
Courtesy of the Erich Fromm Archive, Tübingen.

Sophie's letters are full of emotion, longing, and hope. Yet little by little, her tone changes as opportunities for leaving Germany evaporate. Once the gravity of their situation becomes evident, Sophie turns her focus more and more to her connection with family, friends, and acquaintances, those who were able to leave in time. The sustaining thread throughout the letters is Sophie's heartfelt wish to see her children again. Sophie wrote her last letters in the summer of 1942, when the deportations from Berlin were reaching their height. The entire Jewish community was facing the same fate. The final letter was written the day before she and her husband, David Engländer, were deported to Theresienstadt on September 1, 1942.

In her first letter Sophie thanks Eva for the note her daughter sent en route to Stockholm, where the family would begin their long sea voyage to Bolivia:

Berlin, March 10, 1939

My dear children,

This morning your letter from Stralsund [a German city on the Baltic coast] *arrived and gave us great joy. The children appear to have been exemplary. Hopefully the border crossing with the ferry and the onward trip to Stockholm will be just as uneventful. . . . Because I wrote down all the dates, I was able to follow you in my thoughts and knew that you are now there.*

The letters during the first months of separation are full of longing, and the pain of separation is still very new and raw. It is hard to imagine just how powerful the absence of her children and grandchildren must have been, shaped by the uncertainty of knowing if they would ever see one another again. Details of daily life are interspersed with thoughts about how emigration and a reunion might be achieved:

Berlin, August 11, 1939

Hopefully we can really experience my next birthday with you. I can't even put into words how nice that would be. For us, in any case, it is wonderful to know that you won't mind the sacrifice of having us with you soon—and if it happens or not, we will always thank you for that. It would be important to know how much foreign exchange is necessary. Unfortunately, it will be much more than you needed, because we probably need flagship money and half of the ship tickets must be paid in foreign currency, plus the journey from Africa or from Antofagasta to La Paz. Maybe Erich can contribute something and perhaps with support from an aid society, but just imagine what sums would be necessary to pay for this. I can't imagine that we can get the necessary funds. . . . It will be a while before everything is sorted. In any case, we now have hope and with this hope I am diligently learning Spanish.

In a postcard written the day after Nazi Germany's invasion of Poland, the reality of war is recounted side by side with the effects of Berlin's antisemitic policies:

Berlin, September 2, 1939

Since I don't know if the airmail is still working, I want to at least write you a card. We haven't received any news from you this week. It would be terrible if channels of communication were to falter. . . . We had wanted to be able to remain outside [of Berlin] because of the nice weather at least until the middle of September. But then we suddenly had to return because of the war. You don't need to worry about us. We are healthy and have everything we need.

Berlin, October 8, 1939

Sophie writes to Eva to tell her that she received a letter from a mutual acquaintance who *"just made it out* [of Germany] *before the deadline"* with news about Tante Rosinchen:

Tante Rosinchen has arrived in London . . . what a shame it is that she isn't already with Erich. We are unable to get any news from her directly.

A few months later there is a lag in correspondence with her daughter, presumably as a result of delays in the mail due to the war. Sophie grows increasingly worried and looks for ways to contact her children:

Berlin, November 10, 1939

Because no dispatches can be sent from here without special permission, we will write an airmail letter to Erich today with the request that he telegraph you that we are all well.

After a letter from Eva arrives the next day, Sophie expresses her heartfelt relief that everyone is in good health and adds that she will write another airmail letter to Erich telling him that *"we received news from you"* and that *"he does not need to telegraph you."*

The difficulties in communication continue between November 1939 and March 1940, though Sophie's letters eventually reach Eva. Sophie often raises the question of whether there has been any news of Erich, because she hasn't received any letters from him.[28] As the gravity of the situation for Berlin's Jewish community sets in, Sophie expresses a rare note of despair about ever securing an exit visa:

Berlin, January 11, 1940

In regard to the visa, it seems to be quite hopeless. As I already wrote in the previous letter, don't worry about us in this regard. As long as the war continues it would have been so difficult anyway that it hardly seems as though it could have been possible. Unfortunately, we were not careful in our choice of American relatives and not one of them is wealthy. By the way, at our request Kurt Wertheim [a family member for whom Erich signed an affidavit] *undertook some research to find our relatives in Monroe* [presumably in New York State] *(he happens to be nearby and coincidentally has relationships). But there isn't any wealth there either and the people are in part already much older than I am.*

Sophie's disappointment at not finding sufficient financial support is palpable and was undoubtedly shared by her daughters, who kept searching for ways to help their parents escape from Germany. None of their relatives in the United States appeared to have enough money to pay the steep costs necessary to leave, and as I will describe in Chapter 3, it is worth noting that Fromm was paying for visas and signing affidavits for many different relatives and colleagues at the time.[29]

Over the following months Sophie inquires multiple times with Eva as to whether she has heard anything from Erich. Finally, on March 9, 1940, Sophie writes,

Berlin, March 9, 1940

Just imagine, a few days ago I received a letter from Erich from November 11, 1939, that was en route for over four months. He wrote about Tante Rosinchen's well-being and that he will be writing to you very soon. But you appear not to have received his letter. If you should write him, tell him that his letter took four months. His address is still the same.

Berlin, November 3, 1940

Today Trude [Gertrud Brandt] *wrote that Erich transferred money to her. The bank there needs to confirm with Erich's bank, so it can still take some time. It will of course be a great help for Trude. Write to Erich for us with warmest wishes and don't forget to tell him that his letter was en route for four and a half months.*

Berlin, June 20, 1941

Today we found out that the Heinz [Brandt's] *situation is really hopeless and every effort was in vain. You can tell Tante Rosinchen, in case my*

letter shouldn't reach her. It has all come to naught. Erich has been really wonderful and spared no money or effort. Trude's fate is really awful.

Erich's concern for his family members at the time also included his aunt and uncle, Johanna and Martin Krause. Late in 1941 he signed an affidavit for them to gain entry into the United States. But the hurdles were enormous. On November 1, 1941, Sophie writes Eva to note that *"Uncle Martin and Aunt Johanna have telegraphed Erich in an effort to arrange for travel to Cuba. They received a reply that he initiated the process. Uncle Martin has foreign relations which makes it more possible."*

On December 8, 1941, Sophie wrote a postcard to notify Eva her 124th letter had finally arrived, but that several recent letters were still missing. Sophie was numbering the individual letters, so that she and her daughter could keep track of the post. Sophie adds, with apology, that she is only writing a postcard because it is likely to pass through German censorship more quickly and that there is also an airmail letter on the way. She then adds, *"Next week we will write another letter. Don't worry if you don't get any mail from us. Your post has problems too. For the third time, we wish you both all the very best for your birthdays."*

In fact, there is no record of the letters that Sophie sent. Instead, there is a 6-month gap between Sophie's postcard on December 8, 1941, and her next letter on July 13, 1942. There can be many possible explanations for the interruption. Sophie's letters could have been held back or lost in the process of being mailed. But whatever the reason, they clearly failed to reach Eva. When reflecting on this gap in the communication, it is also hard to overlook the ever-worsening situation faced by Sophie and the remaining members of Berlin's Jewish community, the largest proportion of which were elderly and female. Financial worries were often at the forefront of their minds, but their chief concern was for the well-being of their children. Together, they sought to support one another, creating a community in the midst of fear and longing.[30] At the time, Nazi authorities were forcing Jewish residents to move into so-called Jewish houses and to wear a yellow Star of David. Jewish children who remained in the city were driven out of regular schools and forced into overcrowded Jewish schools. The Jewish population was essentially being segregated and concentrated in preparation for deportation.

What had seemed unimaginable just 3 years earlier, when Sophie's letters to her daughter began, was now a cruel reality: Berlin's Jewish community was being actively arrested and deported to concentration camps and ghettos. The deportations from Berlin increased exponentially in the autumn of 1941 and reached their height in the late spring of 1942. Sophie's final letters are wistful and full of hope for news of her children and grandchildren. Despite her carefully chosen words, the crushing reality of the situation breaks through:

Berlin, July 13, 1942

This is now the fourth airmail letter that we are writing to you. I very much doubt that it will ever reach you . . . previously we had written three steamer letters and two letters to each of you through the Red Cross.

Each and every day, we wait as parents for a letter by airmail, though unfortunately in vain. . . .

We haven't heard anything from Tante Rosinchen, even though we wrote several letters through the Red Cross. . .

I have already written that Uncle Martin and Aunt Johanna have been in Warsaw [Ghetto] since Easter. We often receive news from them. Uncle Martin is struggling with bile disease and Aunt Johanna's health is, as always, shaky. You can imagine how much we miss them. . . .

Will we ever receive letters from you again? What a joy it always was for us! We looked forward to it all week! Now I have only the one wish, to once again receive letters from you. . . .

You can imagine how terribly worried we are about you. Now it's been over three years since you left, and yet we're happy about it and just wish only one thing, that you are well! Do not worry about us. We are old and have lived our lives. We have had a good and meaningful life, because we have good and well-advised children and grandchildren of whom we can be proud. We have had siblings with whom we lived in the greatest harmony. How wonderful it was in our beloved Hohenberge when we were all together.[31] *Don't think me sentimental for writing all of this. But in these times, one doesn't know how much longer one can still correspond.*

Your photos are all sitting on our desk or hanging on the wall above it, and your faces are smiling at me. In my innermost heart there is still a faint hope of seeing you again. Do not lament the fact that we have not been able to join you. We share this fate with so many others. It just wasn't possible and how many others already had visas and were unable to leave.

Greetings to Tante Rosinchen and to Erich... [many additional relatives are mentioned by name]

Once again, all the very, very best! Stay healthy, enjoy every happy minute and don't forget that alongside much sorrow, there is also much beauty in the world. Many, many warm greetings to you all, my beloved big and small ones.

Berlin, August 29, 1942

We are so happy that you are successful and that you are there. How much harder it would be if it was different, although we are so worried about you. For your birthday, dear Wilhelm [Wilhelm Breslauer was the husband of her daughter Anna-Ruth], *we were at your parents and drank coffee to your health. A couple of days later, the parents* [Samuel and Bertha Breslauer] *travelled to Theresienstadt, near Prague.*

We will probably go there [Theresienstadt] *in the next while, but do not know the exact date yet. We are glad that we will see each other there again* [speaking of the Breslauers]. *Father Breslauer's friend, Dr. Alexander, is there too. Likewise, Aunt Flora and countless friends and acquaintances. Aunt Hulda leaves her apartment the day after tomorrow. It is supposed to be good for us old people there, especially with the climate and the surroundings. Regrettably, regrettably, Martin and Johanna are not there* [but in the Warsaw Ghetto.] *We haven't heard from them in weeks and I am terribly worried as Uncle Martin was still weakened by his bile disease.*

Just stay healthy and don't worry about us. I always repeat it in every letter, because I do not know which one will reach you: we have had many good and beautiful things in life, wonderful children and grandchildren, in whom we have the greatest joy. That is worth so much; when you're old, you really know what that means.

At the end of the letter she asks her daughter to send her dearest greetings to Tante Rosinchen and to Erich.

Berlin, September 1, 1942

Tomorrow we won't be in our apartment any longer. We are going to Theresienstadt, to join the Breslauers, Aunt Flora and countless acquaintances.

We still have so much to do that I can't possibly respond to your letter in any detail. We are glad that you are all well and that the children are happy and such good students. The parents Breslauer [Samuel and Bertha Breslauer] *will be happy when we share this news with them.*

We wish with all our heart that you may remain healthy. Maybe there will be a reunion. I greet and kiss you a thousand times and I remain, in love, your Omi und Opa.

This was Sophie's last known communication. Sophie's earlier comment that Theresienstadt *"is supposed to be good for us old people . . . especially with the climate and the surroundings"* was either a reflection of the propaganda surrounding the camp, or more likely, an attempt to conceal the fearsome reality from her daughters. Either way, her words are unimaginably sad. She and her husband, David, were among the 33,000 victims who died at Theresienstadt. Around the same time, Martin and Johanna Krause were sent from the Warsaw Ghetto to the concentration camp of Trawniki, where they were killed.

Before the Nazi rise to power, Berlin's Jewish community had numbered 160,000. When the deportations began, there were 73,000 German Jews still living in Berlin. By the autumn of 1942 most of this number, including the Engländers, their friends, and relatives, had been deported on trains that left from the Grünewald S-Bahn station. On June 16, 1943, the Nazi regime declared that Berlin was officially *Judenfrei* (free of Jews). At war's end in May 1945 only 8,000 members of the original community still lived in Berlin, having survived in hiding or as a result of being married to non-Jews.[32] In her far-reaching study, *Between Dignity and Despair: Jewish Life in Nazi Germany*, the historian Marion Kaplan states that by the war's end, "of the over 500,00 Jews who had lived in Germany at the beginning of the Nazi era, only approximately 15,000 German Jews survived within the pre-1938 borders."[33]

When Fromm died in 1980, a copy of Sophie's letter to her children from August 29, 1942, was found among his personal documents. He had carried Sophie's words with him for nearly 40 years, having moved in that time from New York to Mexico and then to Switzerland.

Afterward

When we encounter the history of Holocaust, it is usually through the sheer weight of numbers—six million Jewish victims, of which over one million were children.[34] We are easily confounded and overwhelmed. In the process, however, the individual experiences of persecution, terror, and suffering often remain in the background. Studying the letters of Gertrud and Sophie challenges our carefully constructed social filters. It helps us to understand the terrible consequences of a society bent on the persecution and destruction of its own citizens. Bearing witness to the experience of Gertrud and Sophie and knowing of the fears and traumas they endured, even if only from afar, breaks through the distance of history. Their lives were as real as our own today. Learning their stories is also vitally important as the last survivors leave us. It gives us a glimpse into the immense and unimaginable suffering that occurred. Narrating what we know about their lives is about not forgetting. How we talk about the Holocaust is important. It informs the way we respond to the catastrophe and shapes what future generations will know and remember.

I felt privileged to be able to translate Gertrud's and Sophie's letters. The women I came to know were highly intelligent, incredibly strong, and immensely caring. We grieve their deaths. But throughout the process of researching their letters and the impact of the Holocaust on Fromm's life and work, there was a question that continued to haunt me: What does it mean for me, a third-generation German, to share the words of Gertrud and Sophie with you? How might my family history implicate me in the very crimes that led to their murders? These are not easy questions to answer, but they are the kinds of questions that we are surely obliged to ask.

A willed and willful amnesia must not be allowed to take the place of informed understanding. Denial and dissociation remain powerful forces, especially in the face of historical trauma. Among my generational peers in

Germany, I encounter an ever-increasing weariness with Germany's memory culture and a wish to avoid any association with its dark history: "It's so long ago. Why ask questions now?" "I'm tired of feeling guilty." "I know it happened. Isn't that enough?" Regardless of who we are or where we live, we are familiar with these kinds of reactions. We don't want to be burdened by a criminal past that is not of our making. But histories of perpetration have long shadows. They reach into the present and shape the world we see around us today.

As Fromm shows us over and over, we simply cannot escape history. The philosopher Alistar MacIntyre (1981) captures this viewpoint when he states, "We are born with a past and, whether we like it or not, whether we recognize it or not, we become the bearers of that history and culture" (pp. 205–206). What will we find if we turn toward that history, rather than away from it? Let me draw on my own German family to illustrate. I learned about the Holocaust from my parents at an early age. When I was a child, they shared with me the horrors committed by Nazi Germany and taught me about the obligation to remember. But as so often happened in German families, just as one door to the past was opened, another remained closed.

When members of my family gathered, talk was of *schreckliche Zeiten*—of the terrible times and the suffering endured by Germans during and after the war. I knew of the destruction, loss, and death that my relatives lived through; of houses destroyed by bombs; of nights in bomb shelters; of fear and of hunger; of fallen fathers, uncles, and brothers; and of the long imprisoned. There seemed to be a tacit agreement among three generations of my family to maintain these familiar narratives, while keeping the stories of Gertrud and Sophie and millions of other victims of the Holocaust at bay.

Nor do I have any comparative memory of talking about what my grandparents actually did or believed in relation to the Nazi regime. My family history, like so many others, remained shrouded in shades of gray, never distinct enough to make out more than a ghostly contour of what might be lurking, waiting to be called out and known. It was only late in life, as if by chance and circumstance, that I spied an unfamiliar photograph of my young grandfather in uniform, the man I had known and loved as a child. I struggled to make room for a history at odds with the fond memories of the time we spent together during my regular childhood visits. I did not know that my grandfather applied to the Nazi Party in 1936, was inducted a year later, and participated in the National Socialist Motor Corps (*Nationalsozialistisches Kraftfahrkorps*; NSKK), the so-called car club used by the Nazi regime to indoctrinate largely middle-class Germans. Historians have demonstrated that NSKK members attended lectures on racial ideology, participated in the November Pogrom, and even provided support for mass exterminations in Eastern Europe.[35] There is little ambiguity in this history, no shades of gray. While my grandfather never directly participated in heinous crimes against humanity, it was the support that he, and millions of other Germans like him, lent Hitler and the Nazi regime that enabled those crimes to occur.

For German descendants like myself, having to reckon with the Nazi past breaks through the defenses created by our families and communities. After glimpsing the photograph of my grandfather, I confronted my mother. Our dialogue began in fits and starts. It turned out we had both been afraid to find words for what had remained unsaid. Soon my mother started to share memories that felt, at times, like an emotional torrent, long-ago experiences that were waiting to be heard. But while my mother was willing to address the Nazi past of her father, there were others who questioned my motivations. Some of my relatives no longer welcomed me into their homes. Even after eight decades, talk of the Nazi past and the Holocaust in German families can still elicit defensive postures, even outright denial.

Finding words for that which remains unspoken can be difficult. But the necessity of confronting the past and speaking out in the present should be clear. The system of perpetration in Germany could only function because of everyday individuals who remained silent and willingly looked away, or joined up and supported the Nazi cause, at least as long as it worked in their favor. The act of enabling poses as grave a threat to our society today as it did so many decades ago.

Fromm understood what it meant to speak out. He felt compelled to take a stand against hatred and destructiveness. In the next chapter, I want to consider the origins of Fromm's resolve. Fromm grew up in the same turbulent social and political contexts that gave rise to the Nazis. On the eve of the Holocaust, when the correspondence with Gertrud and Sophie began, he was 38 years old. How did his determined approach against Nazism emerge?

2
How Is This Possible?

When I first read the Holocaust correspondence, I was living in Berlin, not far from where Fromm's family members once resided. After reflecting on the letters, I wandered aimlessly through the city streets, conscious of the ghostly absence of so many who had called Berlin their home. A sense of grief seemed to emanate from the buildings that were marked by *Stolpersteine*, or "stumbling stones," embedded in the cobblestone sidewalks directly in front of doorways and entrances. There are more than 5,000 *Stolpersteine* in Berlin, each one commemorating a single victim. These markers remind us of the atrocities committed, yet they represent only a tiny fraction of the actual number of individuals who were murdered.

Fromm walked the same streets that are today lined with *Stolpersteine* when he was a child and visited with his aunt Sophie and her family. These are also the streets that Fromm knew as a young man when he lived and worked in Berlin. And only a few years later these same streets would become the marching grounds of brown-shirted paramilitary troops who spread the Nazis' racial ideology, carried out the November Pogrom, and unleashed the Holocaust.

I lived in Berlin's Charlottenburg district, only a short distance from the once-majestic synagogue on Fasanenstrasse. The synagogue, which served the city's liberal Jewish community, was destroyed by belligerent mobs who set it on fire during the night of November 9–10, 1938. But the violent attacks on the synagogue's worshipers actually began much earlier. In 1931, several years before Hitler and the Nazis were elected to power, and while Fromm was still living in Berlin, several hundred SA men stormed the synagogue, committing acts of brutal violence that foreshadowed the terror to come. The synagogue was only a short walk from the psychoanalytic office that Fromm visited each day.[1]

When reflecting on the reality of the Holocaust, it is easy to be overwhelmed by the history that played out on Berlin's streets. The persecution, deportation, and murder of Fromm's family members breaks the bounds of comprehension. When Sophie bids farewell to her daughters and

56   EDGE OF CATASTROPHE

grandchildren, writing "we don't know when we can write again," the grief is overwhelming; it lingers, a tear in the heart of the parent who knows it is likely that she will never see her children again or feel the warmth of their embrace. Gertrud's care for the children in the ghetto, where, as she says, "the misery prevents me from confronting the need," reflects the loss of her own children, whereabouts unknown. After the Holocaust, the families of those who were murdered faced the anguish of irreparable separation and loss. Entire communities were extinguished, leaving a trail of trauma to be carried over generations.

As I struggled with the knowledge of what Fromm's family members endured, I found solace in a local Berlin museum, located not far from where the majestic synagogue on Fasanenstrasse once stood. The museum housed the works of the early 20th-century German expressionist artist Käthe Kollwitz. From that point on, whenever I sought to grapple with horrors that the letters convey, there was a singular image in Kollwitz's work (Figure 2.1) that came to mind, unbidden. I want to start this chapter by reflecting on

Figure 2.1 Käthe Kollwitz, *The Parents*, 1923

what this image, and Kollwitz's powerful portrayal of human suffering, can tell us.

Two human figures, fused together in grief and pain. A man and a woman, collapsed to their knees, lean into one another for support and are enveloped in darkness, signifying despair. Their faces are hidden but their bodies speak for them. The woman's head is slumped down. The man has reached out with his left hand to console her, and with his right he covers his face, the agony too much to bear. The hands seem to express the strain, the bones and veins clearly visible, as if aging has taken place prematurely. The jagged lines where the two figures merge into one highlight their physical discomfort and emotional turmoil. The thin lines on the outsides of their bodies seem to melt into the sense of blackness that surrounds them.

The image we see is of two parents who mourn the death of their child. Their bodies are like physical shells that contain the suffering and trauma that endures within. Together, the parents have become holders of cherished memories that are now unbearably defined by absence and loss. Completed in 1923, *The Parents* is the last and most challenging of the seven woodcut prints that make up Kollwitz's series entitled, simply, "War." Shortly before she finished the series, Kollwitz returned to *The Parents* one more time because, as she wrote in her diary, "Pain is very dark."[2] Kollwitz's hope was to express the "*totality of grief.*"[3]

Kollwitz's work provides a window into a kind of anguish that defies articulation. Her art represents the deep despair that follows the loss of those whose lives are taken unjustly. As the novelist Romain Rolland later said of Kollwitz, "She is the voice of the silence of the sacrificed."[4] Kollwitz knew grief. Following the death of her own son in World War I, the image of the mother grieving her dead child became a forthright statement against the ravages of war. Indeed, Kollwitz's work reflects the social and political landscape in Germany in the aftermath of World War I, which was to play a pivotal role in Fromm's life.

Reflecting on the impact that World War I had on him, Fromm (1962a) remarked that the longer the massive conflict lasted, "the more urgent became the question how is this possible? How is it possible that millions of men continue to stay in the trenches, to kill innocent men of other nations, and to be killed and thus to cause the deepest pain to parents, wives, friends?" (p. 6). It is the same question that Kollwitz surely struggled with as she set herself the task of representing the emotional and physical burdens of loss and despair. Each time I reflect on the deaths of Gertrud and Sophie, I find myself returning to Kollwitz's image and to Fromm's question "How is this possible?" The answer surely alludes us, but as Fromm's life and work show, the struggle to respond is important.

In this chapter, I want to consider the ways in which Fromm's life in Germany shaped his response to Nazism and the Holocaust. Although Kollwitz and Fromm did not, to my knowledge, interact or know one another, Kollwitz's work gives us the means to understand and examine the social, political, and psychological contexts of Fromm's formative years. For Kollwitz, art became a way of effecting social change. For Fromm, writing became a means to educate and foster solidarity with others. Both sought to address the human cost of war and to explore avenues for social and political transformation. These parallels will provide us with a backdrop for examining Fromm's response to World War I and his struggle to live and work in the face of the emerging Nazi threat. Above all, they enable us to gain an understanding of Fromm's determined stance against injustice.

In the Wake of War

Kollwitz's incisive social realism shed light on the political forces that shaped life in interwar Germany and fed the nation's seemingly unstoppable march toward right-wing extremism. Kollwitz was herself directly affected by that history. Having grown up in a progressive household, Kollwitz arrived in Berlin at the turn of the 20th century. It was a city rife with poverty, and in her early art, Kollwitz depicted oppressed workers and women in different states of rebellion. By the outbreak of World War I in 1914, Kollwitz's stance on social justice was well established. Shortly after the start of the war, Kollwitz's youngest son, Peter, was killed in combat in Belgium. In her grief, she turned her focus to the suffering and sorrow that ensued from the savage violence of war.

In 1919, Kollwitz began work on the War series.[5] The seven woodcuts in the series all dealt with the tragedies of World War I and the emotional damage wrought on those who were left behind. In contrast to Kollwitz's earlier works, the War series, and in particular *The Parents*, drew directly from her own life experience, focusing on the pain that she and so many others were forced to endure as a result of losing loved ones. However, rather than depicting the gruesome destruction and violence of battle, Kollwitz depicted women left to face their grief and fears alone, with their partners, or with each other. This enabled her art to become a clear denunciation of war and power of patriarchy. Kollwitz's perspective on the lives of women forced to contend with malnutrition, poverty, and the death of their children evoke for me the kind of experiences described by Gertrud and Sophie in their letters.

By 1919, Kollwitz had become one of the foremost representatives of German expressionism and the first woman to be elected to the prestigious Prussian Academy of Art. Kollwitz continued to labor for many more years before she completed a memorial known as *The Grieving Parents*, which is located at the World War I war cemetery in Roggevelde, Belgium, where Peter was buried. Beginning as a monument for Peter and becoming a memorial to all victims of the war, she sculpted the figures of his mourning parents—her husband Karl and herself—kneeling, arms pressed to their chests, huddled in agony, thus transforming her intensely personal pain into a testimony to the suffering and loss of war. In a diary entry made in November 1922, Kollwitz spoke to the sense of obligation she felt to produce art that could speak to injustice: "Everyone works the way they can. . . I would like to exert influence in these times when human beings are so perplexed and in need of help" (Kollwitz, 1955, p. 104).

Kollwitz's diary entries reveal how her life intersected with her art. By comparison we know relatively little about Fromm's personal experience and thoughts. What is clear is that Fromm shared a similar outlook to Kollwitz and that their lives during the interwar years were shaped by similar social and political forces. In *Beyond the Chains of Illusion* from 1962, in a rare moment of public disclosure, Fromm acknowledged the formative effect of World War I. It was, he said, "the event that determined more than anything else my development" (Fromm, 1962a, p. 5). For the rest of his life, Fromm would theorize about the social and psychological conditions that led nations to go to war. "How is it possible that men stand in trenches for years and live like animals—and for what?" he asked. "The irrationality of human behavior impressed me in this way, and I became curious about the problem" (Fromm, 1962a, p. 7).

At the onset of war in 1914, Fromm was 14 years old, 4 years younger than Kollwitz's son Peter. While Peter was one of the millions who volunteered to fight for their Kaiser, Fromm took a different stance:

> I was a fourteen-year-old boy for whom the excitement of war, the celebration of victories, the tragedy of the death of individual soldiers I knew, were

uppermost in my experience. I was not concerned with the problem of war as such; I was struck by its senseless inhumanity. (Fromm, 1962a, p. 5)

It was at this point that Fromm's deep distrust of nationalism, which would be a guiding theme throughout his life, took root.

Fromm was enrolled in the Frankfurt's Wöhler Gymnasium and witnessed the changes in his teachers and peers. In regard to one of his teachers, Fromm remarked, "How is it possible that a man who always seemed to have been so concerned with the preservation of peace should now be so jubilant about the war?" Fromm would later ask a similar question about Germans who expressed enthusiasm for Hitler. In 1914, Fromm was "struck by the hysteria of hate against the British which swept throughout Germany ... suddenly they had become cheap mercenaries, evil and unscrupulous, trying to destroy our innocent and all too trusting German heroes. We were infected by the hate England mood" (Fromm, 1962a, p. 6). Only 20 years later another "hysteria of hate" would infect Germany, this time in the form of Nazi racial ideology.

Fromm clearly struggled to make sense of what he heard and saw, writing that "Year after year the healthy men of each nation, living like animals in caves, killed each other with rifles, hand grenades, machine-guns, bayonets; the slaughter continued, accompanied by false promises of a speedy victory, false protestations of one's own innocence" (Fromm, 1962a, p. 7). The tragic reality of war was captured by Kollwitz in a diary entry from July 1917, when she poignantly contemplated what epithet to place on Peter's gravestone: "Here lies German youth. Or: Here lie Germany's finest young men. Or: Here lie the youthful dead. Or simply: Here lie the young" (Kollwitz, 1955, pp. 82–83).

While Fromm's comments shed light on his response to the war and the virulent nationalism that fueled it, the effects of the conflict were soon seen and felt on the home front, with far-reaching consequences. Despite being far removed from the trenches, food rationing in Germany began in 1915. By the winter of 1916 there was widespread hunger, a condition that worsened with time. Estimates suggest that well over a half-million Germans died from diseases related to hunger and malnutrition.[6] Urban centers and working-class Germans were especially affected. Soldiers who returned home on furlough told of the bloodshed and carnage; those who were injured or disabled by the war became more visible with time. In the spring of 1918, with the onset of a global pandemic, the so-called Spanish flu, malnourishment, disease, and death increased exponentially.[7]

The impact of the war on Fromm's political development would be long-lasting. As Fromm states,

> When the war ended in 1918, I was a deeply troubled young man who was obsessed by the question of how war was possible, by the wish to understand the irrationality of human mass behavior, by a passionate desire for peace and international understanding. More, I had become deeply suspicious of all official ideologies and declarations, and filled with the conviction "of all one must doubt." (1962a, p. 8)

Fromm reveals that the war also had a direct, personal impact: "A number of my uncles and cousins and older schoolmates were killed in the war" (Fromm, 1962a, p. 7). In addition, Oswald Sussman, who had lived with the Fromm family between 1912 and 1914, died in the conflict. Sussman was a self-declared socialist who fostered Fromm's nascent political awareness. The influence of Sussman, together with the irrationality of the First World War, seems to have drawn Fromm toward Marxism at an early age.[8]

Beyond these various influences on his development, Fromm experienced an intensely religious upbringing. As Fromm tells it, "I was brought up in a religious Jewish family, and the writings of the old testament touched me and exhilarated me more than anything else I was exposed to.... I was moved by the prophetic writings, by Isaiah, Amos, Hosea," particularly the teaching that "nation shall not lift sword against nation, neither shall they learn war anymore; when all nations will be friends" (Fromm, 1962a, pp. 4–5), As Fromm aptly states, "what could be more exciting and beautiful to me than the prophetic vision of universal brotherhood and peace?" (Fromm, 1962a, p. 5). But being Jewish in Germany also meant being confronted with the reality of antisemitism. As Fromm admits,

> Probably the immediate reason for this absorption by the idea of peace and internationalism is to be found in the situation in which I found myself: a Jewish boy in a Christian environment, experiencing small episodes of antisemitism but, more importantly, a feeling of strangeness and of clannishness on both sides. (Fromm, 1962, p. 5)

While Fromm wrote relatively little about antisemitism, Nazi Germany's policies of racial persecution and terror against German Jews would play a determinative role in his life and work.

In the wake of Auschwitz and the untold deaths of World War II, it is easy to overlook the utter devastation wrought by World War I. Mass slaughter, mechanized combat on a scale never before seen, total civilian mobilization, and theaters of war that involved nations around globe all combined to shatter long-standing conceptions of security and continuity. The generation that survived the war was indelibly marked by the destructiveness of the years-long conflict. In Germany, as wounded and dispirited troops returned from battle, the human cost of the war began to settle in: some two million German soldiers had been killed and another 1.5 million were disabled.

Despite 4 years of battle, Germany had little to show for its effort. Poverty, suicide, and substance abuse were widespread among veterans. The Kaiser was forced to abdicate, and a German delegation made up of Social Democratic politicians from the newly minted Weimar Republic traveled to Versailles to sign the peace treaty. Germany was unprepared for the harsh penalties imposed by the Allies, who demanded massive reparation payments, demilitarization, and significant territory. Many Germans believed that they had been let down, if not "stabbed in the back" by their new government, a view that the generals were eager to exploit as they sought to retain power. Those on the political left saw an opportunity to establish a new socialist government. But the attempted proletarian revolution in 1918–1919 was violently suppressed.

In the aftermath, Kollwitz produced a woodcut that depicted the funeral of Karl Liebknecht (Figure 2.2), the socialist leader who was ruthlessly murdered alongside Rosa Luxemburg by right-wing nationalists in Berlin's Tiergarten. Kollwitz was asked by Liebknecht's family to draw his body. On the morning of January 25, 1919, she went to the morgue to make her drawings. Later that day she joined the funeral as Liebknecht was buried together with 31 other political victims. Although Kollwitz was not politically active in a formal sense, the mass demonstration that followed the funeral made a deep impression on her. Kollwitz's woodcut was an evocative and moving memorial to Liebknecht and a powerful indictment of Germany's conservative establishment.

Following the loss of the monarchy, many Germans experienced a kind of psychological and political vacuum. Germany had little experience with democracy, and despite the progressive policies of early Weimar governments, from women's emancipation to social welfare programs, the benefits of parliamentary rule often went unnoted. The economic and social crises of the era meant that the democratic regime struggled to get full support from

HOW IS THIS POSSIBLE? 63

Figure 2.2 Käthe Kollwitz, *In Memoriam Karl Liebknecht*, 1920

the population. The hyperinflation of 1923 and the Great Depression that followed the stock market crash of 1929 exacerbated underlying weaknesses. As the political center fragmented, a divided populace drifted toward the radical extremes. Communists sought revolutionary change and engaged in a bitter political battle with their left-wing rivals, the Social Democratic Party. On the right, ultranationalist sentiment fueled the rise of Hitler and the Nazi Party.

Personal and Political Turbulence

Fromm thus entered into adulthood in a period of social and political upheaval. His deep religious learning inspired a sense of responsibility for others and for a healing of the world in which he lived. His training as a sociologist helped him to understand how human experience is structured by social forces. But it was his introduction to psychoanalysis that proved determinative. Psychoanalysis enabled Fromm to analyze and interpret the lure of authoritarianism and the turbulence that surrounded him, and it offered a means to explore the motivations that spurred people to act in ways that were often against their own interests.

Fromm was introduced to psychoanalysis by Frieda Reichmann. They met through mutual friends, and he began visiting Frieda in the early 1920s while she was working at the Weisser Hirsch Sanatorium in Dresden. Frieda was 11 years his senior, but they shared many interests and were intellectually well matched. Together, Frieda and Erich hatched a plan to establish a psychoanalytic therapeutic community (*das Therapeutikum*) in Heidelberg, which had two noteworthy characteristics. It was intended specifically for a Jewish clientele, and everyone who lived or worked there, including the cook and the cleaners, entered into analysis with Frieda.[9] This included Erich, who thus became one of her patients as well as her lover.[10] Frieda and Erich seemed to recognize the precariousness of their situation and conferred with a senior psychoanalyst, Karl Landauer. He advised them that they could get married once they finished the analysis. By today's standards, of course, Landauer's advice would be manifestly ill-founded and against basic ethical principles. Yet, in the mid-1920s, the limited understanding of power differentials and erotic transferences within a therapeutic relationship seemed to make such marriage a feasible, if ultimately doomed, possibility.

Initially at least, their relationship prospered. Frieda and Erich shared a similar outlook and together made the decision to give up their Jewish orthodoxy. Frieda supported Erich when he underwent an analysis with Wilhelm Wittenberg in Munich, which was subsequently followed by a period of supervision with Landauer at the Southwest German Psychoanalytic Working Group in Frankfurt. In order to finish his psychoanalytic training, Fromm moved to Berlin in 1928, where he completed a training analysis with Hanns Sachs, a personal friend of Freud's and one of the earliest adherents of psychoanalysis.

In the 1920s, Berlin was a city of deep contrasts. By the time Fromm arrived, Berlin had experienced decades of uninterrupted growth. The rapidly industrializing economy lured huge numbers of workers, but the city was unprepared to meet their needs. The plight of Berlin's workers was reflected in their destitute living conditions and the lack of adequate public sanitation. In her art, Kollwitz depicted people enduring illness, hunger or death, scenes that she observed on a daily basis throughout her 49-year marriage to a doctor in one of Berlin's working-class neighborhoods. Berlin's oft-impressive street fronts hid the poverty that lay behind. Apartments buildings were built around a series of inner courtyards, so that only the front of the buildings that abutted the street were open to the air and light. Apartments that faced the inside were small, dark, and frequently overcrowded.

At the same time, Berlin became a European center for innovative arts and culture. The city embraced a culture of permissiveness and experimentation and came to exemplify the liberal and democratic outlook of Weimar Germany. Psychoanalysis in Berlin thrived and reflected the cultural modernism of the city. The Berlin Institute was at the forefront of the growing profession. It was infused with radical and progressive ideas, and many of the analysts who trained at the Institute saw themselves as working toward social transformation. Among the leaders of this outlook was Otto Fenichel, who organized and led a group known as the Children's Seminar, named for its many younger members. It met every 2 weeks until the threat posed by the Nazis forced its members to disperse in 1933. Fromm was a key member of the group and was lauded by Fenichel, who judged his work to be of "fundamental importance" (cited in Jacoby, 1983, p. 71).

In the early 1920s, the Berlin Institute set up the Poliklinik, a free treatment center based on the belief that psychoanalysis should be available to everyone, regardless of income or social class. All of the Berlin analysts were obliged to donate their time or financial support. The Poliklinik was flooded with applications, and by the time Fromm arrived, it had already been expanded. Fromm's association with the free clinic soon led him to establish a similar clinic alongside the new Frankfurt Psychoanalytic Institute. Fromm came to see psychoanalysis as an inherently progressive movement that connected individual well-being with societal well-being. This viewpoint would be at the center of Fromm's professional development, but the rapidly deteriorating political situation in Germany made such a progressive approach increasingly difficult to sustain.

By the late 1920s, the democratic government of the Weimar Republic had survived multiple challenges, so there was no reason to believe it would fail. But the rapid rise of the Nazi Party as a viable political force proved insurmountable. The Nazis were initially a fringe right-wing paramilitary group, made up of disaffected and nationalistic World War I veterans. After the so-called Munich Beer Hall Putsch in 1923, which landed Hitler in prison, the Nazis changed their tactics and became involved in organized politics. Though they had little early success, the mass unemployment that followed the financial crash provided fertile ground for the recruitment of new members.

The economic crisis in Germany was matched by a series of political crises. Political parties sought to promote the interests of their supporters, leading to a host of conflicting economic demands. From 1930 to 1933, parliamentary government functioned in name only. Germany was essentially ruled by a presidential dictatorship as opposing parties took to the streets to express their demands. In working-class districts of Berlin, flags adorned with hammer-and-sickle emblems fought for prominence with swastikas. Radical political factions fought to secure support, and violent confrontations between politically affiliated paramilitary groups, the communist Red Front Fights and Nazi Brown Shirts, played out on the streets.[11]

Fromm found himself at the center of this developing political maelstrom and felt compelled to comment on the events around him. In 1928, he presented a paper on "Psychoanalysis of the Petty Bourgeoisie," a topic that soon found expression in his research on the authoritarian tendencies of German workers. In 1929, Fromm gave a lecture on "Psychoanalysis and Sociology," which pointed toward a synthesis between Freud and Marx. In 1931, he published another essay entitled "Politics and Psychoanalysis". Fromm's cross-disciplinary prowess was recognized by Max Horkheimer, who appointed him the Institute for Social Research's director of social psychology and psychoanalysis.[12]

Dangers in Davos

The start of Fromm's career as a German intellectual thus looked full of promise. But two life-threatening events intervened: a diagnosis of tuberculosis of the lungs in July 1931, and the election of the Nazi Party in January 1933. Over the next decade, Fromm's life was directly shaped by these dual threats; their emotional and physical effects lingered far longer. Fromm's health crisis seemed to mirror the political crisis unfolding in Germany. Within a relatively short period of time, more and more Germans lent their support to Hitler. In September 1930, the Nazi Party gained 18% of the vote and became the second largest party in the Reichstag. In July 1932, they gained 37% and became the largest party. In January 1933, Hitler was appointed chancellor, and in March of that year the Nazi Party gained over 44% of the vote. Decrees creating a one-party state and cementing Hitler's position as dictator were quickly passed. In short order, the Nazis banned all other political parties, outlawed trade unions, imprisoned political opponents, enacted their racial ideology, and began their reign of terror.

As these ominous political events were playing out in Berlin, Fromm was fighting a personal battle against tuberculosis. On the recommendation of his doctors, he traveled to Davos, Switzerland, to convalesce. Prior to the advent of antibiotics, tuberculosis posed a grave threat. For those who could afford it, the sanatoriums of Davos offered hope. In the 1860s, a treatment based on fresh air, sunlight, and generous amounts of food and dairy was pioneered by Dr. Alexander Spengler, who noticed that the population of Davos remained largely unaffected by tuberculosis. Treatments often lasted months on end. Although there was no medical cure, the sanatoriums of Davos at least presented the possibility of containing the disease.[13]

Davos became a place of recovery for Fromm, but he could not escape the shadow of Nazism. Germany's incendiary right-wing politics had embedded themselves in the Swiss town. Among the many Germans who lived and worked in Davos was a fanatical supporter of Hitler, Wilhelm Gustloff. In 1931, Gustloff became leader of the local chapter of the National Socialist German Workers' Party (*Nationalsozialistische Deutsche Arbeiterpartei*; NSDAP), and in 1932, he became the leader of the party for all of Switzerland. The NSDAP had a strong influence on the German community in Davos, invested heavily in local property, and bought numerous sanatoriums where staff and guests were screened according to Nazi racial values. Hitler greetings were common among German expats, and signage for the local branch of the Nazi Party could be seen alongside those for doctors' surgeries.[14]

Gustloff actively agitated against Jewish guests and anyone whom he thought might question the policies of the Nazi Party. As a result of his efforts, Davos became known as Hitler's Spa (*Hitlerbad*). After Gustloff was shot and killed by a Jewish medical student from Yugoslavia in 1936, he was turned into a Nazi martyr. Gustloff was given a state funeral in Germany and lauded by Hitler and the Nazi Party elite. His name was even used to christen the cruise ship, the MV Wilhelm Gustloff, which was sunk in the Baltic Sea by a Soviet submarine in January 1945, with the loss of about 9,400 German refugees and military personnel, a story memorialized in Günter Grass's controversial late-life novel, *Crabwalk*, about German memory and loss (Grass, 2002). Following Gustloff's assassination, local Swiss authorities sought to tamp down Nazi activity, and when the war began, Switzerland declared itself neutral, though it maintained good relations with both Germany and Italy and its banks profited over the course of the Holocaust.

Fromm first traveled to Davos in the fall of 1931 and entered quarantine in the Schatzalp Sanatorium. Until his departure for the United States in the spring of 1934, Fromm primarily resided in Switzerland. The initial phase of Fromm's illness receded in the spring of 1932, and he began to commute back and forth to Geneva to work at the Institute for Social Research, which had just relocated there from Frankfurt. Given its Marxist orientation and the fact that many of its staff were Jewish, the Institute had chosen to leave Germany even before Hitler assumed full power. Fromm's connection with the Institute during these difficult years was a lifeline, providing both intellectual and financial support.

Starting in the summer of 1932, Fromm lived in an apartment in Locarno-Monti in southern Switzerland that belonged to Karen Horney.[15] As Fromm's marriage with Frieda faltered, his friendship with Horney blossomed. Fromm originally met Horney during the regular visits that he and Frieda paid to Georg Groddeck at his sanatorium in Baden Baden beginning in the mid-1920s. Groddeck was known to be a warm and dynamic personality, and it was in Baden Baden that Fromm also got to know the Hungarian psychoanalyst Sandor Ferenczi. Fromm would later remark that Groddeck and Ferenczi had the strongest influence on his work as a psychoanalyst.

After a downturn in his condition, Fromm was forced to return to Davos. He signed a rental contract for an apartment in Davos Platz beginning December 1, 1932. The rental contract lists Fromm's home address as Berlin, though by then he had closed down his psychoanalytic practice and entered into the full employ of the Institute. Fromm witnessed the fateful German elections of January and March 1933 from Davos and clearly hoped to be able to remain in Switzerland. However, like so many Jewish refugees living in Switzerland at the time, both he and the Institute were forced to look elsewhere for safety.

In the fall of 1933, Fromm was well enough to travel to Chicago at Horney's invitation. He gave lectures at the Chicago Psychoanalytic Institute, which was directed by Franz Alexander, and met the American academics Harald Lasswell and John Dollard, both of whom would later become important colleagues. Fromm's visit to the United States proved decisive and in the spring of 1934 he received the valuable visa that permitted him to immigrate. He began his journey in the middle of May 1934. Fromm traveled via Geneva, Paris, and Le Havre. From there he crossed to England, where he set sail from Southampton on the ocean liner George Washington and finally arrived in New York on May 31, 1934.[16] While Fromm was undoubtedly relieved to embark on his journey, he was also faced with a sobering fact: He did not know when he would next see his family members, friends, and colleagues who remained behind in Germany. The new anti-Jewish legislation of the Nazi government portended a dark future.

Toward a Theory of Human Compassion

While tuberculosis presented a constant struggle, Fromm's convalescence in Davos also provided an opportunity for periods of uninterrupted study. Fromm turned his attention to elaborating a critique of patriarchy and a theory of human compassion, two important ideas that would later influence his response to National Socialism. I want to briefly examine Fromm's approach, with the caveat that Fromm's ideas were still in the early stages of development and thus are neither complete nor always entirely clear.

In order to formulate a critique of patriarchy, Fromm focused on the values of duty, fear, and submission to authority that permeated German society. It was in this context that he became interested in the notion of matriarchy and Johann Jacob Bachofen's work *The Mother Right*, which was one of the first attempts to present a study of the evolution of the family as a social institution.[17] Fromm took his cue from Friedrich Engels, whose book *The Origin of the Family* (1884) was strongly indebted to Bachofen. Following Engels, Fromm suggested that the notion of matriarchal society "has a close kinship with the ideals of socialism" (Fromm, 1934, p. 28). He associated compassion and solidarity with the working class and contrasted these values with duty and subordination, which he said were characteristic of patriarchal societies.

Fromm believed that the study of matricentric cultures could shine light on the destructive nature of the patricentric principle. Fromm was highly critical of authoritarian attitudes and the dangers they posed when they kept people docile in the face of authority.[18] This was similar to the argument he would later develop in *Escape From Freedom*. By contrast, the appeal of a matriarchal society could be traced to the fact that "maternal love and compassion are the dominant moral principles, where injury to one's fellowman is the gravest sin, and where private property does not yet exist" (Fromm, 1934, p. 29). As Fromm wrote,

> The patricentric individual—and society—is characterized by a complex of traits in which the following are predominant: a strict superego,

guilt feelings, docile love for paternal authority, desire and pleasure at dominating weaker people, acceptance of suffering as punishment for one's own guilt, and a damaged capacity for happiness. The matricentric complex, by contrast, is characterized by a feeling of optimistic trust in mother's unconditional love, far fewer guilt feelings, a far weaker superego, and a greater capacity for pleasure and happiness. Along with these traits there also develops the ideal of motherly compassion and love for the weak and others in need of help. (Fromm, 1934, p. 41)

From today's perspective, the bifurcation of matriarchy and patriarchy rests on a questionable gender essentialism.[19] We can wonder, moreover, about the source of Fromm's personal interest in matriarchy.[20] Yet it is also important to note that Fromm was not alone in his quest to understand matriarchy. Left-wing intellectuals at the time were attracted to the promise they saw in a matriarchal alternative to patriarchal society. In 1935, Fromm's colleague Walter Benjamin wrote his own essay in praise of Bachofen and acknowledged Fromm's "remarkable study on the sociopsychological meaning of matriarchal theories" (Benjamin, 1935, p. 20; see also p. 311).[21]

The importance that Fromm placed on matriarchy also has a specific historical and situational meaning that is easily overlooked. Fromm's study of matriarchy took place while he was living in Davos. From his vantage point in Switzerland, if Fromm looked south to Italy, he would have observed that Mussolini and fascism were already firmly entrenched, while if he looked north, Hitler and the Nazi Party had just been elected to power in Germany and were in the process of establishing their racialized, totalitarian state. The ideals of fascism were not only pervasive; they were expanding, even on the streets of Davos. Those ideals valorized patriarchy and were highly critical of any notion of female emancipation. For fascists, patriarchy was bound up with an image of hypermasculinity. The leader of a fascist nation was seen as an extension of the father in a traditional patriarchal family, embodying strength and wielding authority over others. Thus, according to the Nazi ideologue Alfred Rosenberg, the Nazi state was based on male warriors and should be entirely free of the influence of women.[22] For the Nazis, the highest duty of women was to give birth and raise children in support of the German racial community, a reinterpretation to the traditional German notion *of Kinder, Küche, Kirche* (children, kitchen, church). While women were denigrated and cast in need of protection, the militarized fascist state was presented as the male embodiment of the power and authority.

It is worth remembering that this is precisely what Kollwitz sought to challenge with her powerful antiwar message. Kollwitz's critique of the fascist ideals of motherhood was surprisingly close to that of Fromm. She focused on strong women and mothers who were forced to grieve their children as a result of wars spurred on by the murderous nationalism espoused by male politicians, military leaders, and monarchs. When the Nazis were elected to power in 1933, they objected to Kollwitz's antiwar message and forced her to resign from the Prussian Academy of Art.[23] In response, Kollwitz joined with other artists to organize in opposition. In 1936, she was arrested by the Gestapo and told that she would be sent to a concentration camp if she did not reveal the names of other German artists with anti-Nazi beliefs. Kollwitz remained silent and was eventually released due to her age. From that point on, she was expressly forbidden to publish or exhibit her work. Her studio was closed, and her art was banned and classified as "degenerate."[24]

Fromm's critique of patriarchy not only challenged the dominant social norms and power structures of the time. He also took aim at Freud's pessimistic and patriarchal account of human sociality. In Freud's account, humans are predatory creatures who are forced to sacrifice their instinctual freedom in order to live together. As Freud wrote in *Civilization and Its Discontents*, "men are not gentle creatures who want to be loved . . . they are, on the contrary, creatures among whose instinctual endowments is to be reckoned a powerful share of aggressiveness" (Freud, 1930/1985, p. 302). Freud's speculative anthropology was heavily gendered. Whereas men were seen as capable of using reason to stem their inclinations, women were given to impulsive action and defined by their passions. The problem, as Carol Gilligan has observed, is that "because his psychology read patriarchy as nature, Freud did not question why sexual love is so problematic and aggression, including war, so irresistible" (Gilligan, 2010, p. 324).

Fromm developed his critique of Freud in *Social Determinants of Psychoanalytic Theory* (1935), which he likewise wrote in Davos. According to Fromm, Freud was "a classical representative of the patricentric character type" (p. 13). In this patricentric perspective, "the meaning of life lies not in the person's happiness or well-being, but in the fulfillment of duty and subordination to authority. There is no unconditional right to love and happiness" (p. 13).[25] Fromm read Freud's technical prescriptions for how psychoanalysts should interact with their patients along similar lines. Freud's emphases on "indifference," on "emotional coldness," and on being "opaque to their patients" (p. 4) were interpreted by Fromm as reflections of the patriarchal bourgeois society in which Freud lived.

By contrast, Fromm sought to emphasize the centrality of compassion in human sociality and found an ally in Ferenczi.[26] Fromm referred to Freud's attitude as a "patricentric-authoritarian, deep down misanthropic 'tolerance'" (p. 18), which he distinguished from Ferenczi's "philanthropic and affirmative attitude towards the patient" (p. 19). According to Fromm, Ferenczi recognized "how decisively important it is for patients that they feel absolutely certain of the unconditional sympathy of the analyst" and that a course of analysis could only end when the patient achieved "a feeling of equality in relation to the physician." (p. 15). Fromm thus underlined the role of "kindness" (p. 16) in the interaction, which, he said, revealed our compassionate nature as human beings.

Fromm's emphasis the quality of compassion also illustrates his proximity to Kollwitz. In her compassionate depictions of human suffering and oppression, Kollwitz sought to recognize women who had been silenced by society by offering them a voice and a face.[27] Given the prominence of such themes as grieving and death in Kollwitz's art, this affirmative aspect of her work has often been neglected. In fact, Kollwitz knew the joys of relating. In March 1928, she wrote in her diary,

> Joy in others and being in harmony with them is one of the deepest pleasures of life. Love or infatuation need not have anything to do with it. I know that in recent years I have been fortunate enough to have this splendid feeling, and I have been quite conscious of what a blessing it is. (Kollwitz, 1955, p. 116)

Kollwitz thus acknowledged the ways in which compassion could foster a deep and meaningful connection with other human beings. In the wake of the Holocaust, this idea would become central to Fromm's writings on love and solidarity and form a necessary counterpoint to human cruelty and destructiveness.

During the late 1920s and early 1930s, as the Nazis were consolidating their power base and spreading their hateful ideology, it must have seemed to Fromm that the human capacity for compassion was becoming increasingly diseased.[28] In the years that followed, events in Germany continued to spiral, and Fromm looked on with concern from his temporary refuge in Switzerland. By 1934, when Fromm boarded a ship for New York, the Nazi regime was actively implementing its anti-Jewish legislation. The contexts that shaped Fromm's early development as a sociologist and psychoanalyst enabled him to address this growing Nazi threat, but neither he nor his family members who remained behind in Germany could possibly imagine what would happen next. As the Holocaust correspondence attests, and as I will show in the next chapter, Fromm's quest to save his relatives, friends, and colleagues would become a central theme of his life as a German Jewish refugee and inalterably shape the direction of his work.

3
Yearning to Submit

"When Fascism came into power, most people were unprepared, both theoretically and practically. They were unable to believe that the human being could exhibit such propensities for evil, such lust for power, such disregard for the rights of the weak, or such yearning for submission" (Fromm, 1941, p. 8). Fromm's comments in *Escape From Freedom* are not just the musings of an intellectual. They are a deeply personal reflection on his first-hand knowledge of the rise of Hitler and National Socialism in Germany. Fromm wrote these words from the safety of New York, but in full recognition of the threat faced by family members who remained behind. While Fromm was composing the chapters of his book and reflecting on the human propensity for evil, he was engaged in a letter-writing campaign and securing affidavits to arrange safe passage out of Germany for relatives, friends, and colleagues who remained behind. The challenges were daunting. The ascendancy of antisemitism, draconian visa restrictions, and the growing drumbeats of war diminished any hope for success. In the midst of it all, writing *Escape From Freedom* provided Fromm with a voice and a sense of agency. The book was the culmination of his study of authoritarianism—the "yearning for submission," as he put it—which he carried out over the course of the 1930s. When *Escape From Freedom* was published in the summer of 1941, the hostilities in Europe had already been raging for 2 years, but the United States had yet to declare war.[1] Fromm spoke directly to an American readership that was eager to learn why Germans expressed overwhelming support for Hitler but that was still hesitant to go to war. Fromm sought to reveal the grave threat posed by fascism.

It is not an exaggeration to say that the publication of *Escape From Freedom* changed the trajectory of Fromm's life. In fact, it is still considered his most essential work and continues to be read by contemporary audiences. That Fromm wrote the book while he was grappling with the existential peril faced by his family members makes it all the more remarkable. It was precisely this unspoken dimension that gave Fromm's book and his psychology of Nazism its far-reaching resonance. As I will suggest in this chapter, it is important to understand *Escape From Freedom* not only as a response to fascism, but also as a highly personal and impassioned work that reflects Fromm's life as a German Jewish refugee.

When Fromm arrived in New York in 1934, he became a resident of Manhattan's Upper West Side, which was a haven for German Jewish refugees. Whereas the Washington Heights area of Manhattan became the most densely populated German Jewish neighborhood in the United States, and ironically named the "Fourth Reich," the Upper West Side was seen by many as the more sophisticated substitute for Weimar Berlin.[2] It was here that Fromm found a new home, surrounded by urbane émigré psychoanalysts and intellectuals. He divided his time between building a psychoanalytic practice, forging professional connections, and establishing a center for the Institute for Social Research at Columbia University. In contrast to his Institute colleagues, Fromm quickly became fluent and learned how to write in English. This enabled him to navigate between the German-speaking refugee community and his American colleagues, a process that could be challenging and complicated. On the one hand, Fromm was a newcomer forced to adjust to a foreign country. On the other, like many German Jewish refugees, Fromm struggled to reconcile his attachment to German culture and language with the fact that Germany was also the source of racial persecution and exclusion.[3] In a letter from the spring of 1936, written to Otto Fenichel, his psychoanalytic colleague from Berlin who had fled to Prague, Fromm acknowledged that "At the moment, I don't really know where I belong."[4] Fromm was speaking as much about his professional affiliation as he was about what it meant to be a German Jewish refugee.

Throughout these formative years, Fromm carried on with his daily work against the backdrop of worsening anti-Jewish legislation in Germany. He received an increasing number of pleas for help from those left behind, which meant that events in Germany were never far from his mind. Fromm sent money, attempted to secure exit visas, and communicated with international aid organizations. In 1935, he sponsored an affidavit for his estranged wife, Frieda Fromm-Reichmann, which enabled her to travel from Palestine to New York. Frieda spent her first weeks living in Erich's apartment, which provided a sense of comfort as she began her new life.[5] This was the first in a long list of affidavits arranged by Fromm. Though the records we have of this period are incomplete, existing documentation shows that from 1937 to 1941, Fromm signed affidavits for a diverse group of individuals who included the economist Peter Glueck; the theater critic and left-wing political activist Hans Siemsen; his relatives Heinz Brandt and Kurt Wertheim; and his uncle and aunt, Martin and Johanna Krause. Many more individuals wrote to Fromm, hoping that he might help them or point them in the direction of someone who could. These letters bring the fearsome reality of the time to bear, and they must have been a constant reminder for Fromm of the ever-increasing threat of fascism.[6]

Thus, by the time *Escape From Freedom* was published in 1941, Fromm had already spent nearly a decade living as a refugee, first in Switzerland and then in New York. He saw the dangers posed by Hitler and the Nazi regime and sought tirelessly to aid those in need. Above all, Fromm understood that any response to fascism needed to be swift, far-reaching, and decisive. The urgency he felt is reflected on the book's opening page, when he writes of the "present political developments and the dangers which they imply" and adds that the psychologist must "contribute to the understanding of the present crisis without delay" (Fromm, 1941, p. vii).

Social Psychoanalysis

Fromm insisted that in order for fascism to be defeated, it first needed to be explained and understood. What set *Escape From Freedom* apart from many other books at the time was Fromm's detailed elaboration of the social, economic, political, and, above all, psychological conditions that led to the rise of National Socialism in Germany. As Fromm tells his readers, "Any attempt to understand the attraction which Fascism exercises upon great nations compels us to recognize the role of psychological factors. For we are dealing here with a political system which, essentially, does not appeal to rational forces of self-interest" (Fromm, 1941, p. 7). In essence, he wanted to understand how it was possible for his fellow Germans to willingly give up their freedoms, submit to authoritarianism, and turn against their neighbors. To do this, Fromm developed a radical new approach known as social psychoanalysis, which combined the insights of sociology and psychoanalysis, the two disciplines in which he trained.

Fromm's social psychoanalysis caught the attention of Walter Benjamin, who maintained that of all the research produced by the Institute for Social Research, "The widest framework has been delineated by the works of Erich Fromm" (Benjamin, 1938, p. 310). According to Benjamin, Fromm moved beyond Freud and his idea of "natural drive structures," in order to understand how human needs were "conditioned in historically given societies." In order to appreciate why Benjamin singled out Fromm, and before engaging in a discussion of *Escape From Freedom* itself, it will be helpful to examine more closely what Fromm actually meant by social psychoanalysis.

Given Fromm's postwar status as a public intellectual, it is easy to overlook the fact that he was first and foremost a practicing psychoanalyst. Indeed, Fromm's concern for human well-being emerged out of his daily work with patients, and his psychoanalytic practice was the basis for many of his ideas about human interaction. Fromm believed that we are each fundamentally social beings and that the mind of the individual can never be understood in separation from the social contexts in which they live. He was especially interested in understanding how political forces effect well-being and pointed to the inherent connection between the health of society and the health of the individual.

In 1929, on the occasion of the opening of the Frankfurt Psychoanalytic Institute (of which he was a cofounder), Fromm presented a lecture entitled "Psychoanalysis and Sociology." There, he described the project that came to define his life's work: namely, to understand how social forces unconsciously shape the individual person, who as Fromm wrote, "in reality exists only as a socialized person" (Fromm, 1929/1989, p. 38). Throughout the 1930s, Fromm examined the determinative influence of socioeconomic class, religion, and ideology on human development. Fromm's approach is evident in a number of works from the period, some of which were written before he arrived in New York. In *The Dogma of Christ* from 1930, Fromm traced the development of religious belief and argued, in effect, that changes in individual belief are the result of broader changes that take place at the level of society. In "The Method and Function of an Analytic Social Psychology" from 1932, Fromm maintained that it is through our families that we come to be formed by the norms and values of society: "The family is the medium through which society or the social class stamps its specific structure on the child, and hence on the adult. *The family is the psychological agency of society*" (1932/1970b, p. 145, original emphasis).

The point, for Fromm, is that society is always at work in the person. In this sense, we might say that our beliefs and actions reflect the societies in which we live. These ideas find their fullest expression in Fromm's article *Man's Impulse Structure and Its Relation to Culture* from 1937, in which he seeks to demonstrate the inherent interconnection between the individual and society:

> Society and the individual are not "opposite" to each other. *Society is nothing but living, concrete individuals, and the individual exists only as a social human being.* His individual life practice is necessarily determined by the life practice of his society or class and, in the last analysis, by the manner of production of his society, that is, how this society produces, how it is organized to satisfy the needs of its members. The differences in the manner of production and life of various societies or classes lead to the development of different character structures typical of the particular society. (Fromm, 1937/2010, p. 58, original italics)

Fromm thus positioned the person within social, cultural, and political relations. Fromm believed that without a critical awareness of the way in which society functions, the therapist, like the profession of psychology as a whole, simply ends up mirroring and reinforcing existing societal norms. For Fromm, mental health was not just an individual problem. It needed to be understood socially and politically. Fromm sought to show how individuals are unconsciously shaped to meet the needs of their society. The result is that they take on the particular roles that society requires of them and learn to contain thoughts and feelings that might otherwise challenge the status quo.[7] The consequences can be disastrous. In the aftermath of Nazi Germany's defeat, and with no small measure of understatement, Fromm remarked, "A culture in which the majority of people fail to realize *the aims* of humanity is not a culture conducive to mental health" (Fromm, 1952, p. 38).

According to Fromm, the profession of psychoanalysis is itself a product of the society and culture in which it is practiced. He maintained that Freud's ideas were a reflection of a specific social and cultural outlook and thus could not be universal in nature. Not surprisingly, Fromm's critical reading of Freud found little sympathy among traditional psychoanalysts or his colleagues at the Institute for Social Research. When Fromm submitted *Man's Impulse Structure and Its Relation to Culture* for publication in the Institute journal, it was rejected by Horkheimer.[8] It was the start of what would become an unbridgeable gap between himself and the Institute. But the further Fromm ventured from Freud, the closer his associations with revisionist psychoanalysts became.

Fromm's publications awakened lively interest in the circle of interdisciplinary clinicians and researchers connected with the American psychiatrist Harry Stack Sullivan. Fromm met Sullivan in 1934, soon after arriving in the United States. Their relationship blossomed as each discovered how much he could learn from the other. Sullivan became acquainted with Fromm's psychological studies of society, and Fromm learned about the ways in which Sullivan conceptualized the self in a nexus of interpersonal relations.[9] When the American Psychoanalytic Association began to require that all its members be medical doctors, Sullivan sought to assure Fromm of a psychoanalytic life outside the Freudian mainstream. In 1936 Fromm was invited to teach at the newly established Washington School of Psychiatry, which he gladly accepted.

Fromm's psychoanalytic associations in New York at the time consisted of friends and colleagues, new and old, including Sullivan, Horney, Fromm-Reichmann, Clara Thompson, and others. It was through Sullivan that Fromm also met and interacted with like-minded interdisciplinary researchers in the culture and personality movement. Among this number were the anthropologists Ruth Benedict, Abram Kardiner, Margaret Mead, and Edward Sapir, along with a host of social scientists.[10] The influence of anthropology on Fromm, Sullivan, and Horney was especially evident, and their combined work became known as "cultural psychoanalysis."[11]

This cross-fertilization of ideas helped Fromm develop the concept of the social character. Fromm's aim was to show how the social character of a group "determines the thinking, feeling and acting of individuals who belong to that group" (Fromm, 1941, p. 278). This was essentially the inverse of a psychology that took as its starting point the individual person and only later accounted for the existence of social factors. Fromm's position at the time was summarized in the following statement:

> The fundamental approach to human personality is the understanding of the human being's relationship to the world, to others, to nature, and to him or herself. We believe that the human being is primarily a social being, and not, as Freud assumes, primarily self-sufficient and only secondarily in need of others in order to satisfy his or her instinctual needs. In this sense, we believe that individual psychology is fundamentally social psychology, or in Sullivan's terms, the psychology of interpersonal relationships. (Fromm, 1941, p. 290)

This was perhaps the best articulation of the "interpersonal approach" that united Fromm and Sullivan and formed the foundation for Fromm's analysis of the psychology of Nazism in *Escape From Freedom*. As Fromm states in the appendix to that book, "Different societies or classes within a society have a specific social character, and on its basis different ideas develop and become powerful" (1941, p. 279).[12] Fromm's aim would be to explain why the idea of authoritarianism became so powerful in Germany, and how the authoritarian character structure fed mass support for Hitler. The problem that concerned Fromm was how it was

> that millions in Germany were as eager to surrender their freedom as their fathers were to fight for it; that instead of wanting freedom they sought for ways to escape from it; [and] that other millions were indifferent and did not believe the defense of freedom worth fighting for. (1941, p. 5)

1938: The Escalating Terror

As important as social psychoanalysis was to the development of *Escape From Freedom*, we must not lose sight of Fromm's personal experience of the time (Figure 3.1), and the way in which the social and political contexts of the late 1930s shaped the arguments of his book. In Europe, the political order was threatened by fascist dictators: Hitler in Germany and Mussolini in Italy. In the Soviet Union, Stalin was orchestrating the Great Purge, which led to

Figure 3.1 Erich Fromm in the Mid-1930s
Courtesy of the Erich Fromm Archive, Tübingen.

the deaths of nearly a million Communist Party members. And in East Asia, Imperial Japan had embarked on a violent invasion of China.

In the midst of this heightened uncertainty, Fromm's health condition was a constant source of worry. Far from being able to settle, Fromm was continually traveling in the search of climates and locations where his tuberculosis might be controlled.[13] During his travels, Fromm wrote regularly to Horkheimer. Despite growing theoretical differences, their correspondence remained cordial and supportive, at least through the start of 1939.[14] The letters between Fromm and Horkheimer in 1938 have survived and give us a good indication of how the troubling political developments were affecting Fromm personally. They also provide an additional perspective on the Holocaust correspondence in Fromm's family, and on the development of *Escape From Freedom*.

The crises in Europe were frequently at the forefront of the Fromm–Horkheimer correspondence. During 1938, Hitler was pressing for the annexation of Austria and the Sudetenland in Czechoslovakia, while Stalin was filling the Gulags and arranging mass executions. In a letter from Arizona on March 9, 1938, Fromm wrote to Horkheimer that *"I am doing well so far; by 'so far' I mean that the political news, and especially that from Russia, often depresses me so much that it takes a lot of effort to get my balance back."* Fromm's obvious disappointment with the direction of communism under Stalin did not dissuade him from its promise. He describes Stalin's purges as *"irrationality that is driven to the point of utter madness"* and contrasts what is happening in Moscow to communist movements in Spain and China. There he finds *"great qualities of humanity, energy, and solidarity, in which the masses spontaneously unfold, guided by the elementary principles of Marxism, or perhaps more simply, reason and humanity."*[15]

By the summer of 1938, Fromm was well enough to join Horney on a trip to Europe. It was the first time he had returned to the continent since he fled in 1934. But their trip took place against the background of Nazi Germany's saber rattling and the persecution of its own citizens. On March 12, 1938, Nazi troops marched through Vienna to the cheers of large crowds, making the Anschluss with Austria a reality. After the Anschluss, Hitler focused his sights on the Sudetenland and threatened invasion in the hope of integrating the region's three million ethnic Germans.

While Fromm was traveling with Horney, he became ill and was eventually hospitalized in Mendrisio, a town in southern Switzerland near the Italian border. On September 1, 1938, Fromm cabled Horkheimer from Mendrisio

Cantonal Hospital, *"Scarlet fever—return about two months."* It took many weeks before the doctors were able to diagnosis the return of tuberculosis. During the month of September 1938, as Fromm was recuperating in hospital, Europe was on a razor's edge. It was also at this time, and from the isolation of his hospital bed in Mendrisio, that Fromm began his correspondence with Gertrud and Heinz Brandt.

Hitler's belligerence was threatening the increasingly fragile European peace that had held since the end of the First World War. Fromm remained sufficiently alert to follow the political events and his concerns were palpable. On September 5, 1938, he contacted Horkheimer: *"Please cable [if] war imminent."* A week later his fever had receded, and Fromm cabled again, this time more urgently, *"Temperature-free—stop—please cable if, after Hitler's speech* [at the Nazi Party Congress in Nuremberg], *a serious risk of war is suspected, since I might try to reach the ship despite the health risk."*

In an effort to avert the outbreak of war, the British Prime Minister, Neville Chamberlain, intervened. He met with Hitler in Berchtesgaden, Germany, on September 15, 1938, to see if an accommodation could be reached. The next day, September 16, 1938, Horkheimer cabled Fromm in an effort to calm his nerves,

> *Dear Fromm, Since you've been ill we've only communicated by telegram and via Mrs. Favez* [the Institute's assistant in Geneva]. *But I would also at least like to let you know with a few lines that we think of you a lot and are sincerely looking forward to having you healthy and back again. Your illness seems, both to us and to you, to be taking its sweet time. Because of the political situation I can only confirm what I've already expressed in the telegrams. The theoretical considerations that for the past five years have repeatedly led me to the conviction that a war in which France and Germany find themselves on opposite sides is highly unlikely also are valid for the coming years. Obviously, such statements can't be made with absolute certainty but only with the degree of probability, even if they are theoretically as well grounded as these are. On the other hand, however, well-grounded views do exist so that they can be clung to not only in relatively peaceful times but even in crises.* (Horkheimer, 2007, pp. 139–140)

With the benefit of hindsight, Horkheimer's "theoretical considerations" of a future without war might seem wholly misguided. But his comments demonstrate how many people, above all Chamberlain himself, fervently held on to a belief in the possibilities for peace. Horkheimer nevertheless ends his letter on a cautious note: *"It's advisable to reserve a cabin on a ship now for the time of your anticipated release from the hospital because places will continue to be scarce in the next few weeks and months"* (Horkheimer, 2007, p. 140). Clearly, the fact that so many thousands of Jewish refugees were searching for a means to leave Europe was a reality no one could overlook.

Fromm responds on the same day, as soon as he receives Horkheimer's communication. His nerves continued to fray as he contended with the exhaustion of illness and the drumbeats of war,

Thank you for your telegrams. Even if I was of the opinion that England would give Hitler the Sudeten Germans and needed the dangerous atmosphere of war in order to save face, I still doubted whether the machinery set in motion did not have a certain power of its own, and furthermore, whether the government in Prague would allow itself to be so calmly forced into suicide. Of course, the isolated situation in the hospital also makes one a little nervous.

Having met Hitler, Chamberlain made the fateful decision that the dictator could be relied upon.[16] Together, the British and French pressured Czechoslovakia into ceding the Sudetenland, but Hitler was not satisfied. In a final effort to avoid a war, the British, Germans, French, and Italians met in Munich on September 29, 1938, and agreed to the immediate German occupation of the Sudetenland. Believing he had averted war, and accepting Hitler's contention that he had no more territorial ambitions, Chamberlain returned to England. In front of a crowd of jubilant onlookers, he declared, "Peace for our time." It was not to be. In March 1939, Germany annexed the remainder of Czechoslovakia. After Hitler invaded Poland on September 1, 1939, Chamberlain was forced to make a solemn declaration of war.

During the intensification of the Sudeten crisis, Fromm remained hospitalized in Mendrisio. Fromm was a fervent antinationalist and opposed to war, yet he seemed to disagree with Chamberlain's actions, not believing that Hitler would be satisfied by the gains he made. Indeed, the Munich Agreement would become synonymous with the failed policy of appeasement. The events of that year made their mark on Fromm. Much of his later work was directed at addressing the cause of extreme nationalism and thus reducing the risk that hostile political relationships would again reach the precipice, as they had in the fall of 1938.

Once Fromm's fever subsided, he traveled to the Schatzalp Sanatorium above Davos, where he would spend the following 6 months in recovery. The sanatorium was already familiar to him since he had stayed there in the early 1930s. Fromm may have been incapacitated by illness, but he continued his correspondence. In the face of the ominous political developments, he began to experience a debilitating sense of powerlessness. On November 4, 1938, he wrote to Horkheimer that

> *It has been a bit too much these last two months, especially regarding what is happening in the world and the horrifying individual misery which you come across in newspapers and letters. Sometimes, during these weeks, it has seemed more than doubtful to me if, under the circumstances, it was still worth holding onto one's life as it were "by force," through doctors, medicines—and the inner will to live. But the feeling "I can make it" stayed more prominent.... We have a responsibility as individuals not to give in. Besides this, there is satisfaction in knowing that even though we might get physically crushed by the steam roller of historical events, we will stay intact spiritually and morally.*

Fromm's remarks give us a window into his increasingly fragile state of mind. The tumult he experienced in the world around him was about to get even worse. As Fromm penned these lines, he could hardly know that only a few days later the Nazis would carry out a massive pogrom against the Jewish communities in Germany and Austria, the so-called Kristallnacht, or Night of Broken Glass, the name given to the destruction by the Nazis. The widespread destruction and bloodshed started on the night of November 9 and carried on into the next day, making clear just how dire the situation really was. On November 11, 1938, Fromm wrote to Horkheimer again, this time sounding a note of alarm regarding his family members.

Drawing directly from the letters that Gertrud sent to him from Posen, Fromm described the situation of Heinz Brandt and laid out possible routes for attaining a visa, asking whether Horkheimer could offer any help. Feeling increasingly anxious, Fromm wrote another letter 2 weeks later, in which he outlined yet more possibilities for getting Heinz a visa. In addition, Fromm described the fate of an unnamed person who had been arrested in the course of the pogrom, adding that *"the Frankfurt Jews seem to be mostly in the Buchenwald concentration camp near Weimar."* Having grown up deeply immersed in Frankfurt's Jewish community, we can only imagine the impact that this news must have had on him. On December 1, 1938, Fromm wrote to Horkheimer with regard to his mother, Rosa,

> *I just received a message from my mother. She absolutely wants to leave.... I feel an obligation to help her as much as I can.... She can go to the USA in about 1½ years (I sent her an affidavit about 2 months ago in any case) but in the meantime she can stay in England or Switzerland (?) if she can make a deposit of about $1000. The money would be quite safe in itself, since it is not for use. I would now like to ask you whether the Institute treasury could lend me $500 (at interest because this "formality" might simplify things. Materially it doesn't matter much). I have asked Mrs. H[orney] for the remaining $500. My wife [Frieda Fromm-Reichmann] just recently raised $5000 for her siblings and therefore does not have it at the moment. If it is not possible, please send me a cable so that I don't give my mother any false hopes.*

Fromm's letter gives us a sense of the challenges involved in helping family members leave Germany and of the significant sums of money needed for exit visas.[17] Like so many other German Jewish refugees at the time, his estranged wife Frieda was struggling to rescue her own relatives. In his reply from December 17, 1938, Horkheimer wrote that he could appreciate the urgency of Fromm's situation, but that the Institute did not have the funds available. Horkheimer added, perhaps to reduce the sting, that in the event he should have to secure $1,000 for his own parents, he would also need to find a way to borrow the money.

Fromm's communications with family members, friends, and colleagues who were trying to find safety led him to reflect on his own situation and gave way to a sense of bewilderment, guilt, and worry. On December 14, 1938, he wrote to Horkheimer,

> *If you only talk to people and hear from people about where they will live, but for whom the question of how they will live and from what they will live no longer seems to be relevant, it begins to feel so unlikely that you have your own visa that solves this problem and you feel (more than you think) that something must just be wrong.*

Fromm's sentiments about something being wrong are captured a few weeks later by Gertrud, when she writes in her letter from December 29, 1938, that her husband Georg is increasingly experiencing an "*alienation from life.*" Disorientation, dissociation, and denial were common responses to a world that had been quite literally turned on its head. It could be hard to know how to go on when one's life was suddenly threatened by racial terror. The world in which one had grown up no longer made sense.

In the midst of experiencing his own doubts about the future, Fromm pushed ahead with his efforts to secure safe passage for Heinz Brandt. On January 6, 1939, he contacted a Swiss lawyer and sent an affidavit:

> *It is my desire to have Mr. Heinz Brandt, born in Posen on August 16, 1909— he is a first cousin of my mother's—in the United States until he becomes self-supporting. I hereby guarantee that Mr. Brandt will at no time become a burden to the United States or any State or subdivision thereof.*

Fromm remained in Switzerland over the following months, where he continued his correspondence with Gertrud and his efforts to secure Heinz's release. As we know, it would all come to naught. After his release from prison, Heinz was taken to Sachsenhausen, the first of several of concentration camps that he was forced to endure.

It took until the spring of 1939 before Fromm was well enough to return to the United States. Fromm booked a birth on a ship to New York, fully aware of how fortunate he was to make the journey when so many were trying desperately to escape Nazi Germany. Fromm's timing was also fortuitous. Had he stayed in Europe much longer he may have faced a far more daunting voyage back to the United States. In June 1939, American authorities turned away the M.S. St. Louis, a ship filled with refugees from Nazi Germany. Its 900 Jewish passengers were forced to return to Europe, where a third of their number would be murdered in the Holocaust. Fromm's departure for New York also coincided with the start of Sophie Engländer's correspondence and spurred his attempts to arrange safe passage for his aunt and uncle. After arriving back in New York, Fromm set to work completing the manuscript for *Escape From Freedom*. There can be little question that his personal experience of the past year shaped the tone and content of his writing.

In Switzerland, Fromm's health had finally begun to stabilize with the advent of new medications, yet there would be no cure for his ailing relationship with the Institute for Social Research. Despite his decade-long relationship with Horkheimer, they would go their separate ways. Fromm's departure was ostensibly initiated by the Institute's financial constraints. Despite being tenured, Fromm was asked to forgo his salary and refused. A financial settlement was eventually reached, but by this time, interactions between Fromm and the Institute had become acrimonious and beyond repair.

Fromm left feeling as though Horkheimer had turned his back on their long and productive collaboration. He was not wrong, though the separation certainly began earlier. The Institute's refusal to publish Fromm's 1937 essay was determinative, as was Adorno's ambition to shape the direction of the Institute after his arrival in New York in 1938. In contrast to Fromm's radical new social psychoanalysis, Adorno emphasized Freud's drive theory, for which he received the full support of Horkheimer and Marcuse. There was no middle ground. The personal antipathy Adorno felt toward Fromm would have a long and deleterious effect on the reception of Fromm's work by succeeding generations of critical theorists.[18] What Fromm could not know when he left the Institute was that the public interest in what he had to say would grant him an independence to move in new and unexpected directions. The publication of *Escape From Freedom* (Figure 3.2) in 1941 was the first step in that direction.

Psychology of Nazism

The arguments in *Escape From Freedom* drew on a variety of Fromm's earlier works. The most important of these was his study of German workers and salaried classes from the late Weimar Republic, which had provided a means to understand the collapse of German workers' parties during the rise of Nazism. In the face of the Nazi Party's ascendancy to power, one of the issues facing the Marxist-oriented Institute for Social Research was why German workers seemed unable to politically alter the course of German society. A pioneering empirical study was organized to address the problem.

During a 3-year period from 1929 through 1932, Fromm directed a group of dedicated Institute associates who handed out 3,300 questionnaires in Berlin and Frankfurt to workers and salaried employees who generally identified as being on the political left. As Fromm later remarked, the chief question that the study sought to answer was: "To what extent do German workers and employees have a character structure which is the opposite to the authoritarian idea of Nazism? And this implied still another question: To what extent will the German workers and employees, in the critical hour fight Nazism?" (Fromm, 1930/1963b, p. 148). The worker's study was extensive.

Figure 3.2 Book Cover to the First Edition of *Escape From Freedom*, 1941: "Freedom is Frightening --Why? A psychologist examines modern man's choice between flight to authoritarianism and achievement of democracy."

Respondents were asked to answer 271 individual questions. However, the political and social turbulence of those years, together with the time commitment asked of respondents to complete the questionnaires, meant that only 1,100 were ultimately collected.[19] The opportunity to analyze and write up the results was postponed until the Institute and its associates found their way to safety in New York. Despite these drawbacks, the information gleaned from the respondents was noteworthy.

The results of the study challenged contemporaneous assumptions about the readiness of workers to stand up against right-wing authoritarianism. Perhaps the most important finding was that only 15% of respondents demonstrated clear anti-authoritarian beliefs. In other words, a great many German workers and employees who were presumed to be solidly of the political left and against authoritarianism either had profascist tendencies or were defined as so-called bystanders, more ready to look away than to stand up against right-wing extremism. In his analysis of the findings, Fromm sought to shed light on the psychological appeal of authoritarianism, which he said

> affirms, seeks out and enjoys the subjugation of human beings under higher external power.... The strong and powerful are simply admired and loved for these qualities, the weak and helpless hated and despised. Sacrifice and duty, and not pleasure in life and happiness, are the guiding aims of the authoritarian attitude. (Fromm, 1984, pp. 209–210)

Not only did the results of the study help to explain the eventual collapse of German left-wing parties in the face of Nazism, but as the sociologist Wolfgang Bonss points out, Fromm's analysis also shows that "despite all the electoral successes of the Weimar Left, its members were not in a position, owing to their character structure, to prevent the victory of National Socialism" (Bonss, 1984, p. 29).

The history of the Worker's Study also reflects Fromm's changing position within the Institute for Social Research. On the one hand, the study played an important role in helping the Institute find a new home at Columbia University. At a time when there was almost no empirical research in the field, Fromm's work drew the interest of the sociologist Robert Lynd, who appealed to the university to find Fromm and the Institute a new home.[20] On the other hand, Horkheimer was concerned that the study's conclusions and limited number of completed questionnaires were not sufficiently representative. An initial overview of the Worker's Study appeared in the Institute's 1936 publication *Studies on Authority and the Family*. But there was never a full reporting, and the results of the Worker's Study were shelved and virtually forgotten. As a result, the publication of the complete study, under the title *The Working Class in Weimar German: A Psychological and Sociological Study*, would have to wait until 1980.[21]

Instead, we find that another of Fromm's works, *Social-Psychological Dimension* (1936), takes prominent place in the *Studies on Authority and the Family*. There he examined the role of socioeconomic factors in the shaping of society and turned his attention to the role of authoritarianism and patriarchy. Fromm suggested that the decrease of influence of the traditional patriarchal family structure in Germany led to a rise to feelings of powerlessness for many Germans, which in turn made authoritarianism especially appealing. Fromm extended this line of thinking in an article he published in 1937 entitled *On the Feeling of Powerlessness*. Commenting on the dangers of authoritarianism, Fromm wrote that "In authoritarian states, the incapacity to have any influence is elevated to a conscious principle." But he adds that a similar dynamic is operative in democracies:

> Average adults in our society are in reality extraordinarily powerless, and this powerlessness has the even more oppressive effect in that they are made to believe that things should actually be completely different, and it is their own fault if they are so weak. They have no power whatsoever to determine their own fate. (Fromm, 1937/2019, p. 326)

Taken together, these two works provided the basis for the arguments that Fromm put forth in *Escape From Freedom*.

When Hitler and the Nazi Party rose to power in Germany, their ascent was generally ascribed to the humiliation many Germans felt as a result of the Versailles Treaty, combined with the economic and societal crises that followed. Fromm accepted these political explanations but asked, in addition, what psychological reasons might account for the fact that Hitler was greeted with such fervor by large segments of the population. According to Fromm, Hitler played on the insecurities he saw within the German populace and seized the opportunity to give expression to his maniacal lust for power. The driving question was why so many Germans willingly gave up their freedoms to embrace the Führer.

Fromm's analysis begins with a broad historical narrative that traces how economic and social changes transformed medieval Europe into a modern capitalist society. Modern Europe ushered in new freedoms that laid the conditions for the emergence of autonomous and rational individuals. But with these changes came a deep-rooted anxiety and a feeling of isolation created by the transformation of society. Fromm maintained that people were faced with a choice: to engage productively with other human beings and garner the benefits of society (democracy) or escape a sense of fear and loneliness by submitting to a greater authority (totalitarianism).

The sweeping nature of Fromm's analysis suggests that he was more concerned with explaining the psychological forces that led people to submit to an authoritarian leader than with establishing the veracity of his historical narrative. Fromm had already drawn links between authoritarianism and the patriarchal family structure in Germany in his earlier works. It remained to show how this family structure was linked to society as a whole. According to Fromm, for many Germans, the loss of the Kaiser and the economic and social crises that followed had, in essence, "shaken the authority of the father." This made them susceptible to Hitler's messaging. Hitler provided millions of Germans with a means of escape by submitting to a larger power. Fromm's perspective was anticipated by Horney, who wrote in her 1939 article *Can You Take a Stand?* that

> Fascist ideology promises to fulfill all their needs. The individual in a fascist state is not supposed to stand up for his own wishes, rights, judgments. Decisions and judgments of value are made for him and he has merely to follow. He can forget about his own weakness by adoring the leader. His ego is bolstered up by being submerged in the greater unity of race and nation. (Horney, 2000, pp. 226–227)

Fromm expands on Horney's perspective by elaborating not only the appeal of submitting to an authoritarian leader, but also the corresponding wish to dominate others. Using quotes from Hitler's writing and speeches, Fromm shows that

> Hitler's personality, his teachings, and the Nazi system express an extreme form of the character structure which we have called 'authoritarian' and that by this very fact he made a powerful appeal to those parts of the population which were—more or less—of the same character. (Fromm, 1941, p. 221)

According to Fromm, the authoritarian character is distinguished by its relationship with power. The authoritarian person willingly submits to those who are more powerful, while showing contempt for those who are perceived as powerless. Fromm argues that the emotional appeal of Nazi ideology lay in "its spirit of blind obedience to a leader and of hatred against racial and political minorities, its craving for conquest and domination, its exaltation of the German people and the 'Nordic Race'" (Fromm, 1941, p. 211). Fromm explains how this psychological process plays out on a societal scale:

> While the "leaders" are the ones to enjoy power in the first place, the masses are by no means deprived of sadistic satisfaction. Racial and political minorities within Germany and eventually other nations which are described as weak or decaying are the objects of sadism upon which the masses are fed. While Hitler and his bureaucracy enjoy power over the German masses, these masses themselves are taught to enjoy power over other nations and to be driven by the passion for domination. (Fromm, 1941, p. 225).

Drawing directly from psychoanalysis, Fromm describes the symbiotic interaction of Hitler and his supporters as a relationship between sadism and masochism:

> The essence of the authoritarian character has been described as the simultaneous presence of sadistic and masochistic drives. Sadism was understood as aiming at unrestricted power over another person more or less mixed with destructiveness; masochism as aiming at dissolving oneself in an overwhelmingly strong power and participating in its strength and glory. (Fromm, 1941, p. 221)[22]

Escape From Freedom was published in 1941, the same year that the murderous campaigns of the Holocaust began. When we read Fromm's analysis today, it is easy to forget that it was written before the deportations of German Jews to concentration camps and ghettos, and before the towns and villages of Eastern Europe were turned into killing fields. Because we encounter the book through the prism of the Holocaust, it may fall short of our wish to make sense of the unfathomable toll of war and genocide. Fromm seems to have shared this concern, especially in the years directly after *Escape From Freedom* was published, when the war was raging and the death camps were murdering many thousands of people each day. The horrors in

Europe may been an ocean away, yet their presence was undeniably close, captured in the words of the letters written by his family members. By early 1943, Sophie had already bid farewell to her daughters. She and her husband were killed in Theresienstadt, and Gertrud would soon write her last words on a postcard from the ghetto in Ostrow-Lubelski. In the face of these tragedies, Fromm took steps to publicly clarify were he stood on the issue of National Socialism.

In the spring of 1943, in one of the few publications from this period, Fromm wrote a short essay entitled *What Shall We Do With Germany?* His aim was to distinguish his account of fascism from the burgeoning number of psychiatric studies that were being published about the German national character. Fromm argued that the problem with these studies was that their authors assumed they could explain cultural patterns by applying the same rational they used to understand their individual patients.[23] In response, he writes that

> It is true, nations have a "social character." They share certain character traits because they share certain fundamental experiences to which all members of the group have been exposed. In order to analyze the social character of any nation, one must study their social, economic, political, and cultural situation in its minute details and then proceed to understand how this total situation molded the character structure of the majority of all members; *one must study the intricate interaction of socio-economic, ideological, and psychological factors which operate in the history of any nation. This can only be done if one is as thoroughly acquainted and concerned with the history of a nation as the psychiatrist is acquainted with the individual life history of their patients.* (Fromm, 1943, p. 10, my emphasis)

As Fromm suggests, a psychiatric diagnosis of cultural patterns is only viable if it is based on detailed study of the contexts and the history from which those patterns arise. Any other approach would fail to grasp the hold that fascism had on its followers. Most importantly, Fromm states that superficial psychiatric diagnoses "*tend to weaken the sense for moral values, by calling something by a psychiatric term when it should be called plainly evil*" (Fromm, 1943, p. 10, my emphasis). The point is that no amount of psychological theorizing can ever take the place of the moral imperative to name and confront sheer evil when we see it. For Fromm, clearly, there was no other way to describe the actions of Hitler and the Nazi state.

My Grandfather and the Nazi Party

Fromm's analysis in *Escape From Freedom* suggests that there is much to be learned by studying the conditions surrounding the rise of fascism. In order to reflect on the implications of Fromm's analysis, and to move our discussion back to the level of lived experience, I want to take the liberty of sharing what I know about the circumstances of my own grandfather and his decision to join the Nazi Party.[24] Born in 1906, my grandfather belonged to the same generation as Fromm and was formed by the aftermath of World War I. In contrast to Fromm, my grandfather experienced the social crises that followed the war in a different way. The evidence suggests that my grandfather moved toward rather than away from nationalism. His father—my great-grandfather—was drafted into the Imperial German Army early in World War I and survived 4 years in the trenches of the Western Front, where he was twice injured. When he finally returned home in 1918, he was by all accounts a different man. My great-grandfather apparently never mentioned the carnage he lived through during the war. The loss of faith in the Kaiser, and the political and economic crises that followed, shook my family's belief in the German nation.

For my grandfather, the rise of the Nazi Party seemed to provide an opportunity to belong to something greater than himself. He may even have believed that the election of Hitler would bring an end to the economic uncertainties of the time. While Hitler's promise of a strong Germany and economic well-being garnered the support of many, Fromm pointed out that these were necessary but not sufficient conditions to explain his rise to power. Nor does it account for my grandfather's choice to become a member of the Nazi Party. There are many reasons why someone may have wanted to be a party member. In a select number of professions, membership even became obligatory. By the start of World War II, the Nazi Party had approximately eight million members, making up some 10% of Germany's total population.

What is clear is that no one could become a member without their active participation.[25] It was the act of applying for party membership that points to the centrality of racial ideology at the heart of the Nazi regime. In the spring of 1936, exactly halfway between the election of Hitler and the start of World War II, my grandfather carefully filled out and submitted his Nazi Party application. This was no trifling matter. The application involved completing a detailed and sworn questionnaire in which the applicant was required to trace back their "Aryan heritage" over several generations. My grandfather was formally inducted on May 1, 1937. His date of admission suggests that he was not an ardent early joiner, and that his decision was variously motivated. But it's impossible to ignore the role of racial ideology in the process. The knowledge that the man whom I knew and loved as a child willingly defined himself and his family in racialized, "Aryan," terms is deeply unsettling to me.

I initially hesitated to visit the federal archives because I was concerned about what I might find there. For many German descendants like myself, the fear of what family members may have believed or done during the Third Reich looms large. My grandfather had been a central figure of my early life, not simply an image of a person I came to know by way of a dusty photograph hanging on the wall. But despite my worries, the moral obligations of memory required me to confront my grandfather's participation in the Nazi regime.

The historical facts that I eventually discovered in my search of multiple archives suggested that my grandfather's story was more complicated than had I initially assumed. Despite my grandfather's avowed loyalty to the Nazi Party, I could find no evidence to suggest that he was anything more than a minor cog in the political machine. At the same time, my grandfather's work in the armaments industry and on the production of the V2 rocket meant that he would have witnessed firsthand the unspeakable conditions endured by forced laborers. My grandfather may never have been directly involved in carrying out the regime's heinous criminal actions, but it was the support that he and so many others lent the regime that enabled and facilitated those crimes. The perpetrators could only carry out their acts of violence with the support of the majority, or at the very least, an active willingness to remain passive and look away. Whether this attitude is described as indifference or willed ignorance, its deadly consequences were the same. As the Holocaust historian Saul Friedlander explained,

> During the Nazi era few domains—with the exception of direct criminal activities—can be considered as entirely abhorrent; on the other hand, very few domains can be considered as entirely untouched by some of the objectionable or even criminal aspect of the core. . . . *In a system whose very core is criminal from the beginning, passivity is, as such, system supporting.* (Friedlander, 1993, p. 73, my emphasis)

To illustrate the point, Friedlander provides the example of the local church community, "which may have remained ideologically untainted," but nonetheless willingly "expels its non-Aryan members and allows them to be transported away without protest" (Friedlander, 1993, p. 73). Seen from this perspective, the history of the Holocaust in Germany was the history of ordinary Germans and their families, those who willingly stood by or turned away.

I also discovered a history of my grandfather that was entirely new to me. While my grandfather's National Socialist German Workers' Party membership card confirmed what I already knew, a different document pointed me in a new direction. It was a so-called Nazi Party correspondence card and was stamped with the date March 31, 1936. The card stated my grandfather's name, occupation, and birthdate, where he lived, and his religion. Under the heading "Organization" there were the two abbreviated words: "*Ehem. Komm.*" My first thought was that the words might stand for *ehemaliger Kommunist* (former communist). My second thought was that this would be quite impossible since my grandfather joined the Nazi Party and his social proclivities during the 1920s did not strike me as those of a communist. However, the archivists' confirmation of my finding suggested that my grandfather was indeed a former communist or a communist sympathizer, at least in the eyes of the Nazi functionaries who were responsible for collating Nazi Party applications and granting memberships. It's quite possible that they defined any political affiliation to the left of center as potentially communist. This meant that my grandfather had evidently transferred his political sympathies from the communists to the Nazis.[26]

During the late 1920s and early 1930s, my grandfather lived and worked in Berlin as an artist and artisan. His years in Berlin paralleled those of Fromm, though they belonged to different social and professional circles. When I was a child, my grandfather loved to tell stories about his youth and drew for me a mental image of late 1920s Berlin: a dynamic city that was teaming with culture and constantly in motion. The dynamism of Berlin can be traced, at least in part, to its progressive politics. It was a left-wing stronghold, and the Nazis struggled to gain traction there, at least initially. What my grandfather never talked about were the pitched street battles that were fought between communist and Nazi paramilitary groups, the chaotic changes that followed as the Nazis gained the upper hand, or the antisemitic acts that were carried out publicly on Berlin's streets.

I later consulted with older family members and learned that my grandfather had indeed been involved with left-wing politics during his years in Berlin. Knowing this gave me pause. How should I make sense of the fact that my grandfather engaged in left-wing and potentially progressive causes, only to end up a Nazi Party member? In light of my discovery, the implications of Fromm's study of German workers and salaried employees became very real for me. Fromm suggested that it was the appeal of nationalism and proclivities toward authoritarianism that led individuals like my grandfather to shift their political allegiance from left to right. Of course, there is much that remains unknown about my grandfather's actions and beliefs. But based on information I was able to glean from multiple sources, he must have looked to authoritarianism to counter the economic, political, and psychological uncertainties of his era. Beyond this, joining the Nazi Party was probably politically expedient for him. But the likely reality, which is far more painful for me to acknowledge, is that my grandfather endorsed the Nazis' worldview. While Fromm helps us to understand the conditions that led people like my grandfather to turn to Nazism, he has little to say about what role the racial ideology at the heart of National Socialism played in this process.

Antisemitism

In explaining German support for Hitler, Fromm's focus is overwhelmingly on social class. He believed that the authoritarian character was most prevalent in Germany's lower middle class. This reveals Fromm's Marxist orientation but was also a limitation. We know today that Nazism appealed to all social classes and support for Hitler was present, to varying degrees, throughout Germany. Of course, it is worth remembering that *Escape From Freedom* was published in 1941, and the full extent of German society's involvement in the Nazi regime only became clear after the war. While Fromm's emphasis on the German lower middle class may have been overhasty, his central concern with "economic issues that make for increasing isolation and powerlessness of the individual" remains relevant. As Fromm explains, these are the conditions that lead to "a kind of escape that we find in the authoritarian character" (Fromm, 1941, p. 241). What Fromm could not foresee, and quite possibly did not recognize, was just how irrational and disastrous the escape into authoritarianism would become once Nazi ideology heralded race as a new kind of religion.

The lack of a thoroughgoing discussion of Nazi ideology and antisemitism in *Escape From Freedom* stands out. Yet it was a problem that effected early critical theory in general.[27] To the extent that antisemitism was acknowledged by the members of the Institute for Social Research, it occurred in a Marxist framework that gave primacy to economic conditions. In 1939, Horkheimer sought to address the issue with his publication of *The Jews and Europe*. On its face, the essay was an attempt to elaborate the Institute's approach to antisemitism, but in reality it was more concerned with the rise of fascism as an outgrowth of capitalism. It starts promisingly enough: "Whoever wants to explain antisemitism must speak of National Socialism" (Horkheimer, p. 77). But Horkheimer goes on to account for National Socialism as the inevitable result of capitalism: "The new antisemitism is the emissary of the totalitarian order, which was developed from the liberal one. One must thus go back to consider the tendencies within capitalism" (Horkheimer, p. 77). It is worth pointing out, moreover, that *The Jews and Europe* was written in German, not English, and was published in the Institute journal. Presumably Horkheimer had an audience of German Jewish émigrés in mind. What he may not have considered was that this audience would quickly see the shortcomings in his analysis. When Benjamin asked his friend, Gershom Scholem, to assess Horkheimer's essay, Scholem showed no hesitation in stating his mind:

> You wish to learn my opinion of Horkheimer's essay, "Die Juden und Europa." After repeated readings, I do not find it difficult to give an easily understood formulation: this is an entirely useless product about which, astonishingly enough, nothing beneficial and new can be discovered. The author has neither any knowledge of nor interest in the Jewish problem. It is obvious that at bottom no such problem exists for him. Thus it is only out of propriety that he deigns to express himself on the subject in passing. (Scholem, 2012, p. 278)[28]

Horkheimer was not alone in his ambivalence about addressing antisemitism. Analyses offered by Leo Lowenthal and Herbert Marcuse during the 1930s made no specific mention of antisemitism.[29] And in his important text *Behemoth: The Structure and Practice of National Socialism* from 1944, Franz Neumann remarked that this "writer's personal conviction, paradoxical as it may seem, is that the German people are the least Anti-Semitic of all" (Neuman, 1944, p. 121). To be sure, Horkheimer's approach would change once the reality of the Holocaust became clear, and especially after the Institute returned to Frankfurt in the 1950s. In addition, with the publication of Adorno's *Guilt and Responsibility* in 1958, the notion of secondary antisemitism became an effective framework for examining how many Germans in the early postwar period either refused to accept responsibility for the Holocaust or sought to minimize its impact. But initially, at least, the absence of any analysis of antisemitism was hard to overlook.

The question of antisemitism was of relevance not just to what was happening in Nazi Germany. Antisemitism was also strongly ascendant in the United States, the very country where the Institute and its members and associates had found a new home. American antisemitism was visible in a number of ways: discrimination in the workplace, restrictions on living in certain neighborhoods, prohibitions on joining social clubs, and quotas imposed by universities that limited the number of Jews who could study or enter into the professions. In addition, there were many antisemitic organizations that propagated the hatred of Jews.

Antisemitism was not limited to the fringes of American society.[30] The famous industrialist Henry Ford was a notorious antisemite, whose four-volume publication from the early 1920s entitled *The International Jew* drew a favorable response from Hitler. In the 1930s, Father Charles Coughlin had a radio audience that numbered in the millions and regularly propagated his antisemitic message. The cultural hero Charles Lindbergh was an avid fan of Hitler and made frequent trips to Nazi Germany. In 1939, Lindbergh wrote in *Reader's Digest* that "We can have peace and security only so long as we band together to preserve that most priceless possession, our inheritance of European blood, only so long as we guard ourselves against attack by foreign armies and dilution by foreign races" (Lindbergh, 1939, p. 65). The perceived threat posed by "foreign races" was captured in an opinion poll that was published by *Fortune Magazine* in November 1938. It asked Americans whether the United States should increase its immigration quotas or encourage political refugees—the largest number of them Jewish—to flee oppression in the fascist states of Europe. Fully two-thirds of the respondents agreed with the proposition that "we should try to keep them out" (Fortune Editors, 2015). In January 1939, less than 3 months after the November Pogrom, two-thirds of respondents to Gallop's American Institute of Public Opinion said they would not take in 10,000 German Jewish refugee children.[31]

In light of the prevailing attitudes, German Jews who found safety in the United States were understandably wary. They did not want to threaten their precarious legal status by expressing their politics, which were often to the left of center. Many were careful about how they spoke out against antisemitism.

In September 1940, the American First Committee, a pressure group that opposed U.S. intervention in the European war, was founded. At its height it had approximately 800,000 members. Although the Committee membership represented a diversity of political perspectives, many of its leading organizers and speakers were profascist and antisemitic. They included Ford and Lindbergh, the latter of whom publicly accused Jews of conspiring to force the United States into war.[32]

This was the American social context in which *Escape From Freedom* was published in the summer of 1941, a book in which Fromm openly rallied his readership to confront the dangers of fascism. Fromm's courage in speaking out was noteworthy, and he was undoubtedly aware of the risks involved. This might also explain his decision to frame the arguments of *Escape From Freedom* in terminology that was familiar to American readers. Most readers would have been more comfortable with Fromm's deliberations on the meaning and nature of freedom than with open discussion of antisemitism and racism. There may also have been a more practical reason for Fromm's decision not to examine antisemitism at any length. Being publicly identified as a left-wing German Jewish refugee who wrote about antisemitism could have made him a target of racial discrimination, which was the reason why Fromm could not stay in Germany to begin with. But given Fromm's willingness to speak out and challenge the status quo throughout his career (a fact that caused the FBI to compile a large dossier on him[33]), I think the more likely reason is that writing about antisemitism at the same time that he was trying to save his family members may simply have proven too painful.

Looking back, we find that it was Fromm's psychoanalytic colleague Harry Stack Sullivan who addressed the threat of antisemitism directly. In November 1938, Sullivan published a detailed editorial on antisemitism in a new interdisciplinary journal called *Psychiatry*. The fact that the editorial's publication coincided with the November Pogrom can only have increased its impact. Sullivan detailed the escalation of contemporary anti-Jewish discrimination and reflected on the historical roots of antisemitism, particularly the role played by Christianity in its propagation. In an important passage, Sullivan states,

> The most widespread hatred of a collectivity in the Western world today is antisemitism. Hatred of Jews has been made a national creed by at least one state. A trend in this direction is being manifested by the other totalitarian powers, and there is a disturbing responsiveness to the formula in many of

the citizens of more democratic countries. Hatred under any circumstances can scarcely be constructive. It is essentially a destructive motivation. Any pervasive enmity within democracy is dangerous. It increases the proportion of people who feel insecure. It intensifies feelings of individual differences. It undermines that general respect for other people which is the real basis for dependable self-respect. Antisemitism is this very sort of pervasive enmity. It is also an enmity peculiarly difficult to combat because of its particular irrational basis. (Sullivan, 1938, pp. 593–594)

What is unspoken in Sullivan's editorial is the personal understanding he brought to the subject. Through his close interactions with German Jewish refugees like Fromm and Fromm-Reichmann, and through his friendship with the ethnologist Edward Sapir, who was also Jewish, Sullivan had a firsthand knowledge of the pernicious effects of antisemitism.[34] We can also justifiably ask whether it was because Sullivan was Catholic and not Jewish that he could more easily engage with the subject. To be sure, Sullivan struggled with societal prejudices in other ways. As a gay man he was careful to hide his sexual orientation from public view, given the high degree of prejudice at the time.[35] Thus, while Sullivan wrote about antisemitism and the effects of racism, he never wrote explicitly about the prejudice he experienced.[36] In a similar sense, Fromm engaged the twin specters of authoritarianism and fascism but did not substantially discuss the Nazis' racial ideology, which was a cause of the murder of his own family members.

Sullivan also became important to Fromm in another way. He immediately recognized the importance of *Escape From Freedom* and arranged for a series of eight separate reviews, including a discussion by the noted anthropologist Ruth Benedict. The reviews were all published in *Psychiatry* in 1942. *Escape From Freedom* received widespread acclaim and was translated into over a dozen languages, even as the war was still raging. The book's chief critics were mainstream psychoanalysts, which is perhaps not surprising given the enmity that had emerged between Fromm and the Freudians. In a particularly caustic review in *The Nation*, the Freudian stalwart, Karl Menninger, remarked, "Erich Fromm was in Germany a distinguished sociologist. His book is written as if he considered himself a psychoanalyst" (Menninger, 1942, p. 154). In his haste to dismiss Fromm's interdisciplinary approach, Menninger ignored a singularly important fact: *Escape From Freedom* was one of the only psychoanalytic books to actually address the reality of fascism at the time![37] A similarly critical review was written by Otto Fenichel (1944).

In Berlin, Fenichel had lauded Fromm for his radical outlook, and they had worked together to integrate Marx with Freud. But now he took umbrage at Fromm's interpretations of Freud. The sad irony was that while Fromm remained outspoken in his left-wing political and psychoanalytic views, Fenichel worked feverishly to be accepted by the conservative American psychoanalytic establishment.

The disapproval unleashed by Fromm's critique of Freud cannot be underestimated. A few years later, Horkheimer offered a negative assessment of Fromm's psychoanalytic perspective that echoed Menninger's. In 1949, Horkheimer was asked by the editors of the journal *Philosophical Review* to describe Fromm's role at the Institute. In his response, Horkheimer noted that

> We worked together for many years and I gladly acknowledge his valuable theoretical and pedagogical contributions. About 1938 our theoretical ways parted, however. He left the Institute and became the head of one of the revisionist schools of psychoanalysis which has tried to "sociologize" depth psychology, thereby, as some of my associates and I felt, actually making it more superficial and losing sight of the decisive social implications of Freud's original conception. (Horkheimer, 2007, p. 271)

Over time, Horkheimer's account of Fromm became codified in the history of the Institute and it still bears influence today. The cordial and productive interaction between Horkheimer and Fromm had clearly come to an end. But in his last recorded letter to Fromm, written on October 18, 1946, the day on which the virulently antisemitic Nazi leader Julius Streicher was hanged, Horkheimer acknowledged their mutual history in the face of the Nazi regime's inhumanity:

> *Recalling that we toasted the demise of symbolic figures of the Nazi Reich on the news of June 30, 1934* [the so-called Night of the Long Knives], *I sent you on Tuesday night a toast to the death of Streicher and his comrades (execution on October 18, 1946.) Even if the circumstances surrounding it are little more cause for celebration today than they were then, the prospect of this latest judgment would have seemed like an impossible dream during the years of terror. Not the innocent, but the hangman is refuted by the hangman.*

Despite their differences, Fromm and Horkheimer shared the experience of being refugees and struggled with the pain of watching from afar as Nazi

Germany carried out its atrocities. It's not hard to imagine that they took satisfaction in learning of the demise of the hateful Nazi leadership. Looking back, what is significant is that Fromm felt compelled to publicly confront the Nazi threat and the political realities in which he lived. The correspondence with Gertrud and Sophie revealed the brutal truth of the Nazi regime and its persecution of German Jews. Fromm simply could not remain silent. *Escape From Freedom* is relevant in other ways too. Fromm's account of authoritarianism, especially in times of uncertainty, helps to explain the attraction of right-wing populism, be it in the past or the present. Fromm's firsthand knowledge of the rise of Nazism strengthened his belief in the need for moral awareness and political activism. It also helps to explain the optimistic note on which Fromm ends his book, when he suggests that democracy will be victorious over "the forces of nihilism" if it can imbue people with "faith in life and in truth and in freedom" (Fromm, 1941, p. 276). Unfortunately, as recent antidemocratic attacks and acts of racial terror suggest, it remains an open question whether democratic institutions can actually provide a sufficient bulwark against the kinds of right-wing authoritarianism, antisemitism, and racial hatred that we see today.

4
Confronting Genocide

In 1945, as the full extent of the catastrophe began to be revealed, Fromm struggled to make sense of the darkness at the heart of fascism. He was reminded of a speech that was given by a fascist general in Spain that ended with the words "Long Live Death!" With that statement, Fromm wrote, "one of the deepest emotional sources of fascist ideology has been touched upon."[1] In the years and decades that followed, Fromm sought to understand the origins of the evil that spawned so much cruelty, suffering, and death. He returned again and again to the question of Germany and its responsibility for the Holocaust, leading him to important insights into the nature of racial narcissism and destructiveness. His interest in these issues was not just academic. It was also deeply personal. Fromm grieved the deaths of Gertrud, Sophie, and many other relatives, friends, and colleagues. The Holocaust correspondence and the knowledge of what they endured would form the unspoken context for many of Fromm's social and political writings. In the wake of the war and genocide, Fromm was strongly committed to building a just society that could secure the voice of all its citizens, regardless of background or identity.

Fromm's postwar life as a German Jewish refugee was shaped by a complex set of political and personal circumstances. As a result of being forced to leave Germany, he became an involuntary member of an international community of refugees. When we read about Fromm today, he is variously referred to as "German," as a "German-born American," or as a "Jewish German-American." While all of these accounts are to some degree correct—Fromm became an American citizen in 1940—it would be more accurate to describe him as a "transnational." In fact, Fromm's life of forced immigration and migration was characteristic of what it meant to be a German Jewish refugee. By September 1939, approximately 280,000 Jews had left Germany and some 115,000 had left Austria. Of these, 90,000 emigrated to the United States, 60,000 to Palestine, 40,000 to Great Britain and about 75,000 to Central and South America. Another 18,000 German Jews found refuge in Shanghai.[2] Being a German Jewish refugee could thus be defined by life in New York, Tel

Aviv, London, or Buenos Aires, or by some combination of different countries, cultures, and languages. What united this diverse group of individuals was a common history of trauma and tragedy as a result of Nazi Germany and the Holocaust.

Fromm found refuge in New York in 1934 and lived there until he moved to Mexico City in 1950. He then spent the next two decades in Mexico, with yearly visits to the United States, and finally retired to Switzerland in the early 1970s. Fromm's movement from one location to the next gave him a unique perspective on the social and political crises that defined the postwar decades in the United States and Europe, and it helps to explain his cosmopolitan outlook as a social critic of capitalism and communism.[3] While Fromm's social and political writings and his work as a public intellectual are widely recognized, the personal dimension of the Holocaust and its impact on the Fromm's life have been neglected. The traumatic effects of the Nazi terror were present in Fromm's marriage to his second wife, Henny Gurland, who had narrowly escaped capture, and in Fromm's continued concern for his cousin Heinz Brandt, who survived Auschwitz against all odds. Like other German Jewish refugees, Fromm would struggle to reconcile his personal fealty to German culture with knowledge of atrocities that were committed by Germans. As he aged, he reflected on the enduring question of antisemitism and the tragic reversal of the German Jewish symbiosis that had shaped his early life. By discussing these interconnected themes, I want to provide the reader with a sense of just how present the legacy of the Holocaust was for Fromm, even if it was never the primary focus of his work. Only thus can we grasp the connection between the deaths of Gertrud, Sophie, and many other members of Fromm's extended family and Fromm's need to address the cruelty and destruction wrought by Hitler and the Nazi regime.

Tragedy in Portbou

While the Holocaust was unfolding across Europe, Fromm was in New York, where he shared the burden of worry with other German Jewish refugees. In 1944, Fromm met his second wife, Henny Gurland, a fellow German Jewish refugee who had escaped Nazi-occupied France with her son in 1940. Henny had fled by night over the Pyrenees to Spain with Walter Benjamin and witnessed his suicide. I want to begin this chapter by recounting Henny's narrow escape and Benjamin's death. The tragedy that unfolded illustrates the extent to which the traumatic reality of the Holocaust formed an integral part of Fromm's awareness. It undoubtedly reinforced the pain associated with the Holocaust correspondence and the loss of his own family members.

In the late 1930s, Fromm and Benjamin were both refugees from Nazi Germany, trying as best they could to master the challenges of their respective situations. Writing from Paris, Benjamin seemed to speak for them both when he stated, "What is required of liberal scholars now is awareness of their special opportunities to call a halt to the retreat of human values in Europe" (Benjamin, 1938, p. 310). Fromm divided his time in New York between the Institute for Social Research and his clinical practice, while for Benjamin, Parisian exile often meant isolation, poverty, and relative lack of publishing venues. Despite their different experiences, both held fast to the importance of speaking out against the dangers of fascism. What neither could know, or indeed possibly imagine, was that their lives would become linked in a tragic circle of fate.

In the years after Hitler and the Nazi Party assumed power, German Jews fled in large numbers to Western Europe. Despite the many difficulties they faced, they still believed or, at any rate, hoped they might be safe. But the German invasion of Belgium, the Netherlands, Luxembourg, and France, which began on May 10, 1940, put them in direct peril. Hundreds of thousands of refugees faced the threat of exposure, arrest, and deportation. In Paris, where Benjamin had lived in exile since 1933, the situation became dire.[4] When the war began in September 1939, his plans to travel to New York in the hope of securing a position at the Institute for Social Research were foiled. After a period of being interned with other German refugees by the French authorities, Benjamin returned to the city. Like Heinz Brandt, Benjamin was rendered "stateless," his German passport having been revoked by the Gestapo because of his antifascist publications. This made finding a way out of France more onerous. Already given to depression, Benjamin experienced a sense of impending doom. He was hardly alone. As Benjamin wrote in his lyrical style to his friend, Gretel Adorno, in April 1939, "Europe is a continent in whose tear-laden atmosphere the signal flares of comfort now ascend only rarely to announce good fortune" (Adorno and Benjamin, 2008, p. 254)

Shortly before the Nazis paraded through the streets of Paris, Benjamin fled south to Marseilles. The collaborationist Vichy regime in France had started to arrest antifascist refugees and hand them over to the Gestapo. Benjamin retained little hope, especially after an attempt to attain a visa for

Switzerland came to naught. As Benjamin remarked to Theodore Adorno in mid-July 1940,

> The complete uncertainty about what the next day, even the next hour may bring has dominated my life for weeks now. I am condemned to read every newspaper (they now come out on a single sheet here) as if it were a summons served on me in particular, to hear the voice of fateful tidings in every radio broadcast. (Adorno and Benjamin, 1999, p. 339)

In the midst of this gloom, Benjamin received a visa to enter the United States, arranged for by Horkheimer in New York. The challenge was how to turn this promise of safety into reality. Benjamin was able to secure transit papers for Spain and Portugal, but an exit visa from France still eluded him.

In Marseilles, Benjamin met Henny and her 16-year-old son, Joseph. Like Benjamin, they too were searching for a way to escape to safety. Before fleeing Germany, Gurland had been an active member of the German Social Democratic Party and worked as a photographer for the party's newspaper, *Vorwärts* (Forwards), where she had been one of a group of women known for their pioneering black-and-white photojournalism and portraiture.[5] Gurland would have faced certain arrest had she remained in Germany. She and Joseph went first to Belgium and then made their way to France. For a time, she lived with her second husband, Rafael Gurland, an antifascist attached to the Spanish embassy in Paris who had fought on the side of the Republicans during the Spanish Civil War.[6] As their marriage came to an end, so too did any sense of safety in France. Like Benjamin, Gurland and her son were able to secure temporary visas to enter the United States, but they lacked exit visas from France.

At the time, Marseilles was filled with many Jewish refugees, all of whom faced similarly dire circumstances. Together, Benjamin and Gurland hatched a plan to risk an illegal crossing over the Pyrenees into Spain. From Spain they hoped to reach Lisbon and then travel by ship to New York. But for their plan to succeed they needed help. Their guide was Lisa Fittko, a young German Jewish refugee from Berlin who had found a potential escape route through the mountains.

Fleeing over the border was dangerous. They faced the possibility of capture by Vichy guards who seemed eager to curry favor with the Gestapo, and hostility from guards on the Spanish side. Spain may not have officially taken sides in the war, but Franco's allegiance clearly lay with Nazi Germany, which had provided military aid during the civil war and was responsible for the carnage at Guernica.[7] Additionally, Henny feared that Rafael Gurland's name could be on a Spanish list of state enemies due to his association with the defeated Republican forces.

After setting out on September 25, they changed their planned route from a moderate to a much steeper and more remote path in order to avoid capture. Benjamin was in poor health as a result of a heart condition. Together, they struggled through the Mediterranean heat and mountainous terrain. Henny described the journey as "a 12 hour ordeal" (Gurland as cited in Scholem, 2012, p. 281). She and Joseph took turns carrying Benjamin's heavy briefcase, which he said contained a manuscript. At one point they even carried Benjamin when he was unable to continue up a steep incline. The next day, the four travelers met a group of women refugees who were also making their way to the small town of Portbou. Together they reached the Spanish border, where they were met by guards.

Unbeknownst to the group, the visa requirements to enter Spain had been changed a few days earlier. As a result, they were all arrested. The Spanish authorities informed them that they would be sent back to France the next day and transferred to the Gestapo. Gurland recounted the traumatic events in a letter she wrote to Adorno on October 11, 1940, after she had arrived in the United States:

> For an hour, four women and the three of us sat before the officials crying, begging and despairing as we showed them perfectly good papers. . . . The only document I had was the American one; for Jose and Benjamin this meant they would be sent to a camp. So all of us went to our rooms in utter despair. (Gurland as cited in Scholem, 2012, p. 282)

Carina Birman, who was one of the group of women who joined Benjamin and Henny on their way down to the Spanish border, remembers her last interaction with the Benjamin:

> I entered the room and found Prof. Benjamin in a desolate state of mind and in a completely exhausted physical condition. He told me that by no means was he willing to return to the border, or move out of this hotel. When I remarked that there was no alternative than to leave, he declared that there was one for him. He hinted that he had some very effective poisonous pills with him. (Birman, 2006, p. 5)

In the privacy of his hotel room, Benjamin swallowed the morphine pills he carried with him and then called for Henny. She was the last person to speak with him. In fact, Henny's son, Joseph, later recalled that his mother nursed Benjamin throughout the night (Gurland, 1998, p. 15). As Henny tells it, "At 7 in the morning Frau Lipmann called me down because Benjamin had asked for me. He told me that he had taken large quantities of morphine at 10 the preceding evening and that I should try to present the matter as illness" (Scholem, 2012, p. 281). Benjamin gave Henny a letter in which he wrote,

> In a situation with no way out, I have no other choice but to make an end of it. It is in a small village in the Pyrenees where no one knows me, that my life will come to a close. I ask you to transmit my thoughts to my friend Adorno and to explain to him the situation in which I find myself. There is not enough time remaining for me to write all the letters I would like to write. (Fittko, 1999, p. 946)

Clearly, Benjamin had reached his mental and physical limit. He was cornered and felt powerless in a situation that would see him returned into the hands of the Gestapo and sent to a concentration camp. Under the circumstances, it is not difficult to assume that he could have been driven to suicide, though over time Benjamin's death became shrouded in mystery. In fact, suicide was often a means for those who faced arrest and deportation to end their lives on their own terms. As Kaplan has noted, the rates of suicide among German Jews correlated with the increase in Nazi persecution and terror:

> Nervous breakdowns, depression and suicides became more and more common. Almost every memoir mentions one or more suicides. . . . The torrents of suicides in the 1930s notwithstanding, the most acute epidemic of suicides occurring during the deportations of 1942 and 1943. These suicides angered the Nazis, who waited for the unsuccessful suicides to recover in order to send them to their state-controlled deaths. (Kaplan, 1998, p. 180)

Benjamin's death certificate was issued by Dr. Vila Moreno, who changed his name to "Benjamin Walter," which concealed his Jewish background and made it possible to bury him in Portbou's Catholic cemetery.[8] Henny paid the rent for a burial niche for 5 years, after which Benjamin's body was moved to the adjoining graveyard.[9] Following Benjamin's death, and after significant sums of money changed hands, the local police chief allowed Henny and Joseph to travel on to Barcelona.

The escape over the Pyrenees would leave an indelible mark on Henny. In accounts of the celebrated philosopher's death, her own nightmare is frequently overlooked. As Henny wrote in her letter to Adorno, she might well have escaped arrest by the Gestapo, but her only child, Joseph, faced certain imprisonment in a concentration camp. The fact that Joseph was not yet an adult made little difference. He was a Jewish, which was reason enough for the Gestapo.

Following the tragedy in Portbou, Henny and Joseph continued on their way through Spain to Portugal. At the Spanish–Portugese border they faced a new threat. Spanish guards questioned them intensely about a foreign exchange they had made. Supposedly they had not secured "the proper receipt" (Gurland, 1998, p. 15). Their papers were taken by the guards, and Henny and Joseph were left not knowing if they would be arrested or allowed to continue. Their anxiety increased after guards entered their train car and removed another group of refugees bound for Great Britain. After an excruciating wait, Henny and Joseph were finally permitted to leave. They traveled on to Lisbon and stayed in the city for 3 months before securing passage on a ship to New York.[10]

In 1941, not long after arriving in New York, Fromm and Gurland met for the first time, through one of the many circles of German Jewish refugees that lived in the city. They shared similar life experiences and political outlooks. But perhaps more than anything else, they shared strong bonds of culture and history: both had been forced to escape their homeland and leave loved ones behind. Erich and Henny quickly became close and married in 1944, following the finalization of Fromm's divorce from Frieda (Figure 4.1).

As the war in Europe raged on and the horrors of the Holocaust began to be revealed, they provided one another with essential support. A letter written by Henny to a friend at the start of 1944 gives us a glimpse into the effect that the unfolding terrors were having on Erich and Henny: "I am very unhappy and depressed, as you can imagine... there is nothing one can do—and I know that we are nevertheless happier than millions of people on the other side."[11] Liberation of the Nazi concentration camps and killing centers in Eastern Europe began with Majdanek in Lublin, Poland, in July 1944. News of what had taken place inside the camps seemed to extinguish any hope that Gertrud, Sophie, and other family members had survived. Erich

Figure 4.1 Henny Gurland, 1945
Courtesy of the Erich Fromm Archive, Tübingen.

and Henny provided each other with comfort and sustenance as they learned of the breadth and barbarity of the crimes. Millions of Jews had already been murdered, and many more would meet the same fate before hostilities in Europe finally ended on May 8, 1945. Erich and Henny must have felt a deep disappointment and anger with a world that first ignored the plight of European Jews and then cruelly refused to take them in, especially when it was clear that so much more could have been done to save lives.

During these years Fromm, who never had children of his own, developed a close relationship with Henny's son, Joseph. Their relationship would span the decades and continue until Fromm's death in 1980. But Fromm's time with Henny was tragically short-lived. Henny's initial happiness at meeting Erich was increasingly overshadowed by long stretches of depression, made worse by severe arthritic pain.[12] For refugees like Henny, who survived the Nazi terror, the emotional traumas and physical trials they were forced to endure often left deep and lasting scars. In 1950, on the advice of physicians, Erich and Henny moved to Mexico City, where it was believed the climate would provide her with some relief. Whether it was the traumatic escape from Vichy France and the harrowing journey through fascist Spain or the cumulative experiences of being a refugee with a history of mental and physical maladies, Henny died 2 years later, in the shadow of the Holocaust and likely by her own hand.

When we consider what happened to Fromm's family, and the brief happiness of his time with Henny, followed by the difficult years of her steady decline, we begin to get a sense of just how personal the tragedy and trauma of the Holocaust really was for him. Whether and to what extent these experiences left a deeper psychological mark on Fromm is not something we can know with certainty, since he never publicly revealed how the Holocaust traumas of his family members, or of his wife's narrow escape, affected him. But we can turn to the experience of Fromm's first wife, Frieda, to gain some insight.

Fromm's affidavit enabled Frieda to reach the safety of New York in 1935. Frieda, like Erich, never appeared to suffer from the kind of serious depression that afflicted many refugees. But as Gail Hornstein, Fromm-Reichmann's biographer has observed, Frieda's distress was nonetheless evident: "Told about the concentration camps, she vomited and ran from the room. Like many German Jews, Frieda and her immediate family members had managed to escape, but more than a hundred of her relatives were murdered by the Nazis. Dozens more survived but lost everything" (Hornstein, 2000, p. 118). In the aftermath, clinical work and writing became a familiar and perhaps comforting way for Erich and Frieda to respond to the horrors. Like many other German Jewish refugees, they were highly productive. Fromm seemed to find sustenance in the structure of his daily life and work, and in reality, there was little more that he or any other refugee could do to manage their memories and the knowledge of the horrors that had occurred.

Reflecting on his own experience as a German Jewish refugee, Peter Gay reminds us that not even the most fortunate refugees from Hitler's Germany could fully escape their past. Gay shared the example of his aging mother to illustrate how the experience of Nazi Germany could still shape the emotional lives of German Jewish refugees, even many decades later. As Gay observes, his mother

> had never been threatened by a Storm Trooper, had never been directly exposed to Nazi violence, but in her errant moments she relived the late

1930s with horrendous immediacy. She interpreted the occasional loudspeaker announcements in her facility [retirement home] as a signal for a pogrom. She imagined that I had been killed. (Gay, 1998, pp. 21–22)

Certainly, Fromm never considered himself as a "survivor," and because he was able to leave for Switzerland early on, his experience of Nazi Germany was different from German Jewish refugees like Gay, who escaped only in the period after the November Pogrom of 1938. In contrast with his relatives, Fromm was also spared the suffering associated with Eastern Europe's ghettos and concentration camps. And yet, Fromm was without a doubt a victim of history. A photograph that Henny took of Erich in 1945 (Figure 4.2), in the last year of the war, speaks for itself: a look of deep sadness and worry, heightened by the toll and exhaustion of many years spent trying to rescue family members, is etched onto Fromm's face. Unlike better known photographs of Fromm that depict the feted public intellectual, the authenticity we find in this photo seems to reflect the unbearable weight of the catastrophe.

Figure 4.2 Erich Fromm, 1945
Photo by Henny Gurland. Courtesy of the Erich Fromm Archive, Tübingen.

States of Denial

While German Jewish refugees were united by their escape from Nazi Germany and the trauma of leaving family members behind, they were an extremely diverse group, distinguished by education, profession, and religiosity. Most lived in the urban centers of Germany, but some also had rural livelihoods. Many were secular and arrived in the United States with only a recent acknowledgment of their Jewishness. Others, like Fromm, grew up with a strong sense of Jewish identity but consciously chose to embrace a secular, humanistic outlook.

After arriving in the United States, German Jewish refugees often retained a strong sense of German culture and language, even though this identity coexisted with the reality of having been cast out by their fellow Germans. Of the 90,000 German Jews who found refuge in the United States, a small number returned to Germany, be it to live in their native culture or to help rebuild a new, democratic county, and there were many more who visited over the decades.[13] Horkheimer and Adorno returned to Frankfurt in 1949 in order to re-establish the Institute of Social Research, but there is no evidence to suggest that Fromm wanted to go back. In general, attitudes among the refugees toward Germans varied, and those refugees who were older when they fled often retained stronger ties to Germany because they identified with the Weimar Republic.[14]

Despite their diversity, virtually all German Jews watched with concern as the contours of postwar Germany took shape. Germany's responsibility for the genocide loomed large. In the aftermath of the war, Fromm saw little initial evidence that the country had changed, let alone that it had confronted its guilt. To be sure, Hitler was dead by his own hand, the Nazi regime was defeated, and wide swaths of the country's cities lay in ruin. In 1946, the Nuremberg trials led to the conviction and execution of Nazi leaders who had, as a group, refused to admit their guilt. The one exception was Albert Speer, Hitler's architect and minister of armaments and war production, who was sentenced to 20 years in prison. His admission managed to convince many, despite the untold suffering and deaths among the eight million forced laborers under his authority.

After the Nuremberg trials, the government of the newly established West German state, the Federal Republic of Germany (FRG), balked at pursuing further criminalization. The Allies were eager to build a bulwark against potential Soviet aggression and supported the status quo in West Germany. In

September 1949, in one of his first speeches to the nation, Chancellor Konrad Adenauer declared, "Denazification has caused much misfortune and much mischief." Where it seemed "defensible," the chancellor said, the federal government was determined "to let bygones be bygones."[15] An attitude of denial became entrenched in Adenauer's government (1949–1963), mirroring the mindset of a nation that was not yet prepared to confront its collective responsibility. The problem was that the beliefs, value system, and prejudices that had shaped the Nazi era were still embedded in German society. As a result, not only did former perpetrators remain free; they also received generous pensions and played an important role in the establishment of the new West German state. A German colleague who grew up in the capital city of Bonn during the 1950s and early 1960s described to me how even as a child, the sight of so many black Mercedes gave rise to a deep sense of unease. The official government vehicles cast an ominous shadow, harking back to a Nazi past that was lurking, barely disguised, beneath the surface of the new democratic state. The silence in Bonn's streets and buildings was repeated in the dynamics of German families, where talk of the past focused on German victimization during and after the war, all but silencing the suffering endured by the victims of the Nazi regime.

For many Germans, indifference to the disappearance of Jewish neighbors in their midst in the years before and during the war gave way to indifference to the question of responsibility after the war. The vast majority believed that responsibility for the Holocaust had nothing to do with them but, instead, lay squarely at the feet of Hitler and his Nazi henchmen who had been tried and hanged in Nuremberg. The average German who participated in the totalitarian Nazi state was hardly innocent. But measured purely on the basis of the denazification process set up by the Allies, neither were they guilty. Indeed, the vast majority of Nazis were easily able to escape justice. Using false statements of support, they received what became known as a *Persilschein*, a certificate of cleanliness named after the German washing detergent. It is no wonder that so many second-generation Germans rebelled in 1968. They were being suffocated by the silence of the politicians and their parents. As Alexander and Magarete Mitscherlich suggested in their well-known book *The Inability to Mourn* (1967), Germans had yet to relinquish their attachment to the Führer.

We don't know exactly when Fromm returned to Germany for the first time, but records show that he attended a congress in Düsseldorf organized by the German Psychoanalytic Society in 1961.[16] There are diverse accounts by

German Jewish refugees that recount just how challenging it could be to visit Germany in the wake of the Holocaust.[17] These difficulties were exacerbated by interactions with individual Germans whose concern about the Nazi past was limited to pleas about their own suffering. These issues were clearly on Fromm's mind as he sought to address Germany's responsibility for the terror and destruction it brought upon European Jewry.

In the early 1950s, hoping to curry favor with its Western allies, the West German government reached an agreement with Israel to pay reparations. The program of restitution, or *Wiedergutmachung* (literally, to make good again), also provided the opportunity for Jewish survivors and refugees to submit claims for individual compensation. Yet the program was deeply unpopular among the German population. Politicians and adjudicators often demonstrated hostility and responded to requests for compensation with implicit and explicit antisemitic stereotyping.[18] As a result, what should have been a straightforward process of acknowledging the emotional suffering of survivors and compensating the financial loss of property became a needlessly complicated and frequently ugly debacle. To be eligible for reparations, individuals had to prove that they had been specifically victimized and that their traumatic injuries were not only disabling but the clear result of racial persecution. Claims for financial loss required proof of the value of property that was most often forcibly sold in haste for sums that were vastly below its actual value. Victims found it difficult if not impossible to meet the rigid and unreasonable requirements and many claims were rejected outright.

In 1958, Fromm helped his mother, Rosa, to submit a so-called restitution claim.[19] She died a year later, and Fromm, as her only heir, became the legal claimant. The grinding process of bureaucratic wrangling meant that it took a total of 7 years before the German government agreed to provide compensation. After countless legal letters, witness statements, and supporting documentation, the government bureaucrats divined a total of 930 marks. This included 300 marks as compensation for Rosa's voyage to England after she fled Nazi Germany, and a further 630 marks for the loss of her property, which was only a fraction of its original value. In a note written in 1958, shortly before her death, Rosa described how in order to leave Germany, she had been forced to sell all her furniture, antique rugs, and silver cutlery sets under duress; they were worth at least 4,000 marks, but she received a mere 400 marks. This was one of countless examples of the way in which Germans directly profited from the racial persecution of their Jewish neighbors. The final amount offered to Fromm was based on a dubious and arbitrary logic that seemed destined only to intensify the original injury. Fromm was asked to sign off on the compensation and thereby bring the restitution claim to an official close. Although he was offered the right of appeal, this would likely have dragged on for many more years. Clearly Fromm wanted only to end the demeaning process. It must have been both infuriating and deeply painful for him and reawakened wounds that had barely begun to heal.

In 1961, in the midst of the struggle to push forward his mother's restitution claim, and in the same year that he first visited Germany, Fromm paused his busy schedule to honor a fellow German Jewish refugee, Adolf Leschnitzer. After the Nazis came to power, Jewish school children were subjected to the Nazi regime's antisemitic policies, which specifically targeted and sought to isolate them. Rather than emigrate early on when he had the chance, Leschnitzer chose to remain Germany in order to organize and supervise a Jewish school system for the tens of thousands of children. In his introduction to a Festschrift for Leschnitzer, Fromm wrote,

> The Jewish youth of Germany, like their elders, were threatened in those early days of the Hitler era not so much with physical violence as with harmful attacks of a psychological nature. Some were at once expelled from the public schools, while others, although permitted to remain temporarily, were exposed—defenseless—to insults, humiliation, and other forms of maltreatment. (Fromm, 1961b, pp. 13–15)

What followed were a series of ever-increasing horrors, which Fromm at the time likened to a kind of "primitive ritual murder." As Fromm explained,

> While a large sector of the adherents of the National Socialist Party was composed simply of secular, opportunistic, ruthless, power-seeking politicians, Junkers, generals, businessmen, and bureaucrats, the core, represented by the triumvirate of Hitler, Himmler and Goebbels, was essentially not different from the primitive "bearshirts," driven by a "sacred fury" and the aim to destroy.... They committed ritual murder first of the Jews, then of foreign populations. (Fromm, 1960b, p. 93)

Societal upheavals in West Germany that began in the late 1960s finally succeeded in creating a new, critical attitude toward the Third Reich. But former Nazi Party members, perpetrators, and enablers still populated the highest ranks of federal and local governments well into the decades of the 1970s and 1980s. Acquitted by the German judiciary, which was itself full of former Nazis, these men and the public that supported them often acted as though the Holocaust never occurred. Questions about their Nazi involvement were not asked and no information was freely offered. The German Jewish journalist Ralph Giordano (1987) referred to this period as "Germany's second guilt," following the Germany's "first guilt" of perpetrating the Holocaust.

Fromm directly addressed the politics and society of West Germany in his book *May Man Prevail* (1961d). He questioned whether the former perpetrator nation would ever truly be able to shed its Nazi past given the role played by former Nazis. As Fromm observed,

> Many former Nazis are still in high government positions. (Dr. Globke, a high civil servant under Hitler and author of the most important commentary on Hitler's racial laws, is chief of Adenauer's chancellory office.) It is characteristic that one of the main attacks against Willy Brandt, the Social Democratic opponent of Adenauer, is the argument that he emigrated from Germany under Hitler, and thus was not a loyal patriot. (Fromm, 1961a, p. 174)

Fromm's assessment was certainly correct, though with the benefit of hindsight, we can observe that his statements were a gross underestimate. Under Adenauer, not only was Hans Globke, coauthor of the Nuremberg Laws, appointed state secretary of the Federal Chancellery, Theodore Oberlaender, who had been in charge of so-called Germanization measures in Poland, which included ethnic cleansing and support for the elimination of Jews, was appointed federal minister for Displaced Persons, Refugees and Victims of War. Throughout the early 1960s (1961a, 1962b), Fromm expressed concern about West Germany's growing sense of nationalism, especially as Adenauer's government pushed for an increase in the West German military, whose generals, as Fromm pointed out, had all "served under Hitler" (Fromm, 1961a, p 3).

In a provocatively titled essay, "Is Germany on the March Again?," Fromm (1966) takes the former defense minister and head of the Bavarian conversative (Christian Social Union; CSU) party, Franz Josef Strauss, to task. Strauss had made a public statement alluding to the possibility of a "new Führer" in connection to the humiliation that he and others felt as a result of the fact that Germany did not possess nuclear weapons. Though

Strauss's utterance was rhetorical in nature, it can't have escaped Fromm's notice that Strauss had been a member of the National Socialist Motor Corps (NSKK), the same paramilitary organization in which my own grandfather participated. As Fromm stated, "a public utterance about a 'new Fuehrer' is disturbing, to say the least. And the sentimental appeal that Germany is humiliated and discriminated against if she has no nuclear weapons is like an echo from the past" (1966, p. 3). Fromm's critique was leveled not just at the politicians, however. He also recognized the role played by the industrialists in supporting Hitler on his road to power (Fromm, 1962a, p. 22). Many in the business elite reassumed their positions in the new West Germany, and the struggle to acknowledge their implication in the Nazi past continues into the present.[20]

It was not until the election of Willy Brandt as chancellor in 1969 that West Germany's relationship with the Nazi era began to change. Brandt defeated Adenauer's successor, Chancellor Kurt Kiesinger, who had been a known member of the Nazi Party and the NSKK. While Kiesinger's Nazi past may have made little difference in earlier years, in November 1968 he was famously confronted by the anti-Nazi activist Beate Klarsfeld. She was captured on film slapping him and shouting "Nazi, Nazi." Her actions came to represent the generational shift at work and captured the zeitgeist that led to Brandt's election. Brandt had been a vocal opponent of the Nazis. Fearing for his life, he escaped to Norway and Sweden, where he spent the duration of the war. Brandt's opposition to Hitler set him apart from most members of his generation, a difference in outlook that made itself felt in his policies.

One of Brandt's first steps as chancellor was to try to ease Cold War tensions between East and West. As part of his "Ostpolitik," Brandt traveled to Poland in December 1970 to sign the Treaty of Warsaw, which relinquished Germany's claims on its former Eastern territories and recognized the border that was created at the close of the war. In Warsaw, Brandt also went to lay a wreath at the monument to the victims of the Warsaw Ghetto Uprising. In an act of personal and public contrition, he spontaneously fell to his knees where he stayed, prone, for almost a minute. The *Kniefall*, or "knee fall" as it was known in Germany, became an important symbol of the willingness to acknowledge and atone for the terrible crimes that had been committed. Brandt's act of contrition garnered much international attention and support, but it was notably criticized by many Germans of his generation. The conservative opposition was particularly incensed, believing that he had embarrassed the nation. They argued that by signing the Warsaw Treaty Brandt had betrayed German national interests.

Comments in the German newspapers immediately following the event were reserved. Even a week later, *Der Spiegel* magazine, one of Germany's leading news weeklies, published an opinion poll in which a majority of Germans deemed Brandt's act of falling to his knees to be an exaggeration (Rauer, 2009, p. 279). Brandt's gesture brought to light the tensions at work in Germany's relationship to its Nazi past. Many of the former Nazis that Fromm pointed to in 1961 were still in positions of power in the early 1970s, and in German society, the myth of so-called good Nazis continued apace. But Brandt's gesture spoke to a younger generation. With time it became a turning point, opening up the door to new forms of collective remembrance and responsibility. Following on the heels of the Auschwitz Trials in Frankfurt (1963–1965), a new sensibility began to shape West Germany's culture of remembrance.

This did not mean, however, that Brandt's own government was free of the past. As the journalist Malte Herwig has shown, "From Konrad Adenauer's cabinet to Helmut Kohl's, former members of the NSDAP had sat at the table in every German government since the war. Under chancellor Willy Brandt alone, 12 former Nazis served as ministers" (Herwig, 2014, p. 140). Indeed, while Brandt was the first Social Democrat to be elected in postwar Germany, there continued to be general agreement among the West German political parties that denazification should remain a thing of the past, a sentiment echoed in 1978, by the soon-to-be chancellor Helmut Kohl, who spoke out publicly against a "new de-Nazification" (Herwig, p. 146). Thus, when Fromm died in 1980, West Germany's confrontation with National Socialism and its perpetration of the Holocaust was still in its infancy.

Hans Brandt's Remarkable Survival

After the war, some left-wing German Jewish survivors believed, or at least hoped, that the East German communist state might hold greater promise than its Western capitalist counterpart. They were attracted above all to its antifascist outlook and the possibility of creating a new and more equitable society that would recognize the rights and equality of all citizens and avoid the terrible mistakes of the past. In comparison with with the Federal Republic of Germany (FRG), the German Democratic Republic (GDR) was more diligent in its denazification process, at least as far as the number of Nazis who were tried and found guilty was concerned.[21] This did not mean, however, that Jews who settled in the GDR openly practiced their religion or identified themselves as Jewish. The sociologist Irene Runge, who together with her parents moved to East Germany as a child in 1949, describes what it was like: "Nobody came to live as a Jew in East Germany—they wanted to live as communists. They repressed everything Jewish." Whether and to what extent this may have been different from the Jewish community in the West is a matter of debate. As Runge states, "I think it was the only way you can live here. You had to stay focused on the political goal. The mindset was: 'We are not going to let Germans stay alone in this country, we will make it a better state than ever.'"[22] The main difference between the postwar Jewish communities in the East and West was thus their relationship to communism. What they both shared is the fact that they were tiny in number and living among Germans who had little interest in confronting their recent past.

One of the German Jews who settled in the GDR after the war was Fromm's cousin Heinz Brandt. Against all odds, he managed to survive three concentration camps and was liberated from Buchenwald by the American army on April 11, 1945. Brandt had been among the few to survive Auschwitz. After arriving there in 1942, Brandt was sent to the satellite farming camp known as Budy. His survival depended on a network of communists whom he knew from his 6 years as a political prisoner. The Kapo in Budy had shared a prison sentence with Heinz in Berlin.[23] Yet this alone could not guarantee Brandt's survival, especially in view of the highly dangerous anti-Nazi activities he undertook while at the camp. In Auschwitz, Brandt participated in the documentation of the extermination process, information that was later smuggled out by the Polish resistance and sent to the government-in-exile in London, and from there to the United States.[24] On January 18, 1945, in advance of the Soviet army, Brandt, along with thousands of other prisoners, was forced on a death march to concentration camps located inside Germany. Anyone who fell behind was shot by SS guards and as a result one in four was killed along the way. When Brandt arrived at Buchenwald, it was already massively overcrowded and he was near death. Brandt received help in the form of extra rations from other communists, which enabled him to survive the catastrophic conditions until he was liberated.

In total, Brandt endured 6 years as a political prisoner followed by another 5 years in three different concentration camps. Despite this history, Brandt chose to remain in Germany. He returned to Berlin, rejoined the Communist

Party, became an employee of the city administration, and worked for a committee called "Victims of Fascism." When the FRG and GDR were established in 1949, Brandt was already firmly embedded in the new East German government, and by 1952, he had become a member of the state leadership. His commitment toward building a communist society was a reflection of his deeply held political beliefs.

Fromm shared his cousin's Marxist outlook, though he seemed to recognize the limitations of the new Soviet-controlled regime. Fromm's strong aversion to Stalin was shared by Brandt. Throughout the 1950s, East Germany went through a period of Stalinization, which prohibited any open discussion about the direction that communism was taking. Brandt's misgivings increased when he learned of the experiences that his sister Lilli Brandt had endured in the Soviet Union under Stalin. She had fled to Moscow in 1932 and become a physician there but was caught up in one of Stalin's many purges and sent to a gulag in Siberia. Lilli Brandt did not return to Moscow until 1956 and was only reunited with her brother in 1957.[25] Until that point, neither knew whether the other had survived. Their brother Richard Brandt had been killed in Moscow many years earlier.

Never a person to be silenced, Brandt challenged the ruling system in East Germany. By 1958, Brandt saw the writing on the wall and fled with his family to Frankfurt, where he planned to continue his political work on behalf of the West German Metalworkers' Trade Union. He was critical of the governments in both East and West, but it was his opposition to the leadership of GDR's Communist Party that proved to be his downfall. At a trade union congress in West Berlin in June 1961, Brandt was kidnapped by the East German State Security Service (Stasi). Brandt was taken back to East Germany, charged with state espionage, and sentenced to 13 years in prison. He was told that if he recanted his critique of the GDR all charges would be dropped. Brandt refused and was thrown into solitary confinement at the infamous, Stasi-controlled Bautzen prison.

Learning of his cousin's disappearance and arrest, Fromm immediately intervened. It would take almost 3 years before Brandt was freed, during which Fromm worked continually to canvass for his release. This must have reawakened memories of the harrowing years of the late 1930s and early 1940s, during which Fromm made every effort to help his cousin flee Nazi Germany. Fromm had succeeded in arranging visas for Heinz for Great Britain and Shanghai, but each time it came to naught. Fifteen years had elapsed, and now he sought to free of his cousin from the clutches of the Stasi.

Fromm's concern for Brandt's well-being was justified. Brandt had already endured 11 grueling years in captivity.

In the intervening period, what had changed was Fromm's rise from academic sociologist and psychoanalyst to public intellectual and peace activist of global renown. Fromm was able to use his connections with other leading activists and politicians and enlisted the support of Bertrand Russel, who helped campaign for Brandt's release. Fromm also convinced Amnesty International's president, Peter Benenson, to take up Brandt's case. In 1963, Amnesty made Brandt their "prisoner of the year," creating international awareness of the unjust arrest and applying pressure on the East German government. At Benenson's request, Fromm wrote a formal letter in support of his cousin:

> Heinz Brandt is a man of faith in the unity of mankind, in human solidarity, in reason and in peace. When Hitler came to power, Brandt fought in the underground; he was arrested and sentenced to prison, and when released he rejoined the ranks of the underground. He was captured again, and altogether spent 11 years in Hitler's prisons and concentration camps. The defeat of the Nazis saved him from death; it also gave him new hope. He believed that the United Socialist Party in East Germany would bring about the realization of equality and freedom. But he became increasingly critical of the Ulbricht regime, until he felt compelled to escape with his wife and three small children to West Germany, where he accepted a position on the publication of the Metalworkers' Trade Union in Frankfurt. But quite in contrast to so many ex-communists, he neither lost his faith in socialism, nor did he sell himself to the right, as a cold war fighter. Even though he made himself unpopular, he passionately fought for coexistence and against West German atomic rearmament. On the occasion of a visit to West Berlin he mysteriously fell into the hands of the East German police. After a year of being held incommunicado, he was sentenced, in a secret trial, to 13 years hard labor. Many outstanding representatives of the peace movement in the West, such as Russell, Collins, Chisholm, Bourdet, Pickett, Riesman, Abendroth, Flechtheim, have approached the government of the G.D.R. with the request of a pardon for Heinz Brandt, to allow him to return to his family and his work for peace in Frankfurt. So far, there has been no reaction. It is most welcome news to all humanitarians that Amnesty has now made Brandt their "prisoner of the year."[26]

It took until 1964 before Brandt was finally released and able to rejoin his family in the West (Figure 4.3). With Fromm's support, Heinz wrote a well-received autobiography, *The Search for a Third Way*, for which Fromm wrote the preface, entitled "Heinz Brandt as a Man of Faith" (Fromm, 1970a). During his years of solitary confinement, Heinz had already done much of the mental work of writing, keeping his mind active by engaging his life's memories. In the decades that followed, Heinz continued to be politically engaged in the new West German "Green" movement and in antinuclear protests. Erich and Heinz shared their political outlook to the last, so it is perhaps not surprising that Fromm's final book, *To Have or To Be* (1976b), helped to inspire the left-wing movements in which Heinz played a leading role. Alongside Fromm's Swiss cousin, Gertrud Hunziker-Fromm, Heinz remained Erich's closest relative and a living connection to their shared heritage of family and loss.

Figure 4.3 Heinz Brandt Being Greeted by His Family After His Release From East German Prison, 1964

Courtesy of the Erich Fromm Archive, Tübingen.

Racial Narcissism

The year that Brandt was released from the East German prison, Fromm published an important book that addressed the insidious effects of political repression. In the early 1960s, as the system of racial laws in the United States known as "Jim Crow" began to be challenged, Fromm was often reminded of the anti-Jewish legislation that had been implemented by the Nazis and portended the genocidal policies to come. Fromm felt obliged to address the parallels. In 1964, at the height of the civil rights movement, he published *The Heart of Man*, which examined the racial terror inflicted on African Americans and drew a direct links to the treatment of Jewish Germans under the Nazis.

During the 1950s and 1960s, the American civil rights movement sought to end the segregation and disenfranchisement of African Americans. The movement met some of its fiercest opposition in the state of Alabama, which had been a center of slavery and the cotton trade. In 1963, the white supremacist bombing of the 16th Street Baptist Church in Birmingham caused the death of four young African American girls. That same year, the state's governor, George Wallace, declared in his infamous inaugural address, "In the name of the greatest people that have ever trod this earth, I draw the line in the dust and toss the gauntlet before the feet of tyranny, and I say segregation now, segregation tomorrow, segregation forever." Fromm was undoubtedly responding to Wallace's statement when he wrote,

> The narcissistic conviction of the superiority of whites over blacks in parts of the United States and in South Africa demonstrates that there is no restraint to the sense of self-superiority or of the inferiority of another group. However, the satisfaction of a group requires also a certain degree of confirmation in reality. As long as the whites in Alabama or in South Africa have the power to demonstrate their superiority over the blacks through social, economic, and political acts of discrimination, their narcissistic beliefs have some element of reality and thus bolster up the entire narcissistic thought-system. The same held true for the Nazis. (Fromm 1964, pp. 82–83)

Fromm was describing, in effect, how Southern white supremacy had enforced racial segregation through the Jim Crow legal system at the state and local level. Once in power in Germany, Hitler and the Nazi Party enacted a series of similar laws, known as the Nuremberg Laws, that were directly based on their study of American race law at the time. However, as the legal scholar James Whitman points out, it was not only "the Jim Crow South that attracted Nazi lawyers. In the early 1930s the Nazis drew on a range of American examples, both federal and state. Their America was not just the South; it was a racist America writ much larger" (Whitman, 2017, p. 5).

Our understanding of the direct connections that exist between Nazi Germany and the United States of the 1930s is relatively recent. Fromm would probably not have known that Nazi lawyers traveled to the United States to study American race law, but he knew enough from living in Germany to draw a direct connection between "racial narcissism which existed in Hitler's Germany, and which is found in the American South" (Fromm, 1964, p. 76). In a manner reminiscent of *Escape From Freedom*, Fromm maintained that the economic and social anxieties experienced by many whites created an especially fertile ground for racism. He argued that "economically and culturally deprived" whites who have no "realistic hope of changing" their situation have "only one satisfaction . . . being superior to another racial group that is singled out as inferior" (Fromm, 1964, p. 76) According to Fromm, members of this group felt that " 'even though I am poor and uncultured I am somebody important because I belong to the most admirable group in the world—I am white;' or, 'I am Aryan' " (Fromm, 1964, p. 76). As Fromm observed, "If one examines the judgement of poor whites regarding blacks, or of the Nazis in regard to Jews, one can easily recognize the distorted character of their respective judgments . . . the lack of objectivity often leads to disastrous circumstances" (Fromm, 1964, p. 81).

Turning to the nature of narcissism itself, Fromm suggested that racial narcissism of groups and the malignant narcissism of individuals are directly related. They are both "crudely solipsistic as well as xenophobic" (1964, p. 74). As Fromm explained, "the group narcissism of the 'whites' or the 'Aryans' is as malignant as the extreme narcissism of a single person can be" (Fromm, 1964, p. 77). The narcissism of the group and the individual are further connected by the way in which the group seeks a leader who can reflect and strengthen the group's narcissism. According to Fromm,

> The highly narcissistic group is eager to have a leader with whom it can identify itself. The leader is then admired by the group which projects its narcissism onto him. In the very act of submission to the powerful leader, which is in depth an act of symbiosis and identification, the narcissism of the individual is transferred onto the leader. The greater the leader, the

greater the follower. Personalities who as individuals are particularly narcissistic are the most qualified to fulfill this function. The narcissism of the leader who is convinced of his greatness, and who has no doubts, is precisely what attracts the narcissism of those who submit to him. The half-insane leader is often the most successful one. (Fromm, 1964, pp. 83–84)

Fromm initially identified how the act of submitting to a powerful leader could assuage a group's anxieties when he was writing *Escape From Freedom* in the late 1930s. But at the time, it was impossible to know how just how dangerous and irrational the symbiotic relationship between a group and its leader could become. Writing in *The Heart of Man*, Fromm described Hitler as "a man of extreme personal narcissism, who stimulated the group narcissism of millions of Germans" (1964, p. 82). According to Fromm, fanatical leaders like Hitler needed "to find believers, to transform reality so that it fits their narcissism and to destroy all critics" (1964, p. 74). As Fromm put it, "Here was an extremely narcissistic person who probably could have suffered a manifest psychosis had he not succeeded in making millions believe in his own self-image, [and] take his grandiose fantasies regarding the millennium of 'the Third Reich' seriously" (1964, p. 74).

Fromm's observations in *Escape From Freedom* and *The Heart of Man* not only help us to understand the psychological dynamics of racism and xenophobia that occurred at the time he was writing those books; his conclusions also have a powerful contemporary resonance. The economic uncertainty and powerlessness that many workers have experienced as a result of neoliberal policies have given rise to leaders and movements eager to harness their anxiety and secure support for their right-wing agendas. This process is reminiscent of the uncertainty that many Germans experienced in the aftermath of World War I and that ultimately hastened the rise of Nazism in the 1930s. Historically distinct periods are of course notoriously difficult to compare. Yet the upsurge in right-wing authoritarianism, and its racist and xenophobic agenda, is common to each. Indeed, it is hard to read Fromm's analysis in *The Heart of Man* without thinking about the way in which the actions of the far-right have been implicitly and explicitly supported by right-wing populist leaders like Donald Trump in the United States, Jair Bolsonaro in Brazil, and Viktor Orban in Hungary. The symbiosis of the narcissism of the group and the narcissism of the individual leader described by Fromm certainly found its expression in the Trump presidency. Trump's leadership used nativism and race baiting to secure support from a base of overwhelmingly white supporters and gave voice to historically entrenched racial divisions in American society. In her recent work *Caste: The Origins of Our Discontents*, the journalist Isabel Wilkerson (2020), sheds light on those divisions. She suggests that Fromm's work on the pathology of racial narcissism not only helps to explain the racism of the past; it also evokes the underlying caste system that supports systemic racism and white supremacy in the United States in the present.[27]

Human Destructiveness

Fromm's discussion of racial narcissism also led him to delve more deeply into the nature of human cruelty and destructiveness. In 1973, he published *The Anatomy of Human Destructiveness*, which appeared first in English and a year later in German, by which time Fromm had retired to Switzerland and closed his clinical practice. Written 40 years after the Nazis took power, *The Anatomy of Human Destructiveness* (1973) was Fromm's attempt to understand the destructive forces that had shaped the course of 20th century and changed the trajectory of his life. It was a highly ambitious book that drew on a host of different disciplines and was arguably his most scholarly work since his tenure at the Institute for Social Research came to an end.

Fromm sought to explain the impulse to be violent and cruel and to answer the question of what makes humans want to kill one another. To this end, he undertook extended analyses of Stalin, Himmler, and Hitler and examined the death and destruction they caused. Fromm argued that aggression could be divided into benign and malignant varieties. He referred to aggression that serves the defensive purpose of preserving life as "benign," while aggression that has no life-preserving function and seeks only to destroy was described as "malignant."

Fromm devoted much of the book to examining different types of malignant aggression. This approach drew on a distinction he introduced in *The Heart of Man* between two orientations: "the biophilic," or love of life, which is oriented toward growth and happiness, and "the necrophilic," or love of death, which is oriented toward decay and destruction. What set *The Anatomy of Human Destructiveness* apart was Fromm's attempt to shed light on the extreme character of sadism, which he defined as the intense desire to control, hurt, and humiliate another person, and necrophilia, which he defined as the unadulterated need to destroy.

Drawing on his earlier works, Fromm developed the link between nationalism, racism, and group narcissism. Fromm reminded his readers that the appeal of authoritarian leaders lay in what they were able to offer their followers:

> Even if one is the most miserable, the poorest, the least respected member of a group, there is compensation for one's miserable condition in feeling 'I am a part of the most wonderful group in the world. I, who in reality am a worm, become a giant through belonging to the group.' Consequently, the degree of group narcissism is commensurate with the lack of real satisfaction in life. (Fromm, 1973, p. 275)

According to Fromm, the narcissism of the group was used by skilled authoritarian leaders to further their political ends. Hitler thus was able to exploit a thirst for vengeance felt by many Germans at the end of World War I:

> A large number of Germans were motivated by the wish for revenge because of the injustice of the Versailles Peace treaty and its material conditions and particularly in its demand that the German government should accept sole responsibility for the outbreak of the war. It is notorious that real or alleged atrocities can ignite the most intense rage and vengefulness. Hitler made the alleged mistreatment of the German minorities in [then] Czechoslovakia the center of the propaganda before he attacked the country. (Fromm, 1973, p. 364)

And in one of few direct references to antisemitism, Fromm went on to state, "One example of thirst for revenge that has lasted almost two thousand years is the reaction to the execution of Jesus allegedly by the Jews; the cry 'Christ-killers' has traditionally been one of the major sources of violent antisemitism" (Fromm, 1973, p. 364). Though Fromm did not spell it out, Hitler was able to tap into this long-standing racial trope and spread the flames of his virulent antisemitism.

As Fromm reminded his readers, it is one thing to exploit the destructive desires and fantasies of others, and quite another to engage in sheer, unadulterated cruelty and destructiveness. To examine this phenomenon, Fromm turned his lens on Himmler, the notorious leader of the SS: "the 'bloodhound of Europe,' as he was called by many, Himmler was, together with Hitler, responsible for the slaughter" (Fromm, 1973, p. 398). Fromm saw Himmler as an extreme example of malignant aggression, a brutally vicious sadist whose actions and entire worldview were shaped by a deep and abiding need to dominate and inflict pain on others. Fromm maintained that Himmler was already a sadistic character before he became leader of the SS, a position "that gave him the power to act out his sadism on the historical stage" (Fromm, 1973, p. 429). Of course, to do so, Himmler depended upon a bureaucratic system and the help of others who were only too willing to follow his murderous wishes.

In a passage that anticipated Zygmunt Bauman's (2000) pathbreaking sociological study of the Holocaust, Fromm described the technical and bureaucratic nature of the genocide:

> The mass murder of Jews was organized like a production process.... The victims were processed methodically, efficiently; the executioners did not have to see the agony; they participated in the economic-political program but were one step removed from direct and immediate killing with their own hands. (Fromm, 1973, pp. 461–462)

This process, in turn, depended upon

> the technicalization of destruction and with it the removal of the full affective recognition of what one is doing. Once this process has been fully established there is no limit to destructiveness because nobody destroys: one only serves the machine for programmed—hence, apparently rational—purposes." (Fromm, 1973, pp. 461–462)

Fromm's point was that Himmler did not act alone. He depended on the likes of Adolf Eichmann and the thousands of other functionaries who made possible the system of mass murder, what Hannah Arendt referred to as the "banality of evil." Fromm's proximity to Arendt's position in *Eichmann in Jerusalem: A Report on the Banality of Evil* (1963) was evident when he wrote that Eichmann was

> fascinated by bureaucratic order and death. His supreme values were obedience and the proper functioning of the organization. He transported Jews as if he would have transported coal. That they were human beings was hardly within the field of his vision, hence even the problem of whether he hated or did not hate his victims is irrelevant." (Fromm, 1964, p. 38)

For Fromm, Hitler came closest to what Arendt (1951) defined as "absolute evil," a person so entirely dominated by the utter need for destruction that he had a love for all that was dead and destroyed.[28] Fromm described Hitler as a person of manifest evil without equal, "entirely without compassion for anyone, their suffering caused him no pain or remorse" (Fromm, 1973, p. 572). Fromm undertook an extended character analysis of Hitler that drew on the biographical information available to him at the time and focused on the social and historical conditions of his development. While Fromm focused on Hitler, he also warned that we must not overlook the presence of evil in other individuals who have the potential to wreak destruction upon their fellow humans:

> The naïve assumption that an evil person is easily recognized results in a great danger: one fails to recognize evil individuals before they have begun their work of destruction. I believe that the majority of people do not have the intensely destructive character of Hitler. But even if one would estimate that such persons formed 10 percent of our population, there were enough of them to be very dangerous if they attain influence and power. To be sure, not every destroyer would become a Hitler . . . he or she might become an efficient member of the SS. But on the other hand, Hitler was no genius, and his talents were not unique. What was unique was the socio-political situation in which he could rise. (Fromm, 1973, p. 574)

Fromm hoped that his research might lead to a better understanding of evil and offer the possibility for future prevention. Fromm knew that there was no single solution to the problem of human destructiveness and recognized that under certain social and political conditions, human beings willingly carried out atrocities. At the same time, he was adamant that malignant forms of aggression, "sadism and necrophilia, are not innate; hence they can be substantially reduced when the socio-economic conditions are replaced by conditions that are favorable to the full development of the person's genuine needs and capacities" (Fromm, 1973, p. 576). Fromm thus reminds us that the potential for evil is directly related to the conditions and contexts in which it emerges. In order to guard against malignant aggression, we must work together toward ensuring a healthy and functioning society.

Fromm's analyses in *The Anatomy of Human Destructiveness* received widespread attention. Perhaps most noteworthy in the context of our study was the reaction of the Austrian Jewish essayist and Holocaust survivor, Jean

Amery. He undertook several reviews, including a lengthy radio discussion on *Sender Freies Berlin* (Amery, 1974, 1975). Amery praised Fromm and argued that *The Anatomy of Human Destructiveness* was without equal in its societal analysis of destructiveness. He even predicted that it would become a standard work in the field. Amery (1975) reiterated Fromm's theses and, like Fromm, ended his review with a warning: "I believe that in fact the ground in which the destructiveness of humankind thrives is the social organization of modern civilization, until its ruin." In this sense, Amery reflected Fromm's bedrock belief that human well-being is dependent upon the well-being of society.

Unrepentant Nazis

Beyond his investigations of Himmler and Hitler, Fromm's inquiry into the Nazi past was evident in his engagement with two important postwar figures: the ethologist Konrad Lorenz and Hitler's confidant, Albert Speer. Fromm began *The Anatomy of Human Destructiveness* with an extended critique Lorenz's theory of an innate aggressive instinct. Lorenz viewed aggression in humans much as he viewed aggression in animals: as an immutable, biologically determined drive. In his bestseller *On Aggression* (1966), Lorenz argued that evolution equipped humans with a biologically programed aggressiveness that had to find release. The parallel with Freud's theory of aggression was obvious, lending an additional edge to Fromm's critique. For Fromm, it amounted to a highly simplistic "instinctivism" that overlooked the social, economic, and political conditions that give rise to malignant aggression. Fromm threw down the gauntlet when he declared that "Nothing short of an analysis in depth of our social system can disclose the reasons for the increase in destructiveness, or suggest ways and means of reducing it" (Fromm, 1973, p. 23).

Fromm warned that Lorenz's facile theorizing could easily morph into ideology. He was not alone. There were many on the German Left at the time who believed that Lorenz was offering Hitler's supporters a ready means of explaining away their actions. What was less known was how much Lorenz had in common with Hitler's supporters. Lorenz was an early joiner of the Nazi Party in Austria and became a member of the Office of Race Policy. In 1940, he penned a notorious statement justifying the destruction of another human being:

It must be the duty of racial hygiene to be attentive to a more severe elimination of morally inferior human beings than is the case today.... This role must be assumed a human organization; otherwise humanity will, for lack of selective factors, be annihilated by the degenerative phenomena that accompany domestication.[29]

After the war Lorenz was so successful in hiding his Nazi past, or at the very least downplaying it, that he became internationally recognized and was awarded the Nobel Prize for Medicine in 1973. When Robert J. Lifton interviewed Lorenz in the late 1970s and pressed him about his Nazi past, Lorenz's response was telling. Seeking to explain his Nazi idealism as a young man, Lorenz remarked, "it is the best people genetically who are the most affected" (p. 287).

Fromm did not call out Lorenz for his Nazi past, but he clearly had Lorenz's self-justifying theorizing in mind when he wrote, "He considers all human aggression, including the passion to kill and to torture, as being an outcome of biologically given aggression" (Fromm, 1973, p. 25). According to Fromm, the notion that we are governed by our aggression undermined "the serious study of the causes of destructiveness, which calls for the questioning of the basic premises of current ideology.... The instinctivist theory offers to relieve us of the hard work of making such an analysis" (Fromm, 1973, p. 23).[30] The hard work of such an analysis was, of course, precisely what Fromm had sought to achieve in his studies of authoritarianism, racial narcissism, and human destructiveness.

The strangest chapter in Fromm's engagement with the Nazi past was undoubtedly his dialogue with Albert Speer. After his release from his 20-year prison sentence in Spandau, Speer published a memoir entitled *Inside the Third Reich* (1970). Fromm read the book and contacted Speer in the hope that a dialogue might enable him to gain insight into the workings of Hitler and the Nazi regime. Fromm and Speer met for the first time in 1972, and the product of their interactions found its way into the pages of *The Anatomy of Human Destructiveness*. As Fromm states in his preface, "I thank Albert Speer, who in conversation and correspondence, was most helpful in enriching my picture of Hitler" (Fromm, 1973, p. 15). Fromm's interaction with Speer came to include personal visits and a correspondence that touched on the past as well as their present.[31] Fromm would even engage in analysis of Speer's dreams, some of which Fromm included in the book (Fromm, 1973, pp. 443–445).

The question, of course, is how to make sense of the relationship between Fromm and Speer. Why would a prominent German Jewish intellectual whose family members had been murdered in the Holocaust and whose life trajectory was inalterably shaped by the Nazis be willing to engage with Speer? We know that Fromm's cousin Gertrud Hunziker-Fromm disapproved of his decision to contact Speer and let her displeasure be known.[32] But it is also important to note that Fromm was hardly alone in his willingness to meet Speer. Robert J. Lifton interviewed Speer numerous times. Lifton himself was introduced to Speer by the doyen of West German postwar psychoanalysis, Alexander Mitscherlich, who commented in regard to Speer, "twenty years in jail 'was enough' and that 'we should not isolate people like him.'" Mitscherlich added that Lifton should pass on his "personal greetings" to Speer (Lifton, p. 307).

Lifton's observations are helpful as we puzzle over Fromm's motivations. According to Lifton, "Speer was attempting to salvage something ethically from the Nazi experience, to demonstrate that 'good men' ('decent Nazis') could function with integrity within the regime" (Lifton, p. 314). The deep-seated contradiction of so-called decent Nazis became evident when Lifton prodded Speer to talk about his knowledge of the genocide. As the minister of armaments and war production, Speer was responsible for authorizing the expansion of Auschwitz. He had submitted documents outlining the construction project. The documents detailed the materials needed, which included "fumigation facilities for special treatment" and "mortuaries with incinerators."[33] As Lifton recalls, Speer "told me of providing certain materials for the work camp in Auschwitz in 1943 and had 'some insight into the bad conditions of such camps' but he insisted . . . sharply that 'I knew nothing of the other'" (Lifton, p. 315). Lifton was renowned for his study of perpetrators and was forced to admit, "I had never before heard anyone claim in this way close knowledge of the slave labor function of Auschwitz and ignorance of its function as a death camp." Lifton concludes that one could either believe that Speer was lying or see him as beset by an inner struggle around "the psychology of knowing and not knowing." Lifton adds, "I favoured the latter view. I thought he was 'living a lie' but that he had not experienced it as a lie."

Following the publication of his second memoir, *Spandau: The Secret Diaries* (1975), Speer was visited by many intellectuals who hoped that he might cast some light on the Nazi regime and the horrors it perpetrated. Speer, for his part, used these interviews to carefully construct an image of himself as a man who deeply regretted his failures, including his inability to recognize the true extent of the crimes of the regime.[34] Speer's pronouncements reflected the unwillingness of his generation to admit their collective responsibility. As the French-German journalist Geraldine Schwartz has observed, "In lying about the extent of his knowledge and sloughing off his own responsibility, Speer encouraged a whole nation to forget its guilt. If Hitler's closest friend, one of the most powerful ministers of the Reich, didn't know, how could other Germans know?" (2020, p. 185). In fact, it would take another several decades of historical research to reveal Speer's full involvement in the Final Solution.

In 1972, when Fromm first engaged Speer, West Germany's highly conservative process of forgetting was still in evidence. German awareness of the Holocaust emerged in stages, beginning with the Frankfurt Auschwitz Trials from 1963 to 1965, and expanding through federal policies for Holocaust education during the 1970s. But it was the broadcast of the television miniseries *Holocaust* in 1979 that brought the Nazi terror directly into people's living rooms. Watched by a third of the nation, the miniseries initiated widespread discussion and turned the word "Holocaust" into a commonly used term in the German language for the first time. In the intervening decades, it became possible to openly acknowledge the widespread complicity of civil society and the military in the genocide.[35]

Fromm's interactions with Speer suggest that his interest in the man went beyond the needs of his book research. Perhaps Speer came to represent for Fromm a repentant Nazi, someone who was willing to acknowledge terrible wrongs. Certainly, Fromm's readiness to write a back-cover endorsement for Speer's English edition of the *Spandau Diaries* suggests that he saw in Speer an example of the human capacity for change. As Fromm (1976a) writes,

> Albert Speer's book is a deeply moving human document. It is also of extraordinary political and psychological interest. His self-analysis of the reasons why and how he could have been involved with the Nazi criminal gang and his remarkably frank account of the change within himself during twenty years are truly convincing.

But knowing that Fromm was a psychoanalyst who was attuned to listening for meaning that remained outside of conscious awareness, we inevitably wonder why he didn't see through Speer's web of half-truths. Perhaps there is also a more subjective element at work. After spending most of the postwar period separated from the culture and language in which he was born and raised, we might wonder whether Fromm's dialogue with Speer offered the possibility of breaking through the caesura of the Nazi past and reflecting on an irretrievable history.

In the final years of his life, Fromm returned to the promise of the prewar German Jewish symbiosis, which was tragically extinguished by the Nazis. Fromm suffered a debilitating heart attack in 1977, and his short essay from 1978, *Remarks on the Relations Between Germans and Jews*, is among his last manuscripts. As Fromm states,

> Hitler's attempt to destroy the Jewish people has so over shadowed the picture of Jewish-German relations that the relationship between Germans and Jews appears to many as having been essentially negative. But one easily forgets that the approximately one hundred years of German Jewish cultural co-living resulted in extraordinary achievement. (1978/1994, p. 105)

Highlighting the works of Marx, Freud, and Einstein, Fromm argues that

> this extraordinary productivity of the German Jewish cultural marriage has its roots in a deep affinity between the Jewish and the German cultures. This affinity is more difficult to grasp today, after we have witnessed the ferocity of anti-Jewish feelings in that part of the German population in which Nazism took its hold. Yet the Jews and the Germans must share some essential qualities that make the fruitfulness of their relationship explainable. (1978/1994, pp. 106–107)

Fromm reveals his own abiding connection to German culture by turning back to the work of Goethe. According to Fromm, until the surge of nationalism that led to the unification of Germany in 1871 and created a power-hungry state,

> Germans could rightly be called "the people of poets and thinkers" ("*das Volk der Dichter und Denker*"), and perhaps nobody represents this anti-nationalistic and anti-militaristic spirit better than one of the greatest Germans living in the period: Goethe, who expressed his scorn for war and nationalism. (1978/1994, p. 107)

It is interesting to consider the contrast between Fromm's comments in *Remarks on the Relations Between Germans and Jews* and those of the

German Jewish historian Dan Diner, who only a few years later, in 1986, famously described the relationship between Germans and Jews in the wake of the Holocaust as a "negative symbiosis." Diner introduced this concept to describe the tragic and systematic reversal of the German Jewish symbiosis, which had been so optimistically anticipated during the Age of Enlightenment. As Diner writes,

> Since Auschwitz—what a sad twist—one can indeed speak about a "German Jewish symbiosis." Of course, it is a negative one: for both Germans as well as Jews, the result of a mass annihilation has become the starting point for their self-understanding. It is a kind of contradictory mutuality, whether they want it or not, for Germans as well as Jews have been linked to one another anew through this event. Such a negative symbiosis, constituted by the Nazis, will stamp the relationship of each group to itself, and above all, each group to another for generations to come. (Diner, 1986, p. 9)[36]

In 1986, the same year that Diner penned his remarks, the Auschwitz survivor and author Primo Levi published his last book, *The Drowned and the Saved*. Levi developed a more differentiated perspective on Speer and the question of German responsibility for the Holocaust. His views provide a helpful addendum to Fromm's work. In the last chapter of *The Drowned and the Saved*, written a year before he died by his own hand, Levi discusses the letters he received from his German readers since the publication of *Survival in Auschwitz* in Germany in 1961 (1988, pp. 166–197). Some of German readers expressed regret for not having had the courage to speak out, but for the most part, Levi tells us, they explained away their actions. The letters convinced Levi that his correspondents, and perhaps Germans in general, failed to engage with the nature of the crimes committed, and probably never would. As Levi (1988) observed, "My book had, it is true, some resonance in Germany, but actually among the Germans who least needed to read it; I had received penitent letters from the innocent, not the guilty. These, understandably, were silent" (Levi, 1988, p. 191).

There was one reader who stood out. Hety Schmitt-Maass was a contemporary of Levi and politically active in opposition to the Nazis. As Levi stated,

> Our friendship was long and fruitful, often cheerful; strange, if I think of the enormous difference between our human itineraries and the geographical

and linguistic distance between us, less strange if I recognize that among all my German readers she was the only one "with clean credentials" and therefore not entangled in guilt feelings, and that her curiosity was and is mine. (1988, p. 197)

The only time that Levi felt distanced from Schmitt-Maass was when she arranged to meet Speer. Schmitt-Maass had read Speer's prison memoirs and, like Fromm, wanted to understand Speer's thinking and the nature of his remorse.

When they met, Schmitt-Maass gave Speer a copy of *Survival in Auschwitz*, and Speer, in turn, gave her a copy of his memoirs to send to Levi. While Levi did not outrightly reject Speer, neither did he endorse him:

> I received and read these diaries, which bear the mark of a cultivated and lucid mind and change of heart that seems sincere (but an intelligent man knows how to simulate). In them Speer comes through as a Shakespearian character of boundless ambition, so great as to blind and contaminate him, but not a barbarian, coward or serf. (Levi, 1986, p. 196)

But Levi was also quick to add that "if I had been forced (as is the custom among civilized persons) to answer a letter from Albert Speer, I would have had some problems" (Levi, 1986, p. 196). Looking back, what Levi could not understand was why Schmitt-Maass would have wanted to meet with Speer. This is undoubtedly also the reaction we may have on learning that Fromm entered into dialogue with Speer. It is noteworthy, then, that after Schmitt-Maass sensed Levi's disapproval, she went to meet Speer a second time. Afterward, she wrote to Levi to report that she found Speer to be "senile, egocentric, pompous, and stupidly proud of his past as a Pharaonic architect" (Levi, 1986, pp. 196–197).

What Germans Knew

Fromm and Schmitt-Maass may both have hoped to see in Speer some redeeming quality or at the very least a genuine change of heart. What we find when we look at Fromm's interviews and writings from the last years of his life, is that he sought to avoid any blanket condemnation Germans. In a 1977 German television interview, following the publication of *To Have or To Be*,

Fromm describes what he believed to be a collective dissociation at work in Germany under Hitler:

> People abroad cannot understand, and I have experienced many such discussions, that most Germans are telling the truth when they say they did not know what Hitler did in terms of killing Jews as well as Russians and Poles and Communists . . . most of the time people didn't know and are quite honest about it. But you have to go a step further: they might have known from some of the signs, if this knowledge had not been dissociated. And this explains why Hitler was able to do such things in the first place. If the German people had known about them, Hitler would undoubtedly not have been able to hold out. The German people in their great majority would have been so repelled by this sadism and this immorality that Hitler had to try everything to keep it a secret from the German people. His attempt was successful because many Germans dissociated that which they could have known. (Fromm, 1977)

Fromm's statement can be understood in a number of ways. First and foremost, he was speaking to the fact that after the war, a great many Germans claimed that they did not know anything about the Holocaust. According to Fromm, this assertation was only possible because Germans engaged in a collective dissociation. By pushing aside evidence of discrimination, deportation, and mass murder, Germans had in essence begun to believe their own lie. The parallel to Speer's denial of having any knowledge about the death camps is noteworthy. At the same time, we find that Fromm was hesitant to attribute blame to Germans as a whole. His stance on the issue was similar to that of Arendt, who reflected on the fallacy of the concept of collective guilt in her 1964 essay, "Personal Responsibility Under Dictatorship". According to Arendt, after the war, talk of collective guilt "turned into a highly effective whitewash of all those who had actually done something, for where all are guilty, no one is" (Arendt, 1964/1965, p. 20). To be sure, Fromm was not averse to discussing questions of ethics or guilt. Nor did he want to minimize the differences between what individual Germans may have done or believed. Ever the sociologist, Fromm wanted to understand which sectors of society were most supportive of the Nazis and thus most willing to submit to authoritarianism and support the murderous policies of Hitler and the Nazi regime.

What we know about these issues today is very different than in the time in which Fromm was speaking and writing on the subject. It is important to be aware of this distinction when considering Fromm's observations. Over the past two decades, the common German postwar claim that "we did not know about anything about it" has been thoroughly examined by historians and has been shown to have little basis in fact.[37] Alexandra Lohse provides a helpful summation of recent historical research when she states,

> The murderers of more than six million European Jews and other victims did not take their "secret" to the grave. And yet, the exculpatory fiction that neither most Nazi leaders nor most "ordinary" Germans knew about Nazi war crimes proved tenacious. For decades into the postwar era, members of the "wartime generation" reflexively denied all knowledge of atrocities and genocide, doggedly insisting "of that we knew nothing." Surviving evidence shows that rumors about atrocities circulated widely among German military and civilian populations just as they embarked on total mobilization to stave off the turning tide of war. Vivid descriptions of the sights, sounds, and smells of mass murder flowed from the military to the civilian populations, where they mingled with information gleaned from Nazi and Allied propaganda. The cumulative effect was that many Germans knew something. Or, as one historian has put it, at the very least, many "knew enough to know it was better not to know." (Lohse, 2021, pp. 73–74)

The process described by Lohse might best be understood as a kind of "simultaneous knowing and not-knowing." Dissociation of knowledge about the Holocaust provided a means of avoiding the question of responsibility. If Germans who engaged in the act of dissociation acknowledged what they saw, heard, and knew, it would have involved recognition of a shared humanity with their fellow Jewish citizens. When we experience a shared humanity, it is much harder to ignore and deny the pain of the other person. We might even feel compelled to act to help them. Instead, the persecution and deportation of the German Jews was quite simply "not seen," and their murder was "not-known," even though the disappearances and deportations were clearly evident and knowledge of the policy of annihilation had become widespread over the course of the war. As the psychoanalytically trained historian Thomas Kohut observes, "It took an act of will for them not to have known what was going on. In a sense they had to avert their eyes to avoid seeing what was right in front of their noses" (2012, p. 139). The act of "looking away" goes to the heart of antisemitism. Looking away "eliminated the possibility of empathy, severing the bond of shared humanity connecting them to persecuted Jews. It was an act of dehumanization, an eradication of Jewish people from consciousness, that mirrored and facilitated their physical annihilation" (2012, p. 137).

This brings us back to the question of how Fromm responded to the problem of antisemitism. In 1979, shortly before his death, the Swiss television journalist Jürg Acklin asked Fromm about the conditions that made Hitler's rule in Germany possible. In response, Fromm offered a summation of his views:

> I think you can see that he didn't succeed in making the German people antisemitic, for example, despite all his propaganda. There are endless examples of Germans who gave protection to Jews. And perhaps there is a better example and that is the millions of packages that were sent to Germany by German Jews in America after the war. That would not be possible if the German people as such had been won over to Hitler's idea. Despite all the propaganda, Hitler did not succeed in really infecting the German people with antisemitism, if I may put it that way. I believe this is a fact that one should really think about when one judges groups of people and when one judges the influence of demagogues. . . . I was outside of Germany at the time and sometimes when I listened to the German radio, then I thought, yes, for God's sake, how can an average person who doesn't know anything about these things, when he hears all these falsehoods, how can he not become antisemitic? But it was like that.
>
> Now you come up against a big problem, and that is: What actually is the root of antisemitism? This is admittedly a somewhat different problem. But if you allow me, I'd like to say something about it. I believe the ultimate root of antisemitism lies in the fact that the Jews have proved that the survival of a group is not necessarily based on power. That is, a completely powerless group can survive through 2000 years. And then in turn can even achieve great cultural achievements, in other words, although they have no power, this has not hindered their survival.
>
> And for those who believe in power, the existence of the Jews is a disavowal, a slap in the face. For if that is possible, then power cannot be of such importance. And as I said, I believe this is the deepest root of

antisemitism: the hatred of a group that has proven that power is not necessary to survive. (Fromm, 1979)[38]

By the time the interview took place, Fromm was struggling with his health. He had just suffered a third heart attack, but his mind was clear. Fromm's statement is striking on several counts. It reveals a willingness to grant his fellow Germans the benefit of the doubt, despite evidence that antisemitism was far more entrenched in German society than Fromm seemed to believe. For example, Kaplan shed lights on the experience of German Jews and their neighbors when she writes,

> After the war, between 3,000 and 5,000 Jews came out of hiding in Germany. In Berlin, a city that once encompassed 160,000 Jewish Berliners, about 5,000 to 7,000 Jews hid, of whom only 1,400 survived. *Fewer than 1 percent of the original Jewish population of Germany in 1933 were rescued by their countrymen or women; most had been persecuted by them.* (Kaplan, 1998, p. 228, my emphasis)

While these statistics may not have been available to Fromm, the tragic reality of life for German Jews during the final years of war was commonly known.

The fact remains that the perpetration of the Holocaust was only possible because a majority of Germans were willing to lend their support to the policies of the regime or, at the very least, to look the other way. This is what Levi was referring to when he states, "The true crime, the collective, general crime of almost all Germans of that time was that of lacking the courage to speak" (Levi, p. 182). In contrast to Levi, certainly, the lack of a comprehensive analysis of antisemitism in Fromm's work stands out. As Levi writes in regard to antisemitism,

> It was the foundation of Nazi doctrine from its beginnings. . . . There's neither a page nor a speech of Hitler's in which hatred against the Jews is not reiterated to the point of obsession. It was not marginal to Nazism: it was its ideological center. (Levi, p. 179)

To be sure, in contrast to Fromm, Levi was unencumbered by a Marxist framework that limited direct engagement with racial ideology. Levi takes us to the very heart of the evil that spawned the Holocaust while Fromm might be described as circling around the edges. But this does not mean he was inattentive.

As we have seen, Fromm returned again and again to the themes of authoritarianism, racism, and destructiveness. His analysis of Hitler and the notion of racial narcissism suggests an intellectual and a personal need to understand the cruelty that was practiced by the Nazi regime and its supporters. Fromm's analysis of Hitler's speeches and writings in *The Anatomy of Human Destructiveness* is an attempt to lay bare the racist ideology that caused the death of millions. Given Fromm's traumatic family history, there is a remarkable lack of animus in these studies, though he neither forgot nor forgave the atrocities that were committed. And yet, in view of Fromm's standing as a public intellectual and social thinker, we may understandably hope to find a greater engagement with the questions of German responsibility and antisemitism. Certainly, from our vantage point today, Fromm's account can appear inadequate, in part because it reflects the norms of the time in which he was writing.

Looking back, we may also wonder whether the less persuasive aspects of Fromm's analysis reflect a hesitancy to fully engage with a subject matter that was unquestionably difficult and painful for him. If this were the case, he would not be alone. In a particularly revealing passage of his memoir, Peter Gay acknowledges his own reluctance to engage with the Holocaust:

> If some refugees have been obsessed with the Holocaust, have I been obsessed with an effort to recoil from it? I do not think so, but I recognize that others might see it this way.... The truth is, I must confess, that I have deliberately refused to dwell on the mass murder of Europe's Jews. I have avoided movies that deal with it, even important ones, like Shoah. I have not yet been to the Holocaust Museum in Washington. When in the mid-1980s, we had an opportunity to visit Auschwitz, my wife went alone. We all have our defences to help us get through life, and these happen to be mine. I am not proud of them, but I see no need to apologize for them. Surely my record of hard work shows that I have not fled to hedonism to erase my past. Freud said that the most effective—or, rather, the least effective—way of dealing with misery is work, and I can testify that Freud was right. (Gay, 1998, p. 204)

Gay's reflections are an important reminder of the diversity of viewpoints that existed among Jewish refugees and survivors. When bringing Levi into discussion with Fromm, it is also worth keeping in mind that when it comes to an analysis of the Holocaust, there are few thinkers who can compare with Levi's profundity. Whatever direction our reflections may take us in, what cannot be doubted is Fromm's steadfast courage in speaking out and holding each of us to account for our actions and beliefs.

Critique of Zionism

Fromm's writings about antisemitism may suffer from a lack of clarity, but there can be little doubt as to where he stands on the negative effects of nationalism. Fromm first developed his concerns about militant nationalism in relation to Germany and World War I. By the 1920s, his concerns about nationalism influenced his perception of Zionism and the attempt to establish a Jewish "homeland." Fromm seemed to fear any kind of ethnonationalism, no matter its source or intent. His discomfort with Zionism grew as the prospect of a Jewish state became more real, and by the mid-1920s Fromm ceased supporting Zionism altogether.

In the immediate aftermath of the Holocaust, Fromm's position on Zionism may have softened somewhat, but his concern for the rights of Palestinians only increased. In 1948, Arendt contacted Fromm to assess his backing for a public statement on the need for a binational state in Palestine. Fromm responded positively and worked through multiple drafts of the declaration, ultimately securing the public support of Albert Einstein and Leo Baeck, both of whom signed the declaration.[39] The statement was published in *New York Times* on April 18, 1948. It called out fanatical nationalism and terror among both Jews and Palestinians and pleaded for their cooperation. Fromm's engagement on the issue also brought him back into contact with Martin Buber, who was a strong and vocal supporter of a binational state.

In the following decades, Fromm's public stance on Israel put him at odds with a majority of Jewish Americans. Fromm expressed concern about the continued growth of Israeli nationalism and argued repeatedly for the need to safeguard the rights of the Palestinians (whom he refers to with the generalized term "Arabs"). He made his position clear in a 1958 edition of the *Jewish Newsletter*:

> It is often said that the Arabs fled, that they left the country voluntarily, and that they therefore bear the responsibility for losing their property

and their land. It is true that in history there are some instances—in Rome and in France during the Revolutions when enemies of the state were proscribed and their property confiscated. But in general international law, the principle holds true that no citizen loses his property or his rights of citizenship; and the citizenship right is de facto a right to which the Arabs in Israel have much more legitimacy than the Jews. Just because the Arabs fled? Since when is that punishable by confiscation of property and by being barred from returning to the land on which a people's forefathers have lived for generations? Thus, the claim of the Jews to the land of Israel cannot be a realistic political claim. If all nations would suddenly claim territories in which their forefathers had lived two thousand years ago, this world would be a madhouse.... I believe that, politically speaking, there is only one solution for Israel, namely, the unilateral acknowledgement of the obligation of the State towards the Arabs—not to use it as a bargaining point, but to acknowledge the complete moral obligation of the Israeli State to its former inhabitants of Palestine. (Fromm, 1958, pp. 1–2)

In 1970, in a dialogue with the Lebanese historian Gérard Khoury, Fromm expanded on this viewpoint:

I do not believe in hate as a constructive sentiment for the liberation of any nation, and of course I am not a friend of nationalism, be it Arab or Israeli. This is something different from understanding deeply the motivation for Arab nationalism and from my severe criticism of Israeli policy, not only since the foundation of the State, but altogether, of a completely Jewish State as such. I think the only solution would have been suggested by Rabbi Magnus, of a bi-national Jewish-Arab State.[40]

Fromm gives perhaps the clearest summation of his position on Israel in a lengthy and revealing letter to the U.S. Senator George McGovern in 1970:

As a Jew and one who is deeply rooted in the Jewish religious tradition and who all his life has followed closely the development of Zionism and since two decades of the State of Israel, I am certainly not without sympathy for the Jewish plight and not without knowledge about the history of Zionism, which has led straight to the present situation.

But at the same time, Fromm states, "the problem of the aggressive spirit which has existed in Israel since the foundation of the State, and before that in the leading figures of Zionism" must be called out. Fromm goes on to write that

> Psychologically speaking, the faith in force and the pride in successful application of force is very understandable. This is a reaction of people who feel not only grieved but also humiliated by the fact that Hitler could slaughter six million Jews. . . . It is natural that they . . . are tremendously sensitive to the dangers of being destroyed another time. But that this attitude is understandable is one thing, its political consequences another. As far as I can see, it has led to an intransigence which runs through the whole history of the State of Israel. Its Israeli government never recognized the moral obligation to compensate the Arab refugees for their property which was seized by Israel after their flight. [41]

Among his former Frankfurt School colleagues, and especially in comparison to Marcuse, Fromm's position on Israel was far and away the most critical. Indeed, Fromm never set foot in Israel. Yet it is also interesting to note that as a young man Fromm was the most religious of the group. Reflecting on his interactions with Fromm during the 1920s at the Free Jewish Learning Center, Scholem remembers Fromm as a strict adherent to orthodoxy and quoted a verse that was circulating about him at the time: "*Mach mich wie den Erich Fromm, dass ich in den Himmel komm*," which translates as "Make me just like Erich Fromm, that into heaven I may come" (Scholem, 2012, p. 143).

By the age of 26, Fromm had given up his orthodoxy, but this hardly meant that he left Judaism behind. As the political scientist, Jack Jacobs, has shown, "Fromm's anti-imperialism does not actually get at the heart of the matter. His dyed-in-the-wool commitment to specific Jewish principles and traditions does" (Jacobs, 2015, p. 132). Fromm's views on Israel emerged out of his commitment to the progressive, socialist tradition of Jewish thought, a perspective that surely remains relevant today. Throughout the remainder of his life, Fromm identified as culturally, but not religiously, Jewish and held fast to the humanistic ideals of Jewish teachings. Those ideals were evident in Fromm's emphasis on human compassion and our ethical obligation to others, which are the topics of my final chapter.

5
Cultivating Love and Hope

In an oft-quoted essay from 1949, Adorno remarked that "To write a poem after Auschwitz is barbaric."[1] In that statement, Adorno captured a feeling that many people struggled with after the Holocaust, namely, whether it was possible to produce art in a culture that gave rise to Auschwitz. To be sure, poetry did in fact provide a means for many survivors and victims to convey their experiences in a way that traditional language could not. The poetry of Paul Celan stands out in this regard, not only because it was written in German, but also because it provides a singularly evocative and deeply moving account of the Holocaust. The larger question, though, was whether there could still be a place for creativity, compassion, and love alongside the unimaginable grief, suffering, and trauma unleashed by the genocide. Reading the letters of Gertrud Brandt and Sophie Engländer, and reflecting on the magnitude of the catastrophe, places this question into stark relief. Gertrud's and Sophie's words communicate the anguish and despair that they were forced to endure. When we learn of their deportations and deaths, we are confronted with the undeniable reality of human cruelty. What must it have been like for Fromm to know of their fate, and still go on to write about love?

Fromm surely struggled with his own doubts about the human condition once he learned of the scale of the atrocities. By chance and circumstance, his life had been spared, while his family members and millions of others had been killed. Yet Fromm remained unwilling to endorse Adorno's pessimism. Nor could he accept the prevailing notion that human beings were innately aggressive, violent beings. For Fromm, the goal of society must be to guard against the social and political conditions that lead to destructiveness, and to foster a sense of solidarity and concern among its citizenry. In short, Fromm retained a deeply held belief in the possibility of compassion and love as countervailing forces to cruelty and destructiveness. This points to the centrality of hope in Fromm's work. Lest his outlook be confused with optimism, it is important to remember the distinction made by Vaclav Havel, who reminds us that "Hope is not the same thing as optimism. It is not the conviction that something will turn out well, but the certainty that something makes sense, regardless of how it turns out" (Havel, 1990, p. 182).

Fromm's thoughts find expression in his best known work, *The Art of Loving*, in which he proclaimed, provocatively perhaps, that "love is the only one sane and satisfactory answer to the problem of human existence" (Fromm, 1956, p. 133). Looking back, it is striking that both of his aunts expressed a similar sentiment in the letters they wrote shortly before their deaths. In the midst of the inhumane circumstances of the ghetto, as she pondered the suffering and misery that surrounded her, Gertrud wrote, "*I believe deeply in the strength of goodness and love and in its eternal and immortal power. It sustains me, when I think about it, that maybe my days will not be entirely pointless, if only a little bit [of goodness and love] can radiate out from me to others.*" Similarly, at the height of the deportations from Berlin, and with a heart-rending sense of finality, Sophie told her children and grandchildren to "*enjoy every happy minute and don't forget that alongside much sorrow, there is also much beauty in the world.*"

Like Gertrud and Sophie, Fromm found meaning in possibilities for human relating and love. Whether he drew these insights directly from the Holocaust letters of his aunts is hard to know, but it is impossible to overlook the connections. Fromm's faith in living and his emphasis on achieving a fullness of life were a critical and necessary response to war and genocide. In this concluding chapter, I want to examine Fromm's account of the human capacity for love against the backdrop of the Holocaust. Fromm saw love and solidarity not only as ideals worth striving for, but as ethical imperatives for living. His approach still has much to teach us about how to engage with one another and respond to destructive social forces.

The Art of Relating

When Fromm's name is mentioned today, it is most commonly in association with the *The Art of Loving*, which was published in 1956. Yet there was little in the preceding two decades of Fromm's life that would have led anyone to believe that he would publish a global bestseller on the nature of love. The Nazi rise to power had forced him to leave Germany and start anew. His tireless attempts to arrange safe passage for his family members ended with the news of their deaths in a genocide that destroyed much of Europe's Jewish population. In the years that followed the war, Henny's worsening illness required Fromm to move yet again. Leaving New York for Mexico in 1950, gave way to a sense of isolation and loneliness. After Henny's tragic death, Fromm entered into a period of grieving. Healing took time and was helped by the relationships he fostered with Mexican psychiatrists and the creation of a community of like-minded clinicians. Perhaps most significantly, he met the woman who would become his third wife. By all accounts, his relationship with Annis Freeman changed him. Those who knew Fromm said that the hard edges of his character began to soften.

It was during this time that Fromm was contacted by Ruth Nanda Anshen, a philosopher and editor with Harper & Row. She suggested to Fromm that he write a book on the nature of love for her series World Perspectives.[2] Fromm took up the challenge and produced the *The Art of Loving*, a short but powerful work that reached an immense audience and continues to be popular today. Fromm's happiness with Annis undoubtedly inspired him, lending his writing a resonance that connected with readers. At the core of the book was Fromm's belief that love is an attitude of concern for the wellbeing of others that orients us toward giving rather than receiving. As such, Fromm's understanding of love had a relevance that went beyond the interaction of two individuals.

The process of writing *The Art of Loving* gave Fromm a chance to reflect on the human condition only a decade after the Holocaust and the Second World War. When the war finally ended, the world struggled to address the human carnage and massive destruction wrought by six years of hostilities. The war had taken the lives of tens of millions, and its impact was imprinted on individuals and societies alike, the physical and emotional injuries clearly visible for all who wished to see. After 1945, it might even have been possible to imagine that people had tired of death. Yet in 1950 the Korean war broke out, which cost nearly four million more lives. The conflict on the Korean peninsula involved major powers from across the globe, and although it ended with an armistice in 1953, it spurred the growth of the Cold War and the nuclear arms race.

Against this background, *The Art of Loving* found a readership that was eager to understand the nature of love and what it meant to "break through the walls" that separate us as human beings (Fromm, 1956, p. 24). Fromm emphasized that our ability to care for others "*is the active concern for the life and the growth of that which we love*" (Fromm, 1956, pp. 28, original emphasis). Fromm maintained that this attitude of concern for another person involves the act of giving: "Giving implies to make the other person a giver also and they both share in the joy of what they have brought to life" (Fromm, 1956, p. 25). It is this mutual act of giving and caring for one another that makes reciprocity possible. A reciprocal relationship is defined by the fact that two persons share equally with one other, while also retaining their individual integrity. This is exactly the opposite of the relationship of domination and submission that Fromm had argued was at the heart of Nazism. Indeed, Fromm's understanding of human sociality formed a direct counterpoint to the destructive forces of fascism, which is why it will be helpful to examine what he says more closely.

In a particularly relevant passage of the book, Fromm suggests that love is an attitude of concern that is based on a set of four individual principles: "care, responsibility, respect and knowledge" (Fromm, 1956, p. 28). *Care* for the other person is the most basic condition of love, and its expression is defined by a sense of responsibility, respect, and knowledge for the other person. Fromm's account is worth quoting in full:

> *Responsibility*, in its true sense, is an entirely voluntary act; it is my response to the needs, expressed or unexpressed, of another human being. To be "responsible" means to be able and ready to "respond." . . . *Respect* means the concern that the other person should grow and unfold as they are. Respect, thus, implies the absence of exploitation. I want the loved person to grow and unfold for their own sake, and in their own ways, and not for the purpose of serving me. . . . To respect a person is not possible without *knowing* them; care and responsibility would be blind if they were not guided by knowledge. *Knowledge* would be empty if it were not motivated by concern. There are many layers of knowledge; the knowledge which is an aspect of love is one which does not stay at the periphery, but penetrates to the core. It is possible only when I can transcend the concern for myself and see the other person in their own terms. (Fromm, 1956, pp. 29–30, my emphasis)

For Fromm, the principles of care, responsibility, respect, and knowledge are not only an essential aspect of a mature loving relationship; they are also a guide to ethical conduct and the basis for a just and equitable society. Admittedly, when we examine these ideas in isolation, they can seem abstract and far removed from the realm of everyday interaction. But if we reflect on the fact that Fromm's approach to love and care emerged out of his daily therapeutic practice with patients, we can better understand the relevance of what he says.[3] Indeed, throughout his career as a psychoanalyst,

Fromm posited love as a normative goal for human life. He believed that healing takes place through a kind of empathic dialogue, an interaction that orients us toward the other person, not as an object, but in their being. Thus, Fromm writes that the psychoanalyst

> must be endowed with a capacity for empathy with another person and strong enough to feel the experience of the other as if it were their own. The condition for such empathy is an optimal of the capacity for love. To understand another means to love them—not in the erotic sense, but in the sense of reaching out to them and of overcoming the fear of losing oneself. Understanding and loving are inseparable. If they are separate, it is a cerebral process and the door to essential understanding remains closed. (Fromm, 2009, pp. 192–193)

The connection that Fromm makes between understanding and loving points us in the direction of Martin Buber's philosophy of dialogue. As we saw in Chapter 1 Fromm became acquainted with Buber's work as a young man, when they both taught at the Jewish Free Learning Center in Frankfurt. At the time, Buber was developing his notion of I and Thou, a relationship that is characterized by a sense of immediacy and an attitude of openness and responsibility toward the other person. In contrast to I and Thou, Buber maintained that when we treat the other person only as a means to an end, we are engaging in an I–It relationship, and that person essentially becomes an object for us.

Fromm later developed the notion of "central relatedness," which has much in common with Buber's I and Thou relationship. As Fromm states, "We understand a person fully, only inasmuch as we are centrally related to them. In these moments we learn as much from the other person as they do from us.... When I use the concept "central relatedness" I mean the relatedness from center to center instead of the relatedness from periphery to periphery" (1959, pp. 177–178). Like Buber, Fromm distinguishes the therapeutic relationship from any kind of human interaction that objectifies the other person. As Fromm explains,

> I can explain the other person as another ego.... Or I can relate to this other person in the sense of being them, in the sense of experiencing, feeling this other person. Then I do not think about myself, then my ego does not stand in my way. But something entirely different happens. *There is what I call a*

central relatedness between me and them. They are not a thing over there which I look at, but they confront me fully and I confront them fully. (1959, p. 174, my emphasis)

The notion of central relatedness not only pertains to Fromm's therapeutic work; it also informs his understanding of human solidarity:

If I see the other person—what happens is not only that I stop judging but also that I have a sense of union, of sharing, of oneness, which is something much stronger than being kind or being nice. There is a feeling of human solidarity when two people—or even one person—can say to the other: "So that is you, and I share this with you." This is a tremendously important experience.... This is also one of the most important therapeutic experiences which we can give to the patient, because at that moment the patient does not feel isolated anymore. (1959, p. 178)

For Fromm, the question of how we relate to and treat the other person is paramount. He believes that solidarity with others begins in our daily experiences, in the acts of consideration we show to others, in short, in the way we perceive and treat one another as fellow human beings whom we meet with an attitude of concern. According to Fromm, we have an ethical obligation not only to other persons, but also to our community and society. When Fromm outlines the characteristics of love and solidarity, he is also describing the qualities of social interaction that are essential for a flourishing democracy. Indeed, Fromm believed that the individual capacity to love and care for others is inherently connected to the well-being of society. He makes this link explicit when he writes,

Society must be organized in such a way that the human being's social, loving nature is not separated from their social existence, but becomes one with it. If it is true, as I have tried to show, that love is the only sane and satisfactory answer to the problem of human existence, then any society which excludes, relatively, the development of love, must in the long run perish of its own contradiction with the basic necessities of human nature. (Fromm, 1956, p. 133)

Fromm's approach to understanding love appealed to a vast number of readers. Yet it was also a trigger for criticism and condescension. For the Freudians, Fromm's emphasis on the centrality of love to human sociality revealed a superficial optimism. They argued that *The Art of Loving* demonstrated the limitations of Fromm's approach because it ignored the biological drives and the role of aggression. Left-wing intellectuals criticized *The Art of Loving* for not being sufficiently emancipatory in his aims. They were understandably wary of any approach that saw love as a vehicle for social change. Other readers pointed out that in contrast to the radical and progressive nature of Fromm's early writings from the 1930s, *The Art of Loving* seemed more in line with existing social conventions and gender norms.

Fromm could hardly have anticipated how popular *The Art of Loving* would become. While he undoubtedly appreciated the praise that his work received, he also recognized the book's limitations. After all, *The Art of Loving* was not a canonical work of scholarship. It was a short treatise on the nature of love that was oriented toward a general audience and published in the midst of the highly conservative decade of the 1950s. It was never meant to be an exploration of the darker side of human nature, which helps to explain why Hitler is mentioned only once and in passing as an exemplary sadist, and the Nazi Party not at all. Fromm would address these issues at length and in considerable detail in *The Anatomy of Human Destructiveness* (Fromm, 1973). But as Fromm's popularity increased, so too did the criticisms of his work. Eventually, he felt compelled to respond:

> As one whose views have often been misrepresented as underestimating the potential of evil in the human being, I want to emphasize that such sentimental optimism is not the mood of my thought. It would be difficult indeed for anyone who has had a long clinical experience as a psychoanalyst to belittle the destructive forces within the human being.... It would be equally difficult for any person who has witnessed the explosive outburst of evil and destructiveness since the beginning of World War I not to see the power and intensity of human destructiveness. Yet there exists the danger that the sense of powerlessness which grips people today—intellectuals as well as average persons—with ever-increasing force, may lead them to accept a ... rationalization for the defeatist view that war cannot be avoided since it is the result of the destructiveness of human nature. Such a view, which sometimes prides itself on its exquisite realism, is unrealistic ... the intensity of destructive strivings by no means implies that they are invincible or even dominant. (Fromm, 1964, p. 17)

Fromm was not a naive idealist. He recognized the human propensity to harm, engage in conflict, and use others for selfish gain. Fromm wrote the *The Art of Loving* in full recognition of the Holocaust and with the knowledge that his own family members had been murdered. In this sense, the book he produced was a direct response to the "explosive outburst of evil and destructiveness" that he describes in the response to his critics. The fact that Fromm does not mention the Holocaust by name was consistent with his approach. Fromm's objective was to shed light on the human capacity to love and care for others and thus to instill a shared respect for humanity. It was precisely this affirmative aspect of *The Art of Loving* that continued to garner interest and support long after the book was published.

A noteworthy extension of Fromm's ideas can be found in the work of the social critic and activist bell hooks. She explored Fromm's ideas in her own book, *All About Love: New Visions* (2001). In a move that would have surprised Fromm's critics, hooks drew a direct link between Fromm and the work of Martin Luther King. As hooks pointed out,

> There is always an emphasis in their work on love as an active force that should lead us into great communion with the world. In their work, loving practice is not aimed at simply giving an individual great life satisfaction; it is extolled as the primary way we end domination and oppression. (hooks, 2001, p. 76)

hooks lamented that the important "politicization of love" in the works of Fromm and King had been neglected. Instead, she wrote, we encounter "popular New Age commentary on love," which fosters a "dangerous narcissism" and "spiritual rhetoric that pays so much attention to individual self-improvement and so little to the practice of love within the context of community" (hooks, 2001, p. 76). The latter point is especially relevant. Given the immense popularity of *The Art of Loving* in the decades after its publication, Fromm's ideas were often reduced to "pop psychology," leading to their outright dismissal by many academics and psychoanalysts. In the process, the wider relevance of his approach was neglected.

For Fromm, love is a vital part of human solidarity. As Gertrud's and Sophie's letters remind us, love enables us to feel a connection with others and can sustain us, even in the darkest moments. The love they describe does not derive out of selfishness or out of need only. It derives from an active willingness to give freely of ourselves to others. The essential nature of love, as Fromm understood it, is dynamic and participatory, a reaching out toward the other person in an attempt to understand, communicate, and meet them as they are, rather than as we would wish them to be. As Fromm wrote, "Love is not a resting place, but a moving, growing, working together" (Fromm, 1956, p. 103).

This brings us back to Fromm's work as a psychoanalyst. Fromm's own relatedness was evident in his work with patients. For example, the Mexican psychoanalyst Jorge Silva Garcia, who was a patient of Fromm's, remarked that their "face-to-face dialogue" was "meaningful, intense, direct. The dialogue happened in the *here and now*" (Silva Garcia, 2009, p. 145, original emphasis). Another of his patients, the psychoanalyst David E. Schechter, wrote that "To be truly with him one felt fully alive and awake" (Schechter, 2009, p. 73). But Fromm's approach was also questioned by those who perceived his therapeutic attitude as judgmental.[4] In point of fact, the notion of central relatedness did not exclude the possibility of disagreement, just as mutuality was not to be confused with sameness. As Fromm wrote in *Escape From Freedom*, "What the concept of equality does not mean is that all human beings are alike" (Fromm, 1941, p. 263). Ruth Lesser, who worked with Fromm for many years, took note and suggested that

> Unlike more cautious, traditional analysts he always focused directly on what he saw as the patient's core orientation. . . . There was no waiting for just the right moment, no hesitation about articulating his judgements, and no equivocation about just the right dosage of truth. With good-humored irony, he noted, "there is nothing polite in anybody's unconscious," including the analyst's. One of his most characteristic phrases after hearing some story from a patient or supervisee was, "Now look here. . ." after which he would explain what he observed about the patient's character. These words, out of context may convey an impression of a moralistic authority. Yet, *as I sat with Fromm, I heard a sense of urgency. Time was precious. . . . His directness, then, was not condemnation but an expression of hope and faith that speaking honestly and clearly to the healthy, striving adult in the patient would foster awareness and ultimately the freedom to fulfill unexplored potentialities.* (Lesser, 2009, p. 98, my emphasis)

There is also another way to understand Fromm's "directness." The sense of urgency described by Lesser has its roots in Fromm's own life experience. His early ideas on compassion and solidarity were developed in response to the dangers posed by authoritarianism. When the Nazi regime took power, unleashed its racial persecution and terror on Germany's Jewish population, and began its war of unbridled aggression, Fromm felt the urgent need to understand the conditions that led to fascism and to rally for its defeat. In the wake of the Holocaust, his resolve to counter the forces of cruelty and destruction strengthened still further. Fromm sought to generate understanding through critical reflection and rational insight, but he also recognized the fundamental necessity for societal and systemic change. Speaking as a psychoanalyst, Fromm maintained that in order to help the individual patient, the therapist also had to be prepared to address the pathologies of society. As Lesser recalled, "Fromm was clearly convinced that analysts should openly support humanistic values both inside and outside the consulting room" (2009, p. 96). In fact, Fromm made this point most succinctly when he declared:

> Private and public life cannot be separated. We cannot split off knowledge of ourselves from our knowledge of society. Both belong together. . . . We have to be political people. I would even say passionately involved political people, each of us in the way that best suits our temperaments, our own working lives, our own capabilities. (Fromm, 1986, pp. 115–116)

In short, we can say that Fromm's goal was to create opportunities for personal *and* political transformation. Simply put, for Fromm, the personal was always political and time was indeed precious. The events he lived through were ample proof of that.

As we confront the racial violence, hatred, and destructiveness that engulfs our own age, I believe that Fromm leaves us with both a warning and a sense of hope. We must not sit back. The threat is real. We can only learn from one another by moving toward human connection rather than away from it. Throughout his life, Fromm held fast to our potential for learning and loving, even in the face of destructiveness. It is an approach that has crucial relevance, not only for how we address the legacy of the Nazi past, but also for how we contend with the hateful present.

In the last year of his life, Fromm was asked whether he thought humanity had learned anything as a result of the Holocaust. His response conveyed none of the optimism with which he was commonly identified:

> Here we confront the question of whether humans actually learn anything on their own. Do they even want to learn, or do they remain tied to their entrenched opinions and insights? . . . I believe the readiness to learn is much

more limited than we assume. . . . Our lives are structured in such a way that people are first of all oriented towards functioning, but not, towards thinking. (Fromm, 1979)

When it came to the possibility for change, Fromm retained a clear-eyed realism. He believed that it was only by addressing how we interact with other people, both on an individual and a societal level, that we could work toward achieving solidary. He was encouraging us to engage with others, to build a more just world, and in essence, to learn and to love.

Fromm died at his home in Muralto, Switzerland, on March 18, 1980, 5 days before his 80th birthday. He became Muralto's first honorary citizen, and a plaque on the building where he lived still commemorates him today.[5] Fromm requested that his ashes be dispersed in Lake Maggiore, which seemed a fitting end for a life that was lived in near constant movement across cultures and continents (Figure 5.1). Yet of all the countries in which Fromm resided, Germany remained the focal point of his journey. Germany was the

Figure 5.1 Erich Fromm, 1970
Courtesy of the Erich Fromm Archive, Tübingen.

place of his birth, the cause of the traumas that shaped his family, and the impetus for his explorations of its tragic failures. Perhaps it is only fitting, therefore, that Germany today is also the location of Fromm's literary estate, of the International Erich Fromm Society and contemporary Fromm studies, and of a large readership that continues to be interested in what he had to say.[6]

Our Ethical Obligation to Others

I began this book with a set of reflections on the recent upsurge of antisemitism and its deadly effects. I have come to this subject not only as a historian interested in the legacy of the Nazi past, or as a psychoanalyst who addresses the traumatic impact of racial violence, but as a grandson of the generation of perpetrators and enablers of the Holocaust. As a German descendant, I found it particularly challenging to research Fromm's family history in full knowledge that my own grandparents supported the Nazi regime. The Holocaust teaches us what happens when people remain silent and cruelty prevails. As a society, and as individuals, we face similar choices today: to be bystanders and enablers or stand up in opposition. As Fromm's life and work attest, we cannot step outside the social and political upheavals that surround us. We cannot remain unaffected. Whether as private individuals or as concerned citizens, we have an obligation to speak out against racism and hate, whatever form it takes.

By sharing aspects of my family history in the context of this book, I have sought to show that histories of perpetration have implications for the present. What we know about the past determines what questions we are willing or able to ask in the present. For German descendants like myself, talk of the Holocaust can still evoke a sense of guilt and shame, feelings that are often associated with half-spoken family histories. We don't want to have to struggle with a past that we did not create. There are many German descendants whose family histories mirror my own: histories of a Nazi past that were never openly discussed or have been disavowed. Among former perpetrator nations, Germany's collective memory culture stands out. Since the 1970s, Germany, as a nation, has worked to confront its collective responsibility for the genocide. Yet many family histories still wait to be reckoned with.[7]

For me, the recognition of a Nazi past in my family lends the Holocaust a terrible and chilling reality that I cannot ignore. It forces me to reflect on the emotional meaning of what occurred and reinforces my obligation to remember and to speak out, just as it has undoubtedly influenced what I have written in this book. When I see the images of the marching right-wing protesters on the streets of contemporary cities and towns, it raises for me the specter of the Nazi past. Knowing about and engaging with this history matters, perhaps now more than ever. This is what Hannah Arendt had in mind when she wrote that

> We can no longer afford to take that which was good in the past and simply call it our heritage, to discard the bad and simply think of it as a dead load which by itself time will bury in oblivion. The subterranean stream of Western history has finally come to the surface and usurped the dignity of our tradition. This is the reality in which we live. (Arendt, 1951, p. 3)

The history of Nazi Germany should be enough to discourage nationalism and xenophobia. Yet in Germany today, as elsewhere, the pervasive threat of racism cannot be denied. Recent events are a warning to us all because they suggest that our belief in an enlightened postwar mentality may have been over-hasty or at the very least, naive. When members of the majority remain passive in the face of racist slogans and antisemitic and Islamophobic remarks that incite violence, then a racist normality has set in. The election of far-right parties to federal parliaments throughout Europe points to an alarming lack of historical awareness. We cannot afford to turn back the clock. History teaches us that complacency begets complicity. This is as relevant in Germany today, with the growth of the far-right Alternative for Germany Party (AfD), as it is for many other nations that struggle with their history and the contemporary reality of racial hatred and violence.

Acts of racial hatred and racially motivated nostalgia for the Third Reich point to a deeply concerning failure to heed the lessons of history. Just as historical crimes pervade individual lives long after they are first committed, the moral obligations to know and remember cross time and place, connecting descendants of perpetrator groups with the crimes committed and enabled by their forebears. We only need to look to see the effects of historical injustice and racism around us—of crimes that were committed long ago and crimes that continue to be committed daily, motivated by hatred and ignorance, seemingly in equal measure. I find myself reflecting on the many forms of denial: forgetting, disavowal, dissociation, willful disregard. As a society, and as individuals, we tend to be highly skilled practitioners of denial.[8]

I have focused my comments in this book chiefly on Germany and the legacy of the Nazi past because it formed the context for much of Fromm's life and work and reflects my own family history. But the conclusions we draw from this study are more broadly applicable. Fromm sought to show that the path to National Socialism in Germany was neither inevitable nor accidental and that fascism can also be a threat in other nations.[9] After a lifetime spent studying the history and politics of Germany, Fritz Stern expressed similar concerns. In his memoir *Five Germanys That I Have Known* (2006), Stern echoed Fromm when he wrote that

> no country is immune to the temptations of pseudo-religious movements of repression such as those to which Germany succumbed. The fragility of freedom is the simplest and deepest lesson. . . . I realized more and more that the lessons I had learned about German history had a frightening relevance to the United States. (Stern, 2006, p. 4)

Fromm reminds us that the freedoms inherent in democratic societies can never be taken for granted. In Nazi Germany, the fragility of freedom was illustrated by the fact that millions of Germans willingly and enthusiastically submitted to Hitler. But as Fromm also sought to show, it would be a mistake to think that authoritarianism was a uniquely German phenomenon. Well before Adorno published *The Authoritarian Personality* (1950), which warned of the possibility of fascism in the United States, Fromm argued that social conditions in the United States could lead to the rise of authoritarianism and a fascist mindset.

According to Fromm, a functioning and healthy society is defined by the active participation of its constituent citizens in democratic forums. When this symbiotic relationship between the individual and society is threatened or breaks down, the consequences can be disastrous. As Fromm tells his readers in *Escape From Freedom*, "there is no greater mistake and no graver danger than not to see that in our own society we are faced with the same phenomenon that is fertile soil for the rise of Fascism anywhere" (Fromm, 1941, p. 240). When a society fosters "the development of a personality which feels powerless and alone, anxious and insecure" (Fromm, 1941, p. 240), it creates conditions in which individuals are not only willing but eager to submit to right-wing, authoritarian leaders.[10]

Fromm's work is clearly resonant today. In his analysis of the rise of Hitler and the Nazis during the 1930s, Fromm exposed the appeal of a politics of denial and destructiveness in the wake of the progressive social and political change that occurred during the Weimar Republic. A politics of denial and destructiveness must not be allowed to flourish again. In the United States, antidemocratic forces and violent racism have been on the rise. The neo-Nazi march in Charlottesville, Virginia, in 2017 and the antisemitic, Islamophobic, and racial attacks that followed were an urgent call to action. The massacre at Pittsburgh's Tree of Life Synagogue in 2018 shone a light on the deadly reality of antisemitism. The murder of George Floyd in 2020 by Minneapolis police officers came to represent the countless African American men and women who have died at the hands of law authorities; some of these crimes have been reported but many remained out of the view of the white majority and media outlets. The Black Lives Matter protests that followed George Floyd's murder seemed, at least for a moment, to break through public indifference to the perennial issue of racist policing. Yet in the wake of the protests, the racial massacre of African Americans in a grocery store in Buffalo in 2022 once again demonstrated the depth of destructiveness that exists in American society. We can justifiably wonder whether the United States, with its history of slavery, lynching, Jim Crow laws, and the genocide of Indigenous peoples, will ever fully confront its dark past, be it through reparations or an honest reckoning with the system of white supremacy and structural racism.

For members of the white North American majority like myself, speaking openly about racism has often proven difficult precisely because it requires us to listen and open ourselves up to the perspective of those who are the victims of injustice. Confronting the reality of racism, be it in the past or present, can give rise to feelings of discomfort and shame that can be difficult to sustain.[11] But it is essential to resist the impulse to shut down the conversation. As Fromm reminds us, a healthy, democratic society requires citizens who are capable of engaging in critical self-reflection and willing to challenge the status quo.

When we recognize the traumatic effects that have followed from histories of deep and abiding injustice, we begin to shed light on historical responsibility. The process of attending to the injuries that follow from historical trauma, while simultaneously acknowledging our own implication in the system that sustains them, is complex. It requires us to acknowledge the limits of what we know and to reflect on our own positions in society.[12] Where do we stand in relation to the suffering in our midst, and how might we benefit from social systems that keep reconciliation and repair at bay? I recognize that there is much I fail to see and understand by virtue of my privileged position in society. I cannot inherently know what it is like to be a victim of racism, to be Black, Indigenous, a person of color, Jewish, a Holocaust survivor, or a descendant of survivors. But these limits do not relinquish me of a responsibility to try to understand the experience of others, to engage with the perpetrator past, and to speak out. On the contrary, they compel me to move out of my comfort zone and look for counternarratives that challenge the assumptions I hold.

I believe that we have an ethical obligation to address violent and traumatic histories, even if they happened before we were born. Indeed, as I have sought to illustrate, and as Fromm shows us over and over, there is much to be gained from treading on unfamiliar ground, even when it creates a sense of discomfort. To understand the Holocaust and other histories of racial violence and genocide, we need to better grasp how our sense of humanity can be imperiled. The paralysis we may feel when we confront the magnitude of human cruelty cannot stand in the way of collective action. The challenge is not only to define destructiveness and its traumatic effects. We also need to inquire into the very nature of resistance.

In the midst of destruction wrought by racial hatreds, genocide, and war, there are those who will still stand up for the victims. Fromm felt compelled to point out that not all Germans supported Hitler. There were some, though small in number, who resisted. How are compassion and courage maintained in the midst of cruelty? What social, political, and psychological processes might contribute to this ethical stance? Exploring these questions is surely where hope lies. At the end of his 1979 interview with Acklin, Fromm (1979) returned to the theme that came to define his life: the quest for human solidarity and a more just society. As Fromm suggests, it is hard to imagine a way forward without activism and resistance, and above all, without a sense of hope:

FROMM: *I'm a naturally hopeful person. And I believe as long as I live, I will not be able to give up my hope for a better world. But I also know that this is a factor, a subjective factor in me. I just can't help it. But objectively speaking, I have to admit that the opportunities are getting smaller and smaller...*

ACKLIN: *But you would believe that at least one hope must remain as a prerequisite for any future at all?*

FROMM: *I think so. Where there is no more hope, there is definitely no more future. Where there is hope, there does not have to be a future. But hope is the condition for all change.*

Notes

Introduction

1. The 1979 Swiss television interview of Fromm was only recently re-discovered. I thank Rainer Funk, Fromm's Literary Executor and Director of the Erich Fromm Archive and Institute in Tübingen, Germany, for alerting me to it. Both the transcription and translation are my own.
2. To date, Funk has written two unpublished essays in German for the membership of the Erich Fromm Society (Funk, 2005, 2009). Funk's essays were the first to introduce a selection of letters (Funk, 2005) and the history of Fromm's family (Funk, 2009). In English, there are two brief descriptions of this chapter in Fromm's life: Friedman (2013), pp. 69–76, and Funk (2019), pp. 85–95. It was as a result of research undertaken by Funk and Friedman that the Holocaust correspondence was donated by family members to the Erich Fromm Archive, Tübingen. The letters were subsequently transcribed.
3. The importance of letters and diaries for our understanding of the Holocaust has been demonstrated by historians (see, for example, Boehling and Larkey, 2011; Garbarini, 2006; and Kaplan, 1998, 2020). This approach draws on Saul Friedlander's (1997, 2007) use of these sources in his groundbreaking two-volume history, *Nazi Germany and the Jews*.
4. This book is about Fromm's experience of and response to fascism. For specific analyses of fascism and its causes, the reader is encouraged to consult such books as: Arendt (1951); Paxton (2004); and Stanley (2018).
5. See Fromm (1973), pp. 573–574. What set Fromm apart from many others scholars and psychoanalysts after the war was his emphasis on understanding the social, economic, and political conditions that gave rise to violence and aggression, rather than viewing aggression as an innate characteristic of the human being. I will examine this theme in Chapter 4.
6. In 1976, the publication of *To Have or To Be* led to a significant increase of interest in Fromm's works in Western Europe. The fall of the Iron Curtain in 1989 led to a rapid expansion of Fromm's readership in Eastern Europe. In Japan, over many decades, Fromm's book *Escape From Freedom* was required reading in high school ethics courses. In China, there has been a strong interest in, and research on, Fromm's writings going back decades. One study (Zimmer, 2015) shows that in the period from 1977 through 2012, year for year, research contributions on Fromm increased. It is also interesting to note that there were a greater number of articles and dissertations produced on Fromm than on Adorno and Horkheimer combined.

7. Over the course of his long career, Fromm cofounded psychoanalytic institutes and organizations including, but not limited to: the Southwest German Institute for Psychoanalysis in Frankfurt in 1929 (later the Frankfurt Psychoanalytic Institute), the William Alanson White Institute of Psychiatry, Psychoanalysis and Psychology in New York in 1943, the psychoanalytic section of the medical school of the National Autonomous University of Mexico City in 1951, the Mexican Institute of Psychoanalysis in 1956, and the International Federation of Psychoanalytic Societies in 1962.
8. As I suggest in *Not in My Family* (Frie, 2017), it is more accurate to use the term "enablers" than "bystanders" or "onlookers." In addition, it is important to note that there were a small number of Germans who were active and passive resisters. I return to these issues at the end of Chapter 5.
9. This was not my first encounter with Fromm's work. I remember seeing his books on shelves at home and hearing avid discussions of Fromm's final book, *To Have or To Be* (Fromm, 1976b), among my relatives during a visit to West Germany in 1977.
10. When psychoanalysts focus only on the therapeutic setting, they have difficulty appreciating the extent to which they and their theories are shaped by society and history. In a similar sense, therapeutic practice always reflects a particular cultural moment in time. Attempts to address the legacy of the Third Reich and its impact on Jewish refugee and émigré psychoanalysts are relatively recent; see Kuriloff (2014) and Prince (2009).
11. A note on terminology: in the secondary literature, there is often an intermingling of two terms: "refugee" and "émigré." In the main, I think "refugee" is the better term since it captures the lived experience of German Jews who were forced to flee. Fromm, to my knowledge, did not tend to use either term to self-identify. Schenderlein (2020, p. 3) suggests that Jews from Germany called themselves refugees, émigrés, or immigrants, but rarely exiles. In order to contextualize Fromm's life experiences and his writings, it is important to understand the extent to which he was a member of the wider German Jewish refugee community that began to take shape immediately after Hitler and the Nazi Party came to power in 1933. On this point, see Grossmann (2008).
12. On the importance of empathy for professional historians, see Kohut (2020).
13. Schenderlein (2020, p. 8) points out that during the 1930s, U.S. immigration policy was based on the National Origins Immigration Act of 1924, which sought to preserve the white, Protestant American majority. In addition, Kaplan (2020, pp. 77–78 and 167) demonstrates that during the 1930s, the U.S. imposed severe entrance limitations and never allowed immigration quotas to be filled. Additionally, on June 26, 1940, Assistant Secretary of State Beckinridge Long sent a memo to State Department Officials advising them "to put every obstacle in the way . . . , which would postpone and postpone and postpone the granting of the visas" (Kaplan, 2020, p. 77).
14. There are, in addition, a number of other important books, among them an edited volume of essays (Durkin and Braune, 2020), a discussion of Fromm's messianic outlook (Braune, 2014), a brief general introduction to Fromm's work (Thomson, 2009) and an overview of Fromm's political theory (Wilde, 2004). With the exception of

two important explorations (Funk, 2009 and Rudnytsky, 2019), there has been limited discussion of Fromm's contribution to psychoanalysis. Earlier relevant works on Fromm include Burston (1991) and Funk (1982).

15. The one exception is a brief autobiographical essay that Fromm wrote when he was in his early 60s, which was published in *Beyond the Chains of Illusion*. See Fromm (1962a). I examine this essay in Chapter 2.

16. Two psychoanalysts who worked closely with Fromm have referred to him as "intensely private" (Landis, 2009, p. 137) and as "always a private person" (Tauber, 2009, p. 131).

17. By prior arrangement with his third wife, Annis Freeman, much of Fromm's early personal correspondence was destroyed after his death. I will return to this issue later in the book. Extant letters are accessible in the Erich Fromm Papers at the New York Public Library (NYPL) and the Erich Fromm Archive in Tübingen.

18. Psychoanalysts would come to play an early and important role in examining the impact of Holocaust trauma on survivors (see, for example, Bruno Bettleheim's 1943 observations of concentration camp prisoners and W. G. Niederland's 1961 concept of survivor syndrome.) However, this interpretative lens was seldom directed at the profession itself, or on those who practiced it. A good example of this process is described by the historian Thomas Kohut in relation to his father, Heinz Kohut. See my dialogue with Kohut in Frie (2018).

19. I had the opportunity to interview Edgar Levenson in early 2024. Levenson interacted with Fromm during the early 1950s, when he was a psychoanalytic candidate at the William Alanson White Institute. In addition, Levenson was analyzed by Edward S. Tauber, who was himself analyzed by Fromm and became one of Fromm's close associates.

20. Sonja Gojman de Millan, personal communication, July 2023. Gojman de Millan also informed me that none of her classmates in the Mexico City psychoanalytic training program knew anything about the history of the Holocaust in Fromm's family. Similarly, Edgar Levenson, who trained as a psychoanalyst at the William Alanson White Institute of Psychiatry, Psychoanalysis and Psychology in New York, during the early 1950s, has no recollection of either Fromm or other European Jewish psychoanalysts ever mentioning the Holocaust (Levenson, personal communication). Levenson took part in several clinical case seminars led by Fromm.

21. The popular narrative of a postwar silence about the Holocaust within Jewish communities, and in North American life more generally (cf. Novick, 1999), has justifiably been questioned and debated (see Cesarani and Sundquist, 2011 and Diner, 2010). It is also important to distinguish between memorialization at the level of family and community, and collective and public memorialization at the level of society. As Diner (2010) has demonstrated, Jewish communities memorialized the victims of the Holocaust long before memories of the Holocaust were addressed at the collective, societal level. On the issue of language and the evolution of terminology related to the Holocaust, see Lipstadt (2016).

22. The way in which we are shaped by time and place is reflected in how we use language. Fromm's writing is a good example of this process, as illustrated by his use of the term

"man" throughout his writings. Yet by the time Fromm died in 1980, second-wave feminism was well established, and perceptions of gender and language had begun to shift. The fact that Fromm continued to use the term "man" in his last publications, whether it was his choice or that of his publishers, is unfortunate. With this in mind, and when appropriate, I have substituted the terms "person" or "human being" for "man." I believe this small but significant step can be undertaken in order to transform the language of the past into the present.

Chapter 1

1. The Fromm family correspondence is housed in the Erich Fromm Papers, New York Public Library (NYPL), and the Erich Fromm Archive, Tübingen. The letters concerning the imprisonment of Heinz Brandt are part of the Fromm Papers, NYPL. The letters written by Gertrud Brandt to Lisa Jacobs, and by Sophie Engländer to her daughter Eva Krakauer, are in the Erich Fromm Archive, Tübingen. I thank Rainer Funk, Fromm's literary executor and director of the Erich Fromm Archive for permission to quote selectively from the correspondence housed at the Erich Fromm Archive. All translations from German are my own.
2. The term "contemporaneous communication" is used by Boehling and Larkey (2011, p. 7).
3. More extensive accounts of Fromm's early life can be found in the following works: Burston (1991), Funk (2000), Friedman (2013), Jacobs (2015), and Jay (1973).
4. Fromm discusses some aspects of his childhood experiences in *Beyond the Chains of Illusion* (Fromm, 1962a).
5. According to Friedman (2013), who met with Gertrud Hunziker-Fromm in 2004, Gertrud's father, Emmanuel Fromm, was a lawyer and ethicist and became an important figure for the young Fromm, introducing him to key works of German literature and music.
6. Fromm offers this account of his childhood to Gérard D. Khoury, in an interview from 1978. See Fromm (2008), p. 34.
7. At the time Fromm attended the school it was known as the Wöhler-Schule. Today it would be designated as a "Gymnasium" (a German senior high school.)
8. Like Rosenzweig and Buber, Fromm would emphasize the centrality of relatedness and love in human experience. I will return to this point in Chapter 5.
9. On this point, and for a detailed overview of the experience of the German Jewish community leading up to and during the Holocaust, see Kaplan (1998).
10. Given that Naphtali was the second youngest in a family of 10 siblings, and that he died in 1933 at the age of 64, it is likely that most of his siblings predeceased him.
11. In line with Fromm's own sentiments, I refer to Gertrud Brandt as Fromm's aunt, even though she is officially Fromm's first cousin once removed. For the same reason, I refer to Gertrud Brandt's son, Heinz Brandt, as Fromm's cousin, rather than his second cousin. Fromm's family tree can be found in Funk (2005).
12. In the late 1930s, Fromm's cousin Charlotte Hirschfeld (née Stein) escaped with her husband to São Paulo, Brazil. From there, Charlotte was able to help rescue her

parents, Martha Stein (née Krause) and Bernhard Stein, by arranging for passage to Brazil. In 1938, Fromm wrote several letters to Charlotte (Lotte), to ask for confirmation that she has received the money he sent to her and her family in São Paulo. This is one of many examples of the way in which Fromm was supporting his relatives financially and working to attain entry and exit visas for them. I will discuss this further in this chapter. See letters to Lotte Hirschfeld, February 16, 1938, and May 11, 1938, Erich Fromm Archive, Tübingen.

13. "Posen" was also the location and the name commonly given to the infamous speech by Heinrich Himmler on October 4, 1943, in which he justified the extermination of European Jews to an audience of SS officers. See: https://www.yadvashem.org/odot_pdf/Microsoft%20Word%20-%204029.pdf

14. Gertrud Brandt feared that starting life anew in Germany would pose serious financial challenges. Nor did she and her husband, Georg, want to leave his parents, who lived in Posen. The Brandts continued to identify as culturally German, and their four children attended German schools in Posen. The Brandts thus belonged to, and identified with, the group of German Jews who lived in a German cultural milieu outside of the official borders of the German Reich. On this point, see Andresen (2007), pp. 46–48.

15. My discussion of Heinz Brandt draws on research carried out by Brandt's German biographer, Knud Andresen, in *Widerspruch als Lebensprinzip: Der undogmatische Sozialist Heinz Brandt (1909–1986)*. See Andresen (2007).

16. The correspondence concerning Heinz Brandt's imprisonment (which includes letters by Fromm, Gertrud Brandt, Georg Brandt, Heinz Brandt, and Juliane Favez) is housed in the Fromm Papers at NYPL.

17. In contemporaneous historical sources, Ostrow-Lubelski is referred to as a "town." Today it is generally referred to as a "village," presumably because of the loss of population. I will use the term "town" in line with historical sources.

18. This is the only letter by Georg Brandt that is included in the correspondence.

19. On this point, see Kaplan (1998), pp. 120–121.

20. In order to avoid the escalating political situation in Germany, the Institute for Social Research moved from Frankfurt to a temporary home in Geneva in 1932. The Institute was increasingly imperiled by right-wing political groups in Germany because of its Marxist orientation and the fact that its membership was identified as Jewish. See Jay (1973).

21. Knowing of Gertrud's difficult situation, and despite the uncertainty of whether she actually was able to receive funds from abroad, Fromm arranged two transfers of $100 through the American Express Company on March 14, 1940, and April 25, 1940. Erich Fromm Archive, Tübingen.

22. The cost of attaining a visa was significant. As Fromm also writes, "Gertrud asks me to get in touch with you to ask you if you could contribute some amount. I myself can give half the sum required. . . . Gertrud writes that you offered to send her money regularly. This will not be necessary, as I am sending her monthly the maximum sum which one is allowed ($16)." Letter to Ernest Leavy on June 19, 1940. Fromm Papers, NYPL.

23. The letters from Gertrud Brandt to Lisa Jacobs are housed at the Erich Fromm Archive, Tübingen.
24. The Oranienburg concentration camp was one of the first to be established in the German state of Prussia. It was closed in 1936 and replaced by the larger Sachsenhausen concentration camp.
25. The first of the so-called killing centers was established in Chelmo in December 1941, followed by Belzec, Sobibor, and Treblinka in 1942. The largest killing center was Auschwitz-Birkenau. By the spring of 1943 it had four gas chambers that were in constant operation. In his book *Ordinary Men*, the historian Christopher Browning (1992, pp. 115–116) provides an account of the killing squads or *Einsatzgruppen*. Browning recounts how in early October 1942, the Reserve Police Battalion 101 rounded up the inhabitants of the ghetto in Konskowola in southeast Poland and took them to a nearby forest and proceeded to murder them. This kind of mass murder was repeated over and over again throughout Nazi-occupied Poland and further east. The most infamous of these mass killings took place at Babi Yar, Ukraine, where 33,771 Jews were slaughtered on September 29–30, 1941.
26. Another record of the destruction of the Jewish population of Ostrow Lubelski has been provided by Isidore Last (1987, p. 413): "In the beginning of May 1942, a secret order was sent to all local police commanders (Kreishauptmanns) to prepare for deportation of Jews from the small towns in the Lublin district. In his answer of May 19th, 1942, Kreishaputmann Ziegenmayer recommended the deportation, in the first place, of Jews from six towns including Ostrow. The number of Ostrow Jews was indicated by Ziegenmayer as amounting to 3062. This number probably includes 300 Slovakian Jews. Since in 1921 there were only 1267 Jews in Ostrow, we may assume that in May 1942, most of the Jews in Ostrow were not of local origin. Any further German orders concerning the fate of Ostrow Jews are unknown to us. According to information provided by survivors, Jews were moved from Ostrow to Lubartow in October 1942. On the way, many of them were killed. The Jews who reached Lubartow were most likely deported together with the Lubartow Jews to the Sobibor and Belzec death camps on October 11th, 1942."
27. See also the detailed and referenced report by Sam Silverman, *An Incident in World War II: The Destruction of Jews in Ostrow-Lubelski*. His unpublished manuscript can be downloaded at: https://www.academia.edu/24415669/An_Incident_in_World_War_II_The_Destruction_of_the_Jews_in_Ostrow_Lubelski
28. The question of whether there has been any news of Erich is raised in letters from December 28, 1939, and January 28, 1940. Erich Fromm Archive, Tübingen.
29. In his biography of Fromm, Friedman (2013, pp. 73–74) suggests that Sophie and her daughter Eva were disgruntled by Fromm's lack of effort to help. However, based on a careful reading of Sophie's letters, I have found no evidence to support Friedman's claim. On the contrary, the letters clearly demonstrate that Sophie had a strong affection for Erich and his mother, Rosa. These sentiments remained, despite Sophie's worsening situation and the recognition that Fromm had limited ability to help.
30. On this point, see Kaplan (1998), pp. 142–144.
31. Hohenberge is a village to the north of the city of Oldenburg in Northern Germany, near the North Sea coastline. The Engländers appear to have had relatives there or

owned a vacation home together with other family members. Hohenberge has since been incorporated into the city of Varel. The Jewish cemetery in Hohenberge still exists and was founded in 1702. It has 120 gravestones, the earliest of which dates back to 1777.

32. On this point see Kaplan (1998), pp. 196–197. A powerful memorial to the deportations of Berlin's Jewish community can be found at Track (*Gleis*) 17 of the Grünewald S-Bahn station.
33. On this point see Kaplan (1998), p. 228.
34. My focus here is specifically on the Jewish victims of the Holocaust. It is thus important to point out that in addition to the six million dead and murdered, there were also half a million Roma and Sinti who were murdered and countless gays and lesbians, the mentally and physically disabled, and political opponents of all stripes who were imprisoned or murdered.
35. See, in particular, Hochstetter (2005).

Chapter 2

1. During the course of his training at the Berlin Psychoanalytic Institute, Fromm's training analyst, Hanns Sachs, had his office in Charlottenberg at Mommsenstraße 7, which is located a short walk from the synagogue on Fasanenstrasse in Berlin. See: https://www.gedenktafeln-in-berlin.de/gedenktafeln/detail/hanns-sachs/1188. Fromm's own office was located at his home in the Schöneberg area of Berlin, at Bayerischer Platz 1. See: https://www.gedenktafeln-in-berlin.de/gedenktafeln/detail/erich-fromm/1800
2. See Bohnke-Kollwitz (2012), p. 548.
3. See Kollwitz (1955), p. 87.
4. Cited in McCausland (1937), p. 20.
5. The power of Kollwitz's woodcuts was magnified by the medium. By cutting and gashing into the wood she found ways to give expression to the raw emotions of war. The first work in the War series, *The Sacrifice*, shows a woman, naked and without protection, giving her child unknowingly as a sacrifice. The second work, *The Volunteers*, is the only one that shows an actual combatant. In it, Kollwitz's son takes his place next to Death, who leads the troops in an ecstatic procession to war. In the third work, *The Parents*, the mother and father are forced to face the unending torment of the loss of their child. The fourth work, *The Widow I*, shows a young pregnant woman deeply alone, with her hands over her body, as if protecting herself. The fifth work, *The Widow II*, shows a war widow in a state of frozen despair, having taken her own life and that of her child. In the sixth work, *The Mothers*, a group of women band together, holding back their children to prevent them from being sacrificed at the altar of war. The last work of the cycle, *The People*, depicts the emotionally and physically wounded victims of war, huddled behind a central woman who evokes the Virgin of Mercy. For helpful accounts of the war series and the themes of death, grief, and mourning they evoke, see Kolb (2018), Murray (2020), Prelinger (1992), Whitner (2016), and the Käthe Kollwitz Museum Köln: https://www.kollwitz.de/en/series-war-overview

6. See Kramer (2020).
7. The Spanish flu spread among German soldiers in the summer of 1918 and then within Germany, where at least 260,000, or every 250th inhabitant, died from the pandemic in 1918 alone. See Förtsch and Rösel (2021).
8. Personal communication, Rainer Funk. See also Friedman (2013), p. 8.
9. Frieda Fromm-Reichmann Autobiographical Tapes (1956). Erich Fromm Archive, Tübingen.
10. My account of the relationship and marriage between Frieda and Erich follows that of Funk (2019 and person communications.) In general, there is some difference of interpretation as to exactly when their relationship began. Hornstein (2000, pp. 59–60), drawing on the work of Ann Silver, suggests that it began when Fromm entered into an analysis with Frieda in Dresden. Friedman (2013, p. 19) is vague, stating only that "When Fromm visited her there [Dresden], the relationship became more serious." Funk maintains that Frieda's analysis of Fromm took place at the *Therapeutikum* in Heidelberg and ended when they "had fallen in love" (2019, p. 21). Regardless of exactly when it began, there can be no doubt about the fact that Erich and Frieda had a romantic relationship, and that following the end of the analysis, they got married.
11. For a helpful description of how this political civil war played out on the streets of working-class Berlin, see Weitz (2007).
12. In 1930, Fromm was formally certified by the German Psychoanalytic Association (Deutsche Psychoanalytische Gesellschaft; DPG). Fromm's pioneering psychoanalytic work during the first 10 years of the Institute remains a generally neglected topic. I will return to Fromm's tenure at the Institute and the reasons for his departure and this neglect in the following chapters.
13. In the late 19th- and early 20th-century Europe, tuberculosis was known as "consumption," "white plague," or "white death." It was an endemic disease, and rates of infection were particularly high in rapidly expanding, poorer urban quarters, where people lived in overcrowded housing. For example, in the 10 years from 1916 to 1925, more than 50,000 people died of pulmonary tuberculosis in Switzerland (van Orsouw, 2020). Over time Davos entered into the popular imagination, especially after Thomas Mann penned his novel *Magic Mountain*, following a stay in Davos for his wife's treatment in 1912. Today, tuberculosis is still considered a serious, if preventable, bacterial infection and most commonly affects the lungs.
14. See Bollier (2016). For photographs of this period that vividly illustrate the Nazi presence in Davos, see: https://www.swissinfo.ch/eng/davos-in-the-1930s-40s/7880780
15. Horney moved to the United States in late 1932 with her three daughters. On September 1, 1932, Fromm signed a lease to stay in the apartment for a full year, through the end of August 1933. However, by the end of October 1932, he returned to Davos. Fromm initially stayed at the Hotel Kurgarten, which proved too expensive, and then found a small apartment at Promenade 35 in Davos Platz. The rental agreements for the apartments in Locarno and Davos, together with the bill from Hotel Kurgarten, are located with other documents from this period at the Erich Fromm Archive in Tübingen. A helpful description of these years can also be found in the illustrated biography of Fromm by Funk (2000).

16. Shortly after arriving in New York, Fromm was forced to travel again in search of a location where he could recuperate from a renewed onset of tuberculosis. Over the coming years, his ill health would continually shape his life and ability to work.
17. Bachofen was a 19th-century Swiss jurist and early anthropological writer whose theorizing was based on his reading of Greek and Roman classics. Bachofen was at base a conservative thinker who positioned matriarchy at an earlier evolutionary stage than patriarchy. Right-wing intellectuals were drawn to his work for its praise of naturalism and anti-intellectualism. Left-wing intellectuals were drawn to Bachofen for the idea that the subordination of women to men in patriarchal societies was the result of social factors, thus providing a foundation for thinking about society in a way that was not determined by biology. For a selection of Bachofen's writings, including *The Mother Right*, see Bachofen (1992).
18. This attitude, as Fromm later wrote to the Marxist humanist Raya Dunayevskaya, had infected the political landscape of Weimar Germany and shaped how the revolutionary Rosa Luxemburg was perceived: "I feel that male Social Democrats could never understand Rosa Luxemburg, nor could she acquire the influence for which she had potential because she was a woman; and the men could not become full revolutionaries because they did not emancipate themselves from their male, patriarchal and hence dominating character structure" (Fromm cited in Dunayevskaya, 1985, p. 242).
19. Bachofen's views on matriarchy have been questioned by anthropologists and feminists alike. For example, Cynthia Eller has raised important questions about the notion of matriarchy when she writes, "Relying on matriarchal myth in the face of the evidence that challenges its veracity leaves feminists open to charges of vacuousness and irrelevance that we cannot afford to court. And the gendered stereotypes upon which matriarchal myth rests persistently work to flatten out differences among women; to exaggerate differences between women and men; and to hand women an identity that is symbolic, timeless, and archetypal, instead of giving them the freedom to craft identities that suit their individual temperaments, skills, preferences, and moral and political commitments" (Eller, 2000, p. 8).
20. As Rudnytsky (2019) suggests, Fromm's perspective on a mother's love was highly idealized and may have reflected his own wishes as the child of a depressed parent. Fromm's singular focus on motherhood also begs the question of what role fathers and nonbinary parents might play in his conception of a more progressive social constellation.
21. During the 1930s, Benjamin was an associate of the Institute for Social Research, which provided him with an important venue in which to publish his work as well as a small (and insufficient) stipend.
22. See Stanley (2018), p. 6, and Durham (2002), p. 13.
23. The Nazi regime was highly critical of the focus on subjectivity and the emotions in modern works of art and in psychoanalysis in particular. The vivid depictions of the horrors of war in the works of Otto Dix or George Grosz were a direct threat to Nazi ideology and its glorification of battle. Kollwitz's art may have been different in style or content from that of Dix or Grosz, but her antiwar message and left-wing social and political views were similarly evident.

24. Kollwitz continued to work privately, focusing on the thematic of the dead child and the grieving mother, the image for which she is most widely recognized today. Her late works depict mothers who refuse to allow their children to be harmed by malignant forces, even, in some cases, merging with their children to create an inseparable union. Kollwitz died shortly before the end of World War II and collapse of the Nazi state, but not before witnessing the destruction of her family home and the loss of her grandson, Peter, named after her own son.
25. See Rudnytsky (2019) for an insightful discussion of Fromm's (1935) article. Rudnytsky also provides a detailed and helpful overview of Fromm's place in the history of psychoanalysis.
26. Fromm's departure for the United States coincided with the end of the psychoanalytic circle that had been important to his development. As Fromm later put it, "In contrast to most other analysts who are mostly concerned with the manipulation of theories, Groddeck and Ferenczi were human beings who empathized with the person they wanted to understand and, I would say, who felt in themselves what the so-called patient was telling them; they were persons of great humanity and for them the patient was not an object but a partner" (Fromm quoted in Funk, 2000, p. 64). Groddeck spent the last year of his life in Switzerland and died in the summer of 1934. Ferenczi died of illness a year earlier in May 1933 at his home in Budapest. Karl Landauer, who had been an important personal and psychoanalytic presence for Fromm in Germany, fled for Sweden in 1933. From Sweden he and his family made their way to the Netherlands, where Landauer worked as a training analyst. The family's escape from the Nazis was short lived. The German invasion of the Netherlands in May 1940 imperiled the lives of every Dutch Jew and Jewish refugee who had sought safe harbor there. In 1943 Landauer and his family were arrested, and a year later they were deported to the concentration camp of Bergen-Belsen. Landauer died there in January 1945; his wife and daughter survived.
27. On this point, see McVeigh (2016), p. 27.
28. Martha Nussbaum (2007, 2010) writes about the notion that compassion can be "diseased."

Chapter 3

1. These publications were also the last to be written in German and mark the shift away from Fromm's earlier Freudian perspective to the interpersonal and social psychoanalytic approach for which he became known.
2. On this point see Grossmann (2008), p. 165.
3. For a detailed account of the struggle faced by many German Jewish refugees, see Schenderlein (2020).
4. Letter to Otto Fenichel, March 19, 1936. Erich Fromm Archive, Tübingen.
5. On Fromm-Reichmann's life as a refugee during the period from 1934 to 1935 in France (Strasbourg), Palestine, and New York, see Hornstein (2000), pp. 80–82.

6. Requests for help received by Fromm in the form of written letters, as well as documentation of his attempts to help family members, friends, and colleagues, can be found in the Erich Fromm Papers, New York Public Library (NYPL).
7. Shortly after the war, Fromm described this process as follows: "It is the function of social character to shape the energies of the members of society in such a way that their behavior is not left to conscious decisions whether or not to follow the social pattern but that *people want to act as they have to act*" (Fromm, 1949, p. 5, original emphasis). In the early 1950s, the interpersonal psychoanalyst Edgar Levenson participated in several clinical case seminars that were led by Fromm at the William Alanson White Institute. Levenson recalls that when a clinical case was presented to Fromm, he was particularly interested in examining the way in which society impacted on the patient's well-being (Edgar Levenson, personal communication).
8. It is worth noting that the original title of Fromm's 1937 study was "A Contribution to the Method and Function of an Analytical Social Psychology". It was changed by Rainer Funk, editor of the English collection of essays in which it first appeared (see Funk in Fromm, 1937/2010, p. 13) to "Man's Impulse Structure and its Relation to Culture". As Funk points out in his brief introduction to the essay, the reason for this change was to avoid confusion with the title of Fromm's earlier 1932 publication, "The Method and Function of an Analytical Social Psychology".
9. As Clara Thompson later remarked in her 1956 article on Sullivan and Fromm, "The work of each supplements the other, and their basic assumptions about human beings are similar. The chief area which they share in common is the interest in the impact of cultural pressures on personality development" (Thompson, 1956/1979, p. 195).
10. On this point see Wake (2011).
11. On this point see Frie (2014) and Frie and Sauvayre (2022).
12. In this sense we can justifiably say that *Escape From Freedom* marks the foundation of a combined social and political turn in psychoanalysis.
13. The unsettled nature of Fromm's life was reflected in the course of his life up to that point. By the time Fromm arrived in New York at the age of 34, he had already lived through World War I, the pandemic known as the Spanish flu, the social and political crises of the Weimar Republic, the rise of the Nazis and their virulent antisemitism, and a diagnosis of tuberculosis.
14. The Fromm–Horkheimer correspondence provides a full accounting of these events. Fromm's letters can be found at the Erich Fromm Archive, Tübingen; the Fromm Papers, NYPL; and the Max Horkheimer Archive in Frankfurt. As I indicate in the text, a selection of Horkheimer's letters were published in the *Gesammelten Schriften von Max Horkheimer*, Vols. 15 and 16.
15. Fromm's comment here anticipates his later distinction between "totalitarian socialism" and "Marxist humanist socialism." See Fromm (1961c), p. viii.
16. This was a comment that Chamberlain made in a letter to his sister when he described meeting Hitler. Chamberlain went to Germany and met Hitler three times in the course of September 1938. Chamberlain seemed willing to believe Hitler, even after spending significant time with him.

17. Based on the inflation index, 1,000 U.S. dollars in 1938 is roughly equivalent to 22,000 dollars in 2024.
18. On this point see Durkin (2019), Friedman (2013), Jay (1973), and McLaughlin (1999) and (2021). Immediately following the war, it was Adorno who first articulated the Institute's differences with Fromm. As Martin Jay points out in his classic history of the Institute, *The Dialectical Imagination*, Adorno's attack "revealed a bitterness of tone very different from that of the Institute's work in the past" (Jay, 1973, p. 103). Adorno's tone would also be reflected in Marcuse's dismissal of Fromm's psychoanalytic approach during the 1950s. The personal animosity felt toward Fromm helps to explain why Fromm's essential early role in bridging sociology, psychoanalysis, and Marxism went largely unacknowledged by Institute members after his departure.
19. The secondary literature on the Worker's Study often notes that some of the completed questionnaires were missing. However, in a 1975 German radio interview, Fromm explicitly disputes this suggestion and goes on to detail the study's importance. See Fromm (1975).
20. See Bonss (1984), McLaughlin (2021), and Wheatland (2009).
21. The Worker's Study remained unpublished until 1977, when Fromm asked Bonss whether he would be able to bring the research to light. It was published as a German monograph in 1980 and appeared in German in *Fromm's Collected Works* (Vol. III) in 1981. It was published in English for the first time in 1984, under the title *The Working Class in Weimar Germany: A Psychological and Sociological Study*. After the partial publication of worker's study in 1936, its results came to be overshadowed by *The Authoritarian Personality*, written by Theodore Adorno, Else Frenkel-Brunswick, Daniel J. Levinson, and R. Nevitt Sanford in 1950. Like the Worker's Study, *The Authoritarian Personality* revealed the presence of fascist tendencies, though it focused on the United States, not Germany. The fact that there is no reference to the Worker's Study in *The Authoritarian Personality*, despite the obvious link between them, can presumably be traced back to the troubled relationship between Adorno and Fromm.
22. As the sociologist Lynn Chancer (2020, p. 105) points out, it is important to note that Fromm does not equate a specific gender with either sadism and masochism. For Fromm, neither pathway is biologically determined, so that a person may exhibit either one of these psychological characteristics, regardless of their gender identification. Rather, as Chancer suggests, it would seem that Fromm's aim is to help us to understand how society shapes people in specific directions.
23. Fromm's argument is directed specifically at Richard Brickner's 1943 article "Is Germany Incurable?" See Brickner (1943).
24. A fuller account of my grandfather's history can be found in Frie (2017).
25. On this point see Herwig (2014), p. 233.
26. On this point see Fromm (1984) and Abromeit (2021).
27. For helpful discussions of how members of the Institute of Social Research approached the issue of antisemitism, see Jacobs (2015) and Rensmann (2017).
28. For background on Scholem's response to the essay and to Benjamin, as well as Scholem's impressions of Horkheimer, see Jacobs (2015), pp. 48–51.

29. See Jacobs (2015), especially Chapter 2, "The Significance of Antisemitism: The Exile Years."
30. A similar phenomenon was present in other Western nations, though in different ways. For a discussion of fascism and antisemitism in Canada at the time, see Théorêt (2017).
31. On this point see Tharoor (2015).
32. Lindbergh gave the infamous speech in which he accused Jews of being war agitators on September 11, 1941, in Des Moines, Iowa. See https://exhibitions.ushmm.org/americans-and-the-holocaust/main/us-public-opinion-about-entering-world-war-ii-1940
33. Portions of Fromm's FBI file are accessible through the FBI records portal; see: https://vault.fbi.gov/Erich%20Fromm
34. While we don't know to what extent Fromm may have shared with Sullivan the peril faced by his family members who remained in Germany, we do know that Sullivan was frequently at Yale University to visit with Sapir. At the time, Sapir was one of only four Jewish faculty members at the university and he experienced discrimination. On this point see Perry (1982).
35. Regarding the question of Sullivan's sexuality and its centrality to his life and work, see Wake (2011).
36. Sullivan wrote two important articles about the effects of racism on young African American men. See Sullivan (1940/1964a) and (1941/1964b). These articles are discussed in Stephens (2022).
37. Wilhelm Reich's *The Mass Psychology of Fascism* was published in German in 1933 but did not appear in English until 1946. In contrast to Fromm, who was concerned with the social forces that shape individuals and groups, Reich used a more traditional psychoanalytic lens to explain fascism as a consequence of sexual repression at the level of family and community. Another German Jewish psychiatrist and refugee, W. G. Niederland, gave a series of lectures in the United States on the subject of fascism in Germany and other European countries. These lectures took place before he became a psychoanalyst in 1953. On Niederland's efforts, see https://archives.cjh.org//repositories/5/resources/12075

Chapter 4

1. Fromm discussed this in several places. See letter to Horkheimer, March 9, 1938. Erich Fromm Archive, Tübingen. See also Fromm (1964), pp. 33–35.
2. For a more detailed account of these and other important statistics, see: United States Holocaust Memorial Museum, "German Jewish Refugees, 1933–1939." Holocaust Encyclopedia. https://encyclopedia.ushmm.org/content/en/article/german-jewish-refugees-1933-1939
3. It is important to note that many of Fromm's well-known books were written during his years in Mexico City, a cultural context that provided him with a critical distance to reflect on the systemic issues facing the United States.

4. Our understanding of what transpired on the fateful border crossing relies on the following sources: Henny Gurland's firsthand account, which she shared in a letter to Adorno (in Scholem, 2012, pp. 281–283); an essay and a memoir by Lisa Fittko (1999 and 2005), who guided Benjamin, Gurland, and her son through the Pyrenees; and a short memoir by Celia Birman (2006), who was a member of the party of four women refugees that Benjamin and Gurland met on the second day of their escape from France. Additionally, there is a detailed, but unpublished, memoir by Joseph Gurland (1998) that is housed at the Erich Fromm Archive, Tübingen. Joseph Gurland's memoir recounts the life of his mother in Germany, their time as refugees in France, and their escape through Spain to Portugal and then on to the United States. I do not know of any other secondary account of Benjamin's death that draws on all four of these sources.
5. On this point see Joseph Gurland (1998), p. 17, Erich Fromm Archive, Tübingen.
6. Rafael Gurland hailed from a Russian Jewish family and was the cousin of Arkardij Gurland, who worked at the Institute for Social Research in New York during the period 1940–1945. Arkardij helped to secure temporary U.S. visas for Henny and Joseph. When Henny Gurland sent a note to Adorno with Benjamin's last words, it was mailed first to Arkardij Gurland and then passed on to Adorno. In the secondary literature, the names of Rafael Gurland and Arkardij Gurland are often confused.
7. German aerial bombers infamously provided support for Franco in the form of the bombing of Madrid in 1936 and of Guernica in 1937.
8. Gurland's letter to Adorno was written in October 1940. She destroyed Benjamin's note after committing it to memory. Gurland feared that if his death was seen as a suicide, it would further complicate the situation for everyone. The physician agreed to support the notion that his death was due to physical illness, not suicide.
9. A memorial to Benjamin by the Israeli artist Dani Karavan was inaugurated in 1994 and looks out from the cemetery in Port Bou toward the harbor and Mediterranean Sea beyond. See: https://walterbenjaminportbou.org/en/passages-karavan/
10. On the life of Jewish refugees in Lisbon, and in Portugal more generally, see Kaplan (2020).
11. Letter to Izette de Forest, February 20, 1944. Erich Fromm Archive, Tübingen.
12. In his biography of Fromm, Friedman (2013) recounts his 2009 interview with Doris Gurland (Joseph Gurland's spouse and Henny Gurland's daughter-in-law). Drawing on Doris's account, Friedman writes that the group of escaping refugees was "strafed by hostile planes" before reaching the Spanish border (Friedman, 2013, p. 133). However, none of the other three eyewitness reports of the escape, Birman, Fittko, or Joseph Gurland, make any mention of being attacked by planes, thus casting doubt on this account. These sources would have been available to Friedman when he wrote his biography. Curiously, he makes no mention of this conflict.
13. On the experience of German Jewish refugees in the United States and different attitudes toward Germany, see Grossman (2008) and Schenderlein (2020).
14. On this point see Gay (1998), p. 4, and Schenderlein (2020), pp. 186 and 195.
15. Cited in Schwarz (2020), p. 72.

NOTES 179

16. On this point, see Funk (2000), p. 135. It would take another 20 years before the German profession of psychoanalysis began to confront its own entanglement in the Nazi regime. See Lockot (1985) and (1994).
17. Arendt (1950); Gay (1998); Schenderlein (2020).
18. On the relationship of West Germany to Israel, and German attitudes toward Israel, see Marwecki (2020). On the prevalence of antisemitism in relation to claims for compensation, see Herzog (2016), p. 96.
19. A copy of the Rosa Fromm's restitution claim (*Entschädigungsakte, 54343*), along with letters from the lawyer, Paul Simon, who was hired to handle the claim that was submitted on March 19, 1958, and officially closed on May 3, 1965, can be found at the Erich Fromm Archive, Tübingen.
20. On this point, see de Jong (2022).
21. On this point, see Herwig (2014) and Nieman (2019).
22. Cited in Rozanes (2021).
23. A "Kapo" was a prisoner, frequently with a criminal record, who was assigned by the SS to supervise forced labor. On Brandt's years as a prisoner in concentration camps, see Andresen (2007), pp. 109–126; on his captivity in Auschwitz, see Andresen (2007), especially pp. 119–122.
24. On this point see: https://www.deutscheundpolen.de/personen/person_jsp/key=heinz_brandt.html
25. See Andresen (2007), p. 207.
26. This letter is part of the documentation on Heinz Brandt that is housed at the Erich Fromm Archive, Tübingen.
27. In her focus on caste, Wilkerson draws on the earlier work of the psychologist and social scientist John Dollard and his influential study, *Caste and Class in a Southern Town* (1937), in which he argued that economically insecure Southern whites displaced their aggression onto African Americans. Dollard and Fromm worked together as part of the culture and personality movement in the late 1930s and 1940s.
28. There are no references to Arendt in *The Anatomy of Human Destructiveness*, but a brief letter exchange between Arendt and Fromm from the late 1940s demonstrates that they knew one another (located at the Erich Fromm Archive, Tübingen). I will discuss their letter exchange further in relation to their mutual response to the establishment of the State of Israel.
29. Cited in Lifton (2011), p. 285.
30. For more on the debates surrounding Lorenz's work and its impact at the time, see Weideman (2021). As Weideman observes, feminists have pointed to the sexism inherent in ethologists' claims that innate aggression was a driver of human evolution. Psychoanalysts who explicitly paired Freud's and Lorenz's views on aggression generally had negative reactions to *The Anatomy of Human Destructiveness*. See Herzog (2016) for discussion of Lorenz and postwar psychoanalysis.
31. The correspondence between Fromm and Speer is housed at the Erich Fromm Archive, Tübingen. My comments here draw specifically on evidence that is found in *The Anatomy of Human Destructiveness*.
32. Personal communication, Rainer Funk.

33. Schwartz (2020), p. 185.
34. As strange as the dialogue between Fromm and Speer may seem to us today, other examples of interactions between Jewish Germans and German Nazis have been documented. The Israeli documentarian Arnold Goldfinger explores the interaction between his Jewish German grandparents and a German SS officer in his film *The Flat* (2011). The documentary concerns the hidden postwar relationship between Goldfinger's maternal grandparents, the Tuchlers, and the pro-Zionist SS officer Leopold von Mildenstein and his wife. Their interactions continued well after 1945, when the horrors of the Holocaust were widely known. For an analysis of the relationship between the Tuchlers and Mildensteins, see Munk (2016).
35. A parallel process was taking place in North America. In the decades after the Second World War public accounts of immigration by European Jewish refugees were often framed in terms of freedom from oppression and the opportunity to prosper. The immediate postwar decades were a defining period for Jewish refugee families. As the sociologist Arlene Stein (2014) points out, the focus on cultural adaptation, perseverance, and financial success shaped the ways that many refugees talked about the past. Once in the United States, refugees often found themselves in a cultural milieu where there was limited opportunity for talk of hardship, suffering, or trauma. Adaptation to this new setting often meant focusing on the future while revealing relatively little about the past. Lipstadt (1996) suggests that it was not until the 1960s that Jewish communities and scholars began to use the term "Holocaust." And it was not until the airing of the television miniseries of the same name, *Holocaust*, in 1978 that the term entered into general usage in the American public.
36. In a noteworthy demographic shift, thousands of young, educated, secular, and politically left-leaning Israelis have emigrated to Germany, and especially Berlin, in the past two decades. Estimates of the number of Israeli immigrants are between 10,000 and 20,000. Many are descended from German Jewish Holocaust survivors, and some hold European citizenship through their parents and grandparents, facilitating their residency in Germany. On this point see Estrin (2019).
37. On this point see the following works: Dörner (2007), Herf (2006), and Longerich (2006).
38. As Jack Jacobs points out (2015, p. 130), Fromm's claim, that from the Nazi perspective Jews were a danger because they proved they could survive without power, was inherently linked to his critique of Israel, which I will discuss further. David Feldman, Director of the Birkbeck Institute for the Study of Antisemitism, elaborates this point when he discusses how the foundation of Israel transformed the relationship of Jews to state power. As Feldman states, "It fundamentally changed the relationship of Jews to the question of minorities. For in Israel, Jews constitute the majority population, and the state is defined as 'Jewish' notwithstanding the presence of a large minority population" (Feldman, 2018, p. 1149) At risk of reducing a highly complex situation to a simple statement, Fromm argued that the power of the State of Israel was used to the advantage of Jews over the Palestinians, thereby neglecting Palestinian needs and rights. On Fromm's relationship to and criticism of Israel, see Jacobs (2015), pp. 125–130.

39. Fromm's correspondence with Leo Baeck concerning the public statement can be viewed at the Erich Fromm Archive, Tübingen. Fromm knew Baeck personally from their early years of working at the Free Jewish Learning Center in Frankfurt. While Fromm's earlier drafts were more critical of Jewish actions in Palestine than the eventual published statement, his general criticisms remained.
40. Cited in Khoury, 2009, p. 167. An additional perspective can be found in an essay that Fromm wrote in response to the Six Day War in 1967, in which he offered a critical analysis of the Israeli actions toward the Palestinians. Entitled "Martyrs and Heroes" (Fromm, 1967/1999), it was published posthumously in German in Fromm's collected works. An English translation is available through the Erich Fromm Archive, Tübingen.
41. Letter to George McGovern, July 18, 1970. Erich Fromm Archive, Tübingen.

Chapter 5

1. See Adorno (1955/1982), p. 17. Adorno's statement is often taken out of the specific context in which it was written and misquoted as suggesting that poetry is impossible after Auschwitz. Adorno later sought to correct these misunderstandings. In the *Negative Dialectics*, Adorno wrote that "Perennial suffering has as much right to expression as a tortured man has to scream; hence it may have been wrong to say that after Auschwitz you could no longer write poems. But it is not wrong to raise the less cultural question whether after Auschwitz you can go on living—especially whether one who escaped by accident, one who by rights should have been killed, may go on living. His mere survival calls for the coldness, the basic principle of bourgeois subjectivity, without which there could have been no Auschwitz; this is the drastic guilt put on him who has been spared" (Adorno, 1990, pp. 362–363).
2. Ruth Nanda Anshen's role in the publication of *The Art of Loving* was communicated to me by Rainer Funk.
3. Because Fromm wrote little about his therapeutic work, his contributions to the field of clinical psychoanalysis are generally overlooked. In a letter from 1974 to David Schechter, Fromm acknowledged the "peculiar discrepancy" that he had "written very little about immediate detailed clinical experience when this is the main basis of my thinking and the one in which I find the greatest satisfaction." Letter to David Schechter, May 28, 1974. Erich Fromm Archive, Tübingen.
4. The best known report of this kind is by one of Fromm's former analysands, Michael Maccoby (1995). It is interesting to note that Maccoby's account is not shared by Fromm's other patients who have disclosed aspects of their work with him. On this point see Horney Eckardt (2009) and Tauber (2009). This discrepancy is an illustration of the fact that each therapeutic relationship is unique and reflects the particular personal dynamics evoked by the interaction between the patient and analyst.
5. Fromm had an apartment in Casa La Monda at 4 Via Stefano Franscini in Muralto, Switzerland. See Rues (2020).

6. In addition to the Erich Fromm Institute and Erich Fromm Archive in Tübingen, the International Psychoanalytic University in Berlin is home to the Erich Fromm Study Center and the Erich Fromm Professorship. The International Erich Fromm Society, which regularly hosts workshops and conferences, is likewise located in Germany. Studies on Erich Fromm have been published in the German-language journal *Fromm Forum* since 1996. There is also an abridged English-language version of the *Fromm Forum*, which contains a selection of English articles and articles that have been translated from German.
7. My argument here parallels those of Angelika Bammer in her book *Born After: Reckoning With the German Past* (2019). Although Bammer is second-generation German and I am third-generation German, our approaches to the discoveries we each made in our families are similar. See Frie (2017).
8. For a more detailed discussion of these themes, see Frie (2019).
9. I am paraphrasing Fritz Stern (2006, p. 4). Although there are obvious differences between the work of Fromm and Stern, there are also points of intersection. As German Jewish refugees, albeit from different generations, they both spent much of their careers seeking to address and understand Germany's history and politics.
10. In *Escape From Freedom*, Fromm wrote that "we have pointed out the economic conditions that make for increasing isolation and powerlessness.... We have shown that this powerlessness leads either to the kind of escape that we find in the authoritarian character, or else to a compulsive conforming in the process of which the isolated individual becomes an automaton" (Fromm, 1941, pp. 318–319). In the immediate postwar years, especially in *Man for Himself*, Fromm (1947/1960a) considered the consequences of conformism and proposed the notion of a "marketing character." The "marketing character" was one of four types of "non-productive character orientations" that Fromm compared with what he called a "productive character orientation." A productive orientation referred to our ability to realize our potential for creativity and solidarity with others and was oriented toward the development of love, reason, and productive work. With the publication of *The Sane Society* in 1955, Fromm identified what he called the "pathology of normalcy" that governed capitalist societies. The basic premise of the pathology of normalcy was first developed by Fromm in 1944 in a short article called "Individual and Social Origins of Neurosis." There he used the term "socially patterned defects" (Fromm, 1944, p. 383).
11. On the issue of confronting historical responsibility and racism in the present, and the emotional challenges this process can present, whether in Germany or the United States, see Frie (2023).
12. On this point, see Frie (2019) and (2020).

References

Abromeit, J. (2021). Siegfried Kracauer and the early Frankfurt School's analysis of fascism as right-wing populism. In P. F. Noppen and G. Roulet (Eds.), *Theorie Critique de la Propoganda* (pp. 251–277). Paris: Éditions de la Maison des sciences de l'homme.
Adorno, G., and Benjamin, W. (2008). *Correspondence 1930–1940*. Cambridge: Polity Press.
Adorno, T. W. (1982). An essay on cultural criticism and society. In *Prisms* (pp. 17–34). Cambridge, MA: MIT Press. (Original work published 1955)
Adorno, T. W. (1955/2010). *Guilt and defense: On the legacies of National Socialism in postwar Germany*. Cambridge, MA: Harvard University Press.
Adorno, T. W. (1990) *Negative dialectics*. London: Routledge.
Adorno, T. W., and Benjamin, W. (1999). *The complete correspondence, 1928–1940*. Cambridge, MA: Harvard University Press.
Adorno, T. W., Frenkel-Brunswik, E., Levinson, D. J., & Sanford, R. N. (1950). *The authoritarian personality*. New York: Harper and Row.
Amery, J. (1974, December 31). Fromm und die Lebensfrömmigkeit. [Fromm and the Piety of Life.] *Die Weltwoche*, 52.
Amery, J. (1975, February 16). Destruktivität und Radikaler Humanismus: Über Erich Fromm, "Anatomie der menschlichen Destruktivität [Unpublished manuscript]." *Sender Freies Berlin*. Erich Fromm Archive, Tübingen.
Andresen, K. (2007). *Widerspruch als Lebensprinzip. Der undogmatische Sozialist Heinz Brandt (1909–1986)*. [Contradiction as a Principle of Life. The Undogmatic Socialist Heinz Brandt.] Bonn: Dietz Verlag.
Arendt, H. (1950). The aftermath of Nazi rule: Report from Germany. *Commentary*, 10, 342–353.
Arendt, H. (1951). *The origins of totalitarianism*. London: George Allen and Unwin.
Arendt, H. (1963). *Eichmann in Jerusalem: A report on the banality of evil*. New York: Viking Press.
Arendt, H. (1964). Personal responsibility under dictatorship. In H. Arendt, *Personality and Judgement* (pp. 17–48). Ed. J. Kohn. New York: Schocken Books, 2003.
Bachofen, J. J. (1992). *Myth, religion and the mother right*. Princeton, NJ: Princeton University Press.
Bahr, E. (1984). The antisemitism studies of the Frankfurt School: The failure of critical theory. In J. Marcus and Z. Tar (Eds.), *Foundations of the Frankfurt School of Social Research* (pp. 311–321). New York: Routledge.
Bammer, A. (2019). *Born after: Reckoning with the German past*. London: Bloomsbury Academic.
Benjamin, W. (1935). Johann Jakob Bachofen. In H. Eiland and M. W. Jennings (Eds.), *Walter Benjamin: Selected Writings Volume 3, 1935–1938* (pp. 11–24). Cambridge, MA: Harvard University Press, 2002.
Benjamin, W. (1938). A German Institute for Independent Research. In H. Eiland and M. W. Jennings (Eds.), *Walter Benjamin: Selected Writings Volume 3, 1935–1938* (pp. 307–316). Cambridge, MA: Harvard University Press, 2002.

Benjamin, W., and Scholem, G. (1989). The correspondence of Walter Benjamin and Gershom Scholem, 1932–1940 (Gary Smith and Andre Lefevere, Trans.). New York: Schocken Books.

Bettelheim, B. (1943). Individual and mass behavior in extreme situations. *Journal of Abnormal and Social Psychology, 38,* 417–452.

Birman, C. (2006). *The narrow foothold.* London: Hearing Eye.

Boehling, R., and Larkey, U. (2011). *Life and loss in the shadow of the Holocaust: A Jewish family's untold story.* Cambridge: Cambridge University Press.

Bohnke-Kollwitz, J. (Ed.). (2012). *Käthe Kollwitz. Die Tagebücher 1908–1943* (New edition). [Käthe Kollwitz. The diaries 1908–1943.] Munich: btb.

Bollier, P. (2016). *Die NSDAP unter dem Alpenfirn. Geschichte einer existenziellen Herausforderung für Davos, Graubünden und die Schweiz.* [The NSDAP under the *Alpinefirn.* History of an existential challenge for Davos, Graubünden, and Switzerland.] Chur, Switzerland: Verlag Desertina.

Bonss, W. (1984). Introduction. In E. Fromm, *The Working Class in Weimar Germany* (pp. 1–38). Cambridge, MA: Harvard University Press.

Brandt, H. (1970). *The Search for a third way: My path between East and West.* (Foreword by Erich Fromm). New York: Double Day and Co.

Braune, J. (2014). *Erich Fromm's revolutionary hope: Towards a critical theory of the future.* New York; Rotterdam, Netherlands: Sense Publishers.

Brickner, R. (1943). *Is Germany incurable?* New York: J. B. Lippincott Co.

Browning, C. (1992). *Ordinary men: Reserve Police Battalion 101 and the Final Solution in Poland.* New York: HarperCollins.

Buber, M. (1923). *I and Thou.* New York: Scribner, 1970.

Burston, D. (1991). The legacy of Erich Fromm. Cambridge, MA: Harvard University Press.

Cesarani, D., and Sundquist E. J. (Eds.) (2011). *After the Holocaust: Challenging the myth of silence.* London: Routledge.

Chancer, L. (2020). Feminism, humanism and Erich Fromm. *Fromm Forum, 24,* 101–114.

De Jong, D. (2022). *Nazi billionaires: The dark history of Germany's wealthiest dynasties.* Boston: Mariner Books.

Diner, H. (2010). *Remember with reverence and love: American Jews and the myth of silence after the Holocaust, 1945–1962.* New York: University Press.

Dollard, J. (1937). *Caste and class in a southern town.* New Haven, CT: Yale University Press.

Dörner, B. (2007). *Die Deutschen und der Holocaust. Was niemand wissen wollte, aber jeder wissen konnte.* Berlin: Propyläen.

Dunayevskaya, R. (1985). *Women's liberation and the dialectics of revolution: Reaching for the future.* Atlantic Highlands, NJ: Humanities Press.

Durham, M. (2002). *Women and fascism.* London: Routledge.

Durkin, K. (2014). *The radical humanism of Erich Fromm.* New York: Palgrave Macmillan.

Durkin, K. (2019). Erich Fromm and Theodore Adorno reconsidered: A case study in intellectual history. *New German Critique, 46,* 103–126

Durkin, K., and Braune, J. (Eds.). (2020). Erich Fromm's critical theory: Hope, humanism and the future. London: Bloomsbury Academic.

Eckhaus, M. (1987a). Living through two world wars. In D. Shtokfish (Ed.), *Ostrow-Lubleski Memorial-Book* (pp. 383–398). New York: The New York Public Library—National Yiddish Book Center, Yizkor Book Project.

Eckhaus, B. (1987b). To remember and to tells [sic]. In D. Shtokfish (Ed.), *Ostrow-Lubleski Memorial-Book* (pp. 380–383). New York: The New York Public Library—National Yiddish Book Center, Yizkor Book Project.

Eller, C. (2000). *The myth of matriarchal prehistory: Why an invented past won't give women a future.* Boston: Beacon Press.

Engels, F. (1884). *The origin of the family, private property and the state.* London: Penguin Books.

Engelsing, T. (2007, January 23). Das Hitlerbad. *Die Zeit.* https://www.zeit.de/2007/04/A-Davos/komplettansicht

Estrin, D. (2019, March 7). Thousands of Israelis now call Berlin home and make their cultural mark. *NPR.* https://www.npr.org/2019/03/07/700356426/thousands-of-israelis-now-call-berlin-home-and-make-their-cultural-mark

Feldman, D. (2018). Toward a history of the term "antisemitism." *American Historical Review, 123,* 1139–1150.

Fenichel, O. (1944). Psychoanalytic remarks on Fromm's "Escape From Freedom." *The Psychoanalytic Review, 31,* 133–152.

Fittko, L. (1999). *The story of old Benjamin.* In Walter Benjamin, *The Arcades Project* (pp. 946–954). trans. Howard Eiland and Kevin McLaughlin. Cambridge, MA: Harvard University Press.

Fittko, L. (2005). *Escape through the Pyrenees.* Evanston, IL: Northwestern University Press.

Förtsch, M., and Rösel, M. (2021). The Spanish flu killed 260,000 in Germany in 1918. *ifo Dresden berichtet, 28*(3), 6–9. https://www.ifo.de/en/publikationen/2021/article-journal/spanish-flu-killed-260000-germany-1918

Fortune Editors. (Nov. 18, 2015). Here's *Fortune's* survey on how Americans viewed Jewish refugees in 1938. *Fortune Magazine.* https://fortune.com/2015/11/18/fortune-survey-jewish-refugees/

Freud, S. (1985). *Civilization and its discontents* (J. Strachey, Trans.). London: Pelican. (Original work published 1930)

Frie, R. (2014). What is cultural psychoanalysis? Psychoanalytic anthropology and the interpersonal tradition. *Contemporary Psychoanalysis, 50,* 371–394.

Frie, R. (2017). *Not in my family: German memory and responsibility after the Holocaust.* New York: Oxford University Press.

Frie, R. (Ed.) (2018). *History flows through us: Germany, the Holocaust and the importance of empathy.* New York: Routledge.

Frie, R. (2019). History's ethical demand: Memory, denial and responsibility in the wake of the Holocaust. *Psychoanalytic Dialogues, 29,* 122–142.

Frie, R. (2020). Recognizing racism in Canada. *Psychoanalysis, Self and Context, 15,* 276–280.

Frie, R. (2023). Learning to embrace our discomfort: Accepting our historical responsibility and implication in systemic racism. *The Humanistic Psychologist,* https://doi.org/10.1037/hum0000331

Frie, R., and Sauvayre, P. (Eds.) (2022). *Culture, politics and race in the making of interpersonal psychoanalysis.* New York: Routledge.

Friedlander, S. (1993). *Memory, history and the extermination of the Jews of Europe.* Bloomington: Indiana University Press.

Friedlander. S. (1997). *Nazi Germany and the Jews, volume 1: The years of persecution, 1933–1939.* New York: HarperCollins.

Friedlander. S. (2007). *Nazi Germany and the Jews, volume 2: The years of extermination, 1939–1945.* New York: HarperCollins.

Friedman, L. J. (2013). *The lives of Erich Fromm: Love's prophet.* New York: Columbia University Press.

Fromm, E. (1931). Politik und Psychoanalyse. [Politics and Psychoanalysis.] In *Psychoanalytische Bewegung*, Band 3 (pp. 440-447). Wien: Internationaler Psychoanalystischer Verlag.

Fromm, E. (1934). The theory of mother right and its relevance for social psychology. In R. Funk (Ed.), *Love, Sexuality, and Matriarchy: About Gender* (pp. 19-45). New York: Fromm International Publishing Corporation.

Fromm, E. (1935). The social determinants of psychoanalytic therapy. *International Forum of Psychoanalysis*, 9(2000), 149-165.

Fromm, E. (1936). Studies on authority and the family. Sociopsychological dimensions. *Fromm Forum*, 24(2020), 9-58.

Fromm, E. (1941). *Escape From Freedom*. New York: Farrar & Rinehart, Inc.

Fromm, E. (1943, June 29). What shall we do with Germany? *Saturday Review of Literature*, 26, 10.

Fromm, E. (1944). Individual and social origins of neurosis. *American Sociological Review*, 9, 380-384.

Fromm, E. (1949). Psychoanalytic characterology and its application to the understanding of culture. In S. S. Sargent & M. W. Smith (Eds.), *Culture and Personality* (pp. 1-12). New York: Viking Fund.

Fromm, E. (1952). The contribution of the social sciences to mental hygiene. In A. Millan (Ed.), *Proceedings of the Fourth Congress of Mental Hygiene* (pp. 38-42). Mexico City: La Prensa Médica Méxicana.

Fromm, E. (1956). *The art of loving*. New York: Harper & Brothers.

Fromm, E. (1958, May 19). The Problem of Power in Israel. *Jewish Newsletter*, XIV(10), 1-2.

Fromm, E. (1959). Dealing with the unconscious in psychotherapeutic practice. *International Forum of Psychoanalysis*, 9(2000), 167-186.

Fromm, E. (1960a). *Man for himself: An inquiry into the psychology of ethics*. London: Routledge and Kegan Paul, 1960. (Original work published 1947).

Fromm, E. (1960b). Psychoanalysis and Zen Buddhism. In D. T. Suzuki, E. Fromm, and R. De Martino, *Zen Buddhism and Psychoanalysis* (pp. 77-141). New York: Harper and Row.

Fromm, E. (1961a, July). Facts and fictions about Berlin. *Committee of Correspondence*, 2-6.

Fromm, E. (1961b). Introduction. In E. Fromm and H. Herzfeld (Eds.), *Der Friede. Idee und Verwirklichung. Festgabe fuer Adolf Leschnitzer* (pp. 13-16). [Peace. Idea and Realization. Commemorative publication for Adolf Leschnitzer.] Heidelberg: Lambert Schneider.

Fromm, E. (1961c). *Marx's concept of man*. New York: Frederick Ungar.

Fromm, E. (1961d). *May man prevail: An inquiry into the facts and fictions of foreign policy*. New York: Doubleday Anchor Books.

Fromm, E. (1962a). *Beyond the chains of illusion: My encounter with Marx and Freud*. New York: Simon and Schuster, Inc.

Fromm, E. (1962b, July). Dissenting voices from Germany, old and new. *Committee of Correspondence*, 16-19.

Fromm, E. (1963a). The dogma of Christ. In E. Fromm, *The Dogma of Christ and Other Essays on Religion, Psychology and Culture* (pp. 15-94). New York: Holt, Rinehart and Winston. (Original work published 1930)

Fromm, E. (1963b). The revolutionary character. In E. Fromm, *The Dogma of Christ and Other Essays on Religion, Psychology and Culture* (pp. 145-167). New York: Holt, Rinehart and Winston.

Fromm, E. (1964). *The heart of man: Its genius for good and evil*. New York: Harper & Row.
Fromm, E. (1966). Is Germany on the march again? *War/Peace Report, 6*, 3-4.
Fromm, E. (1970a). Heinz Brandt as a man of faith. In H. Brandt, *The Search for a Third Way: My Path Between East and West* (pp. xi-xvi). Garden City, NY: Doubleday.
Fromm, E. (1970b). The method and function of an analytic social psychology. In E. Fromm, *The Crisis of Psychoanalysis* (pp. 137-162). New York: Henry Holt. (Original work published 1932)
Fromm, E. (1973). *The anatomy of human destructiveness*. New York: Holt, Rinehart and Winston.
Fromm, E. (1975, April 20). *Hitler—wer war er und was heißt Widerstand gegen diesen Menschen?* [Radio broadcast]. [Hitler—who was he and what does resistance to this man mean?] https://www.youtube.com/watch?v=vkQhs5a_RaY&t=696s
Fromm, E. (1976a). Back cover book endorsement. *Spandau: The Secret Diaries*, by Albert Speer. New York: Macmillan.
Fromm, E. (1976b). *To have or to be*. New York: Harper and Row.
Fromm, E. (1977, December 24). Das Zusichkommen des Menschen. Interview von Michaela Lämmle und Jürgen Lodemann mit Erich Fromm. [The Coming Together of Man. Interview by Michaela Lämmle and Jürgen Lodemann with Erich Fromm.] *Basler Magazin, 47*, 3.
Fromm, E. (1979). Keine Zukunft ohne Hoffnung. Interview von Jürg Acklin mit Erich Fromm. Erstsendung 28. Oktober 1979, Swiss Television (SRF) und DRS Zürich [Unpublished manuscript]. [No Future Without Hope. Interview by Jürg Acklin with Erich Fromm. First broadcast October 28, 1979.] Fromm Archive, Tübingen, Germany.
Fromm, E. (1984). *The working class in Weimar Germany: A psychological and sociological study*. Cambridge, MA: Harvard University Press.
Fromm, E. (1986). For the love of life. In H. J. Schulz (Ed.). New York: Free Press.
Fromm, E. (1989). Psychoanalysis and sociology. In S. E. Bronner and D. Kellner (Eds.), *Critical Theory and Society: A reader* (pp. 37-39). London: Routledge, 1989. (Original work published 1929)
Fromm, E. (1990). *The sane society*. New York: Holt, Rinehart and Winston. (Original work published 1955)
Fromm, E. (1994). Remarks on the relations between Germans and Jews. In R. Funk (Ed.), *On Being Human* (pp. 105-110). New York: Continuum. (Original work published 1978)
Fromm, E. (1999). *Märtyrer und Helden*. [Martyrs and Heroes.] In R. Funk (Ed.), *Erich-Fromm-Gesamtausgabe in zwölf Bänden* (Vol. XI, pp. 514-520). Munich: dtv Verlag. (Original work published 1967)
Fromm, E. (2008). Interview by Gérard D. Khoury, part 1. *Fromm Forum, 12*, 33-40.
Fromm, E. (2009). *The art of listening* (R. Funk, Ed.). New York: Continuum.
Fromm, E. (2010). Man's impulse structure and its relation to culture. In R. Funk (Ed.), *Beyond Freud: From Individual to Social Psychology* (pp. 17-74). New York: American Mental Health Foundation. (Original work published 1937)
Fromm, E. (2019). On the feeling of powerlessness. *Psychoanalysis and History, 21*, 311-329. (Original work published 1937)
Funk, R. (1982). *Erich Fromm: The courage to be human*. New York: Continuum.
Funk. R. (2000). *Erich Fromm: His life and ideas: An illustrated biography*. London: Continuum.

Funk, R. (2005). *Erleben von Ohnmacht im Dritten Reich: Das Schicksal der juedischen Verwandtschaft Erich Fromms aufgezeigt an Dokumenten* [Unpublished manuscript]. [Experiencing Powerlessness in the Third Reich: The Fate of Erich Fromm's Jewish Relatives Revealed in Documents.]. Erich Fromm Archiv, Tübingen.

Funk, R. (Ed.). (2009a). *The clinical Erich Fromm: Personal accounts and papers on therapeutic technique*. Amsterdam: Brill.

Funk, R. (2009b). *Erich Fromm und der Holocaust: Ein Beitrag zur Deutsch-Jüdischen Kulturgeschichte* [Unpublished manuscript]. [Erich Fromm and the Holocaust: A Contribution to German-Jewish Cultural History.] Fromm Archiv, Tübingen.

Funk, R. (2019). *Life itself is an art: The life and work of Erich Fromm*. London: Bloombury Academic.

Garbarini, A. (2006). *Numbered days: Diary writing and the Holocaust*. New Haven, CT: Yale University Press.

Gay, P. (1998). *My German question: Growing up in Nazi Berlin*. New Haven, CT: Yale University Press.

Gay, P. (2008). Reflections on Hitler's refugees in the United States. Keynote speech. *The Leo Baeck Institute Year Book*, 53, 117–126.

Gilligan, C. (1986). Remapping the moral domain: New images of the self in relationship. In T. Heller, M. Sosna, & D. Wellbery (Eds.), *Reconstructing Individualism: Autonomy, Individuality and the Self in Western Thought*. Stanford, CA: Stanford University Press.

Gilligan, C. (2010). Free association and the grand inquisitor: A drama in four acts. *Contemporary Psychoanalysis*, 46, 311–333.

Giordano, R. (1987). *Die Zweite Schuld; Oder, Von der Last, ein Deutscher zu sein*. [The second guilt; Or, On the burden of being German.] Hamburg: Rasch und Roehring Verlag.

Goldfinger, A. (2011). *The Flat*. Ruth Films.

Grass, G. (2002). *Crabwalk*. New York: Harcourt.

Grossmann, A. (2008). German Jews as provincial cosmopolitans: Reflections from the Upper West Side. *The Leo Baeck Institute Year Book*, 53, 157–168.

Gurland, J. (1998). *Henny (Meyer) Gurland, 1900-1952: The story of my mother* [Unpublished manuscript]. Erich Fromm Archive, Tübingen.

Havel, V. (1990). *Disturbing the peace: A conversation with Karel Huizdala*. London: Faber.

Herf, J. (2006). *The Jewish enemy. Nazi propaganda during World War II and the Holocaust*. Cambridge, MA: Harvard University Press.

Herwig, M. (2014). *Post-war lies: Germany and Hitler's long shadow*. London: Scribe.

Herzog, D. (2016). *Cold War Freud: Psychoanalysis in the age of catastrophes*. Cambridge: Cambridge University Press.

Hess, H. (2011). *German expressionism: Works from the collection*. https://www.moma.org/s/ge/curated_ge/

Hobbes, T. (1982). *Leviathan*. London: Penguin. (Original work published 1651)

Hochstetter, D. (2005). *Motorisierung und "Volksgemeinschaft": Das Nationalsozialistische Kraftfahrkorps (NSKK) 1931–1945*. [Motorization and the "people's community": The National Socialist Motor Corps.] Munich: R. Oldenbourg Verlag.

hooks, b. (2001). *All about love: New visions*. New York: HarperCollins.

Horkheimer, M. (1939/1989). The Jews of Europe. In S. E. Bronner and D. MacKay Kellner (Eds.), *Critical Theory and Society: A Reader* (pp. 77–94). London: Routledge.

Horkheimer, M. (2007). *A life and letters: Selected correspondence*. Manfred R Jacobson and Evelyn M. Jacobson (Ed. and Trans.). Lincoln: University of Nebraska Press.

Horney, K. (2000). Can you take a stand? In B. J. Paris (Ed.), *The Unknown Karen Horney: Essays on Gender, Culture and Psychoanalysis* (pp. 222–227). New Haven, CT: Yale University Press.

Horney Eckardt, M. (2009). From couch to chair. In R. Funk (Ed.), *The Clinical Erich Fromm* (pp. 71–73). Amsterdam: Brill.

Hornstein, G. (2000). *To redeem one person is to redeem the world. The Life of Frieda Fromm-Reichmann.* New York: The Free Press.

Jacobs, J. (2015). *The Frankfurt school, Jewish lives, and antisemitism.* Cambridge: Cambridge University Press.

Jacoby, R. (1983). *The repression of psychoanalysis: Otto Fenichel and the political Freudians.* Chicago: University of Chicago Press.

Jay, M. (1973). *The dialectical imagination: A history of the Frankfurt School and the Institute of Social Research, 1923–1950.* Boston: Little, Brown.

Kaplan, M. A. (1998). *Between dignity and despair: Jewish life in Nazi Germany.* New York: Oxford University Press.

Kaplan, M. A. (2020). *Hitler's Jewish refugees: Hope and anxiety in Portugal.* New Haven, CT: Yale University Press.

Kohut, T. A. (2012). *A German generation: An experiential history of the twentieth century.* New Haven, CT: Yale University Press.

Kohut, T. A. (2020). *Empathy and the historical understanding of the past.* New York: Routledge.

Kolb, M. (2018). Intimations of mortality from recollections of atrocity. Käthe Kollwitz and the art of mourning. In K. Hammerstein, B. Kosta, & J. Shoults (Eds.), *Women Writing War: From German Colonialism Through World War I* (pp. 305–328). Berlin; Boston: De Gruyter. https://doi.org/10.1515/9783110572001-015

Kollwitz, H. (Ed.). (1955). *Diary and letters of Käthe Kollwitz.* Chicago, IL: Regnery.

Kramer, A. (2020). Naval blockade (of Germany). In U. Daniel, P. Gatrell, O. Janz, H. Jones, J. Keene, A. Kramer, and B. Nasson (Eds.), *1914-1918—Online. International Encyclopedia of the First World War.* Freie Universität Berlin. DOI: 10.15463/ie1418.11451. Retrieved January 22, 2020 from https://encyclopedia.1914-1918-online.net/pdf/1914-1918-Online-naval_blockade_of_germany-2020-01-22.pdf

Kuriloff, E. (2014). *Contemporary psychoanalysis and the legacy of the Third Reich: History, memory, tradition.* New York: Routledge.

Landis, B. (2009). When you hear the word, the reality is lost. In R. Funk (Ed.), *The Clinical Erich Fromm* (pp. 137–140). Amsterdam: Brill.

Last, I. (1987). Ostrow Lubelski. In D. Shtokfish (Ed.), *Ostrow-Lubleski Memorial-Book* (pp. 410–419). New York: The New York Public Library—National Yiddish Book Center, Yizkor Book Project.

Lesser, R. (2009). There is nothing polite in anybody's unconscious. In R. Funk (Ed.), *The Clinical Erich Fromm* (pp. 91–99). Amsterdam: Brill.

Levi, P. (1988). *The drowned and the saved.* New York: Vintage International.

Lifton, R. J. (2011). *Witness to an extreme century.* New York: Free Press.

Lindbergh, C. (1939, November). Aviation, geography, and race. *The Reader's Digest,* 35(211), 64–67.

Lipstadt, D. (1996). America and the memory of the Holocaust, 1950–1965. *Modern Judaism, 16,* 195–214.

Lipstadt, D. (2016). *Holocaust: An American understanding.* New Brunswick, NJ: Rutgers University Press.

Lockot, R. (1985). *Erinnern und Durcharbeiten: Zur Geschichte der Psychoanlyse und Psychotherapie im Nationalsozialismus.* [Remembering and working through: On the history of psychoanalysis and psychotherapy in National Socialism.] Frankfurt: Fisher Taschenbuch.

Lockot, R. (1994). *Die Reinigung der Psychoanalyse. Die Deutsche Psychoanalystische Gesellschaft im Spiegel von Dokumenten und Zeitzeugen. (1933–1951).* [The cleansing of psychoanalysis. The German Psychoanalytic Society as reflected in documents and by witnesses to history. (1933–1951).] Tübingen: Edition Diskord.

Lohse, A. *Prevail until the bitter end: Germans in the waning years of World War II.* Ithaca, NY: Cornell University Press.

Longerich, P. (2006). *"Davon haben wir nichts gewusst!" Die Deutschen und die Judenverfolgung 1933–1945.* ["We knew nothing about that!" The Germans and the Persecution of the Jews 1933–1945.] Munich: Siedler.

Maccoby, M. (1995). The two voices of Erich Fromm: The prophetic and the analytic. *Society, 32,* 72–82.

MacIntyre, A. (1981). *After virtue: A study in moral theory.* Notre Dame, IN: University of Notre Dame Press.

Malinowski, B. (1924). Psycho-analysis and anthropology. *Psyche, 4,* 293–332.

Marwecki, D. (2020). *Germany and Israel: Whitewashing and statebuilding.* Oxford: Oxford University Press.

McCausland, E. (1937). Käthe Kollwitz. *Parnassus, 9,* 20–25.

McLaughlin, N. (1999). Origin myths in social science: Erich Fromm, the Frankfurt School and the emergence of critical theory. *Canadian Journal of Sociology, 24,* 109–139.

McLaughlin, N. (2021). *Erich Fromm and global public sociology.* Bristol, UK: Bristol University Press.

McVeigh, J. (2016). "They were all deceived": Art, women and propaganda in the life and work of Käthe Kollwitz. In C. C. Whitner (Ed.), *Käthe Kollwitz and the Women of War: Femininity, Identity, and Art in Germany During World Wars I and II* (pp. 21–30). New Haven, CT: Yale University Press.

Munk, Y. (2016). Arnon Goldfinger's *The Flat*: Holocaust memory, film noir, and the pain of others. *Jewish Film & New Media, 4,* 25–42.

Murray, A. (2020). Käthe Kollwitz: Memorialization as anti-militarist weapon. *Arts, 9*(1), 36. http://dx.doi.org/10.3390/arts9010036

Neiman, S. (2019). *Learning from the Germans: Race and the memory of evil.* New York: Farrar, Straus and Giroux.

Neuman, F. (1944). *Behemoth: The structure and practice of National Socialism 1933–1944.* New York: Harper & Row Publishers.

Niederland, W. G. (1961). The problem of the survivor. *Journal of the Hillside Hospital, 10,* 233–247.

Nietzsche, F. (2004). *Beyond good and evil.* New York: Firstworld Library. (Original work published 1886)

Novick, P. (1999). *The Holocaust in American life.* New York: Houghton Mifflin.

Nussbaum, M. (2007). *The clash within: Democracy, religious violence, and India's future.* Cambridge, MA: Harvard University Press.

Nussbaum, M. (2010). Compassion: Human and animal. In A. Davis, R. Keshan, and J. McMahan (Eds.), *Festschrift in Honor of Jonathan Glover* (pp. 202–228). Oxford: Oxford University Press.

Paxton, R. O. (2004). *The anatomy of fascism*. New York: Random House.
Perry, H. S. (1982). *Psychiatrist of America: The life of Harry Stack Sullivan*. Cambridge, MA: Harvard University Press.
Prelinger, E. (1992). *Käthe Kollwitz*. Washington, DC: National Gallery of Art.
Prince, R. (2009). Psychoanalysis traumatized: The legacy of the Holocaust. *The American Journal of Psychoanalysis*, 69, 179–194.
Rauer, V. (2009). Symbols in action: Willy Brandt's kneefall at the Warsaw Memorial. In J. C. Alexander, B. Giesen, and J. Mast (Eds.), *Social Performance: Symbolic Action, Cultural Pragmatics, and Ritual* (pp. 257–282). Cambridge: Cambridge University Press.
Reich, W. (1970). *The mass psychology of fascism*. New York: Farrar, Straus & Giroux. (Original work published 1946)
Rensmann, L. (2017). *The politics of unreason: The Frankfurt School and the origins of modern antisemitism*. Albany: SUNY Press.
Rozanes, S. (2021, February 21). How Jewish life developed in Germany after the Holocaust. *Deutsche Welle* (DW.com). https://www.dw.com/en/how-jewish-life-developed-in-germany-after-the-holocaust/a-56604526
Rudnystky, P. (2019). *Formulated experiences: Hidden realities and emergent meanings from Shakespeare to Fromm*. New York: Routledge.
Rues, R. (2020, March 15). Omaggio a Erich Fromm: 40esimo anniversario della sua scomparsa. [Tribute to Erich Fromm: 40th anniversary of his death.] *insubricahistorica.ch*. https://insubricahistorica.ch/blog/2020/03/15/omaggio-a-erich-fromm-40esimo-anniversario-della-sua-scomparsa/
Schechter, D. E. (2009). Awakening the patient. In R. Funk (Ed.), *The Clinical Erich Fromm* (pp. 73–78). Amsterdam: Brill.
Schenderlein, A. C. (2020). *Germany on their minds: German Jewish refugees in the United States and their relationships with Germany, 1938–1988*. New York: Berghahn Books.
Scholem, G. (2012). *Walter Benjamin: The story of a friendship*. New York: New York Review of Books.
Schwartz, G. (2020). *Those who forget: My family's story in Nazi Europe—A memoir, a history, a warning*. New York: Scribner.
Silva Garcia, J. (2009). His way to clarity and humaneness. In R. Funk (Ed.), *The Clinical Erich Fromm* (pp. 145–152). Amsterdam: Brill.
Stanley, J. (2018). *How fascism works: The politics of us and them*. New York: Penguin Random House.
Stein, A. (2014). *Reluctant witnesses: Survivors, their children and the rise of Holocaust consciousness*. New York: Oxford University Press.
Stephens, M. (2022). More simply human than otherwise: Interpersonal psychoanalysis and the field of the Negro problem. In R. Frie and P. Sauvayre (Eds.), *Culture, Politics and Race in the Making of Interpersonal Psychoanalysis* (pp. 83–110). New York: Routledge.
Stern, F. (2006). *Five Germanys I have known*. New York: Farrar, Straus and Giroux.
Sullivan, H. S. (1938). Antisemitism. *Psychiatry*, 1, 593–598.
Sullivan, H. S. (1964a). Discussion of the case of Warren Wall. In *The Fusion of Psychiatry and Social Science* (pp. 100–107). New York: Norton. (Original work published 1940)
Sullivan, H. S. (1964b). Memorandum on a psychiatric renaissance. In *The Fusion of Psychiatry and Social Science* (pp. 89–95). New York: Norton. (Original work published 1940)
Tauber, E. S. (2009). Words are ways. In R. Funk (Ed.), *The Clinical Erich Fromm* (pp. 131–134). Amsterdam: Brill.

Tharoor, I. (2015, Nov. 7). What Americans thought of Jewish Refugees on the eve of World War II. *The Washington Post.* Retrieved from: https://www.washingtonpost.com

Théorêt, H. (2017). *The blue shirts: Adrien Arcand and fascist antisemitism in Canada.* Ottawa, ON: University of Ottawa Press.

Thomson, A. (2009). *Erich Fromm: Explorer of the human condition.* London: Palgrave Macmillan.

Thompson, C. (1979). Sullivan and Fromm. *Contemporary Psychoanalysis, 15,* 195–200. (Original work published 1956).

United States Holocaust Memorial Museum. German Jewish Refugees, 1933–1939. In *Holocaust Encyclopedia.* https://encyclopedia.ushmm.org/content/en/article/german-jewish-refugees-1933-1939

van Orsouw, M. (2020). The White Plague. National Museum. https://blog.nationalmuseum.ch/en/2020/07/pestilence/

Wake, N. (2011). Private practices: Harry Stack Sullivan, the science of homosexuality, and American liberalism. New Brunswick, NJ: Rutgers University Press.

Weideman, N. (2021). *Killer instinct: The popular science of human nature in twentieth-century America.* Cambridge, MA: Harvard University Press.

Weitz, E. (2007). *Weimar Germany: Promise and tragedy.* Princeton, NJ: Princeton University Press.

Wheatland, T. (2009). *Frankfurt School in exile.* Minneapolis: University of Minnesota Press.

Whitner, C. C. (2016). Käthe Kollwitz and the Krieg cycle: The genesis, creation, and legacy of an iconic plate series. In C. C. Whitner (Ed.), *Käthe Kollwitz and the Women of War: Femininity, Identity, and Art in Germany during World Wars I and II* (pp. 21–30). New Haven, CT: Yale University Press.

Wiggershaus, R. (1995). *The Frankfurt School: Its history, theories, and political significance.* Cambridge, MA: MIT Press.

Wilde, L. (2004). *Erich Fromm and the quest for solidarity.* New York: Palgrave Macmillan.

Wilkerson, I. (2020). *Caste: The origin of our discontents.* New York: Random House.

Zimmer, M. (2015). Erich Fromm in China—Overview of the reception of his thinking (1961–2014). In R. Funk and N. McLaughlin (Eds.), *Towards a Human Science: The Relevance of Erich Fromm for Today* (pp. 301–312). Frankfurt: Psychosozial Verlag.

Index

For the benefit of digital users, indexed terms that span two pages (e.g., 52–53) may, on occasion, appear on only one of those pages.

Figures are indicated by an italic *f* following the page/paragraph number.

Acklin, Jürg
   Fromm on views of, 142–43
   interview with Fromm, 164
Adenauer, Konrad (Chancellor), 115–16, 119
Adorno, Gretel, 107
Adorno, Theodor, 13, 88, 99–100, 149
   Gurland's letter to, 109
Age of Enlightenment, 137–38
aggression
   Fromm on, 134
   Lorenz on evolution and, 133–34
Aktionenen, 41
Alexander, Franz, 68–69
alienation from life, 86–87
All About Love (hooks), 156
Alternative for Germany party (AfD), 161
American antisemitism
   upsurge in 1930s 24
   visibility of, 100
   see also United States
American Institute of Public Opinion, Gallop, 100
American Psychoanalytic Association, 79–80
Amery, Jean, 132–33
Amnesty International, 124
Anatomy of Human Destructiveness, The (Fromm), 6, 15, 18, 129, 132–33, 134, 144, 155
Anschluss, 22, 82
Anshen, Ruth Nanda, 151
antisemitism, 18
   American, 24, 100
   ascendancy in Berlin, 25–26
   Christianity and, 101–2

   Fromm on reality of, 61
   German culture and, 106
   Holocaust denialism, 4
   incidents of, 1
   Nazi ideology and, 102, 103–4
   Nazism ideology and, 98–100
   policies in Germany, 28
   reality of, 2
   Sullivan on threat of, 101–2
   United States and, 100–1, 162–64
Arendt, Hannah, 140, 145, 161
   on banality of evil, 131–32
Art of Loving, The (Fromm), 3, 18, 150–52, 154–55, 156
Auschwitz
   Heinz Brandt's survival of, 122
   Speer authorizing expansion of, 135
   trials in Frankfurt (1963-1965), 121
Austria, 22, 23, 85, 105–6, 133
   German annexation of, 82
authoritarian character, Fromm on, 92–93
authoritarianism, 3
   appeal of, 63–64, 90, 97–98
   fascism and, 102, 162
   Fromm study, 6, 8–9, 15, 75, 103–4, 134
   German submission to, 77, 140
   patriarchal family and, 92
   right-wing, 90, 103–4, 128–29
   rise of, 162
   role of, 91
   theme of, 144
   yearning for submission, 75
Authoritarian Personality, The (Adorno), 162

Bachofen, Johann Jacob, 69, 70
Baeck, Leo, 21, 145
Bamberger, Selig Bär, 21
Bauman, Zygmunt, on Holocaust, 131
Behemoth (Neumann), 99–100
Benedict, Ruth, 80, 102–3
Benenson, Peter, 124
Benjamin, Walter, 17–18, 70, 98–99
   Adorno (Gretel) and, 107
   Adorno (Theodore) and, 108
   burial of, 110–11
   Carina's interaction with, 109
   Fromm and, 77–78
   Institute for Social Research, 107
   living in exile, 107
   morphine pills and death of, 110–11
   "stateless", 107
   tragedy in Portbou, 106, 109–11
   transit papers for, 108
Berlin, 55–56
   Deportation of Jewish community from, 50–51
   Fromm's childhood visits to, 20–21
   Fromm's family in, 24, 26
   Fromm's life and training in, 22, 54, 64, 68
   Holocaust letters from, 42–50
   Jewish survivors of, 51, 143
   Poverty and revolution in, 62–63, 64–65
   Rise of Nazis in, 66
   Weimar years of the 1920s, 64–66, 97
Berlin, Kollwitz depicting, 64–65
Berlin Aid Association, 31–32
Berlin Institute, 65
Between Dignity and Despair (Kaplan), 50–51
Beyond the Chains of Illusion (Fromm), 59
Birman, Carina, on interactions with Benjamin, 109
Black Lives Matter, 162–63
Bolsonaro, Jair, 128–29
Bonss, Wolfgang, 90
Brandt, Georg, 24–26
   alienation from life, 86–87
   letter to Erich, 27
   photograph of, 26*f*
Brandt, Gertrud (née Krause), 16, 18, 19, 20, 23–25, 111–12
   death of, 57–58
   final letters of, 41–42
   letter from Favez on assistance request, 33–34
   letters from, 149, 150
   letters of, 25, 156–57
   letter to Favez, 30
   letter to Fromm, 27–28, 30–33
   letter to Fromm seeking to speed things along, 36–37
   Lisa Jacobs' correspondence with, 38–40
   photograph of, 26*f*
Brandt, Heinz, 16, 17–18, 25–27, 46–47, 76–77
   deportation to Auschwitz, 38
   Favez assisting, 30
   Fromm on, 85–86
   Fromm's efforts to support, 87
   Fromm's formal letter of support for, 124–25
   Gertrud seeking visa for, in England, 31, 32–33
   letters to Fromm on, 27, 28
   on need for transit visa, 37–38
   Oranienburg concentration camp, 39
   photograph on release from East German prison, 125*f*
   release from East German prison, 126
   survival of, 121
   surviving Auschwitz, 106
   visa for Shanghai, 37
Brandt, Lilli, 25–26, 123
Brandt, Richard, 25–26
Brandt, Willy
   as chancellor, 120–21
   election of, 120
Brandt, Wolfgang, 24–26, 33, 37, 42
Breslauer, Anna-Ruth, 42, 49
Breslauer, Bertha, 49
Breslauer, Samuel, 49
Breslauer, Wilhelm, 42, 49
Buber, Martin, 21, 145, 153
   I and Thou relationship, 153
   philosophy of dialogue, 153
Buchenwald, 23, 85–86, 122
   Heinz Brandt's liberation from, 122
Budy, Heinz Brandt at farming camp, 122

Cambridge University, 9
Can You Take a Stand? (Horney), 92
capitalism, 99, 106
care, loving relationships, 152–53
Caste (Wilkerson), 128–29
Celan, Paul, 149
Central American visa, 35–36
central relatedness, Fromm's notion of, 153–54
Chamberlain, Neville, 83–84
Chemnitz, racially motivated riots in, 1
Chicago Psychoanalytic Institute, 68–69
Children's Seminar, 65
China, Imperial Japan's invasion of, 81–82
Christianity, antisemitism and, 101–2
Christian Social Union (CSU), 119–20
Civilization and Its Discontents (Freud), 71
civil rights movement, American, 126
Cold War, 151
collective memory culture, Germany's, 160
Columbia University, 76
communism, 82, 106, 122–23
contemporaneous communication, letters as, 20
correspondence. *See* Holocaust correspondence
Coughlin, Charles (Father), 100
Crabwalk (Grass), 67
Cuba, 29, 30–31, 47
Czechoslovakia, 22, 82, 84, 130

Dachau, 23
Davos
  dangers in, 66
  as Hitler's Spa (*Hitlerbad*), 67
Der Spiegel (magazine), 121
destructiveness. *See* human destructiveness
Diner, Dan, 137–38
Dogma of Christ, The (Fromm), 78
Dollard, John, 68–69
Drowned and the Saved, The (Levi), 138

East German State Security Service (Stasi), 123
Eckhaus, Mechl, 33, 41
  on arrival of Posen's deportees, 33
Eichmann, Adolf, 131

Eichmann in Jerusalem (Arendt), 131
Einstein, Albert, 145
Engels, Friedrich, 69
Engländer, David, 24–25, 39–40, 43
  death of, 93–94
  photograph of, 43f
Engländer, Sophie (née Krause), 16, 18, 19, 20, 24–25, 55–56, 87, 111–12
  death of, 57–58, 93–94
  letters from, 149, 150
  letters of, 19, 42, 156–57
  letters to children, 43–51
  photograph of, 43f
Erich Fromm Papers, Holocaust correspondence, 12–13
Escape From Freedom (Fromm), 5–7, 8, 9, 17, 69, 75–76, 77–78, 80–82, 87, 88, 89f, 91, 93–94, 95, 98–99, 101, 102–4, 127, 128–29, 157

Fasanenstrasse synagogue, 55
fascism
  analysis of, 4
  authoritarianism and, 102, 162
  Fromm on, 7, 17, 75–77, 94, 102–3, 105, 157–58, 162
  growth of, 8
  hold on followers, 94
  ideals of, 70
  Mussolini and, 70
  National Socialism as extreme form of, 6
  rise of, 95, 98–99, 162
  threat of, 5–6, 12–13, 101, 107, 151–52
fascist ideology, "Long Live Death!", 105
Favez, Juliane, 30–31
  letter from Gertrud Brandt, 30
  letter to Fromm, 32–33
  letter to Gertrud on requests, 33–34
  sharing Gertrud's postcard with Fromm, 34
  updating Fromm on inquiry with Jewish World Congress and Red Cross, 34–35
Federal Republic of Germany (FRG or West Germany), 115, 121, 124
Fenichel, Otto, 65, 76, 102–3
Ferenczi, Sandor, 68, 72

Final Solution, 18, 23
  Nazi Germany's implementation of, 40
  Speer's involvement in, 135–36
First World War. *See* World War I
Five Germanys That I Have Known (Stern), 162
Floyd, George, 162–63
Ford, Henry, 100–1
Fortune Magazine (magazine), 100
Fourth Reich, 76
France, Nazis parading through Paris' streets, 107–8
Frankfurt, Institute for Social Research, 3
Frankfurt Auschwitz Trials, 136
Frankfurt Psychoanalytic Institute, 65, 78
Frankfurt School of Critical Theory, 9
Freeman, Annis, 150–51
Freud's drive theory, 88
Freud, Sigmund, 9–10, 71–72, 77–79, 103, 144
Friedlander, Saul, on Holocaust history, 96–97
Friedman, Lawrence, Fromm's biographer, 13–14
Fromm, Erich, 39–40
  on American civil rights movement, 126
  arrival in New York, 75–77, 87
  on art of relating, 150
  beginnings of, 20–22
  comments on nationalism, 59–60
  critique of Freud, 71–72
  death of, 14–15, 159–60
  education of, 21–22
  encountering, 6
  Freeman (Annis) and, 150–51
  as German Jewish refugee, 105–6
  grieving relatives and colleagues, 105
  Holocaust history of family, 4–5
  Holocaust letters of family, 12–13
  Horkheimer and, 103–4
  human destructiveness, 129
  impact of war on political development, 61
  Institute for Social Research, 3, 5, 7
  interview with Acklin, 164
  on knowledge of Germans, 139
  Kollwitz's art work and, 57–58
  marriage to Henny Gurland, 111–13
  personal and political turbulence, 63
  photograph (1970), 159*f*
  photograph (mid-1930s) 81*f*
  photography (1945), 114*f*
  position on Israel, 145–47
  as purveyor of hope, 3
  on racial narcissism, 126
  refuge in New York, 106
  Reichmann and, 64, 68
  self and society, 2–3
  social psychoanalysis, 77
  survey of Berlin and Frankfurt workers, 88–90
  Swiss television interview with, 3
  tuberculosis, 66–67, 69, 82–83
  on unrepentant Nazis, 133
  on Zionism, 145–47
Fromm, Erich (letters)
  efforts to support Heinz Brandt, 87
  Favez updating, on seeking assistance, 34–35
  formal letter supporting cousin Heinz Brandt, 124–25
  Georg Brandt to, 27
  Gertrud Brandt to, 27–29, 30–32, 36–37
  Horkheimer and, 82, 83–84, 85–86, 87–88
  letter to Favez regarding visa for Heinz, 35–36
  position on Israel to Senator McGovern, 146
Fromm, Naphtali, 20–21, 23–24
Fromm, Rosa (née Krause), 20–21, 23–25, 31, 42, 117–18
Fromm, Seligmann Pinchas, 21
Fromm Institute and Archive, 14–15
Fromm-Reichmann, Frieda, 76–77, 80, 86
  depression and distress, 113
  see also Reichmann, Frieda
Funk, Rainer, 14–15

Garcia, Jorge Silva, 157
Gay, Peter, 9–10
  emotional lives of German Jewish refugees, 113–14
  on Fromm's critique of Freud, 9–10
  memoir *My German Question*, 13

on reluctance to engage with
  Holocaust, 144–45
 on work of Freud, 10
gender essentialism, 70
genocide, 2, 6, 12, 23
 Bauman on Holocaust, 131
 German's responsibility for, 115, 160
 of Indigenous people, 162–63
 Lohse on, 141
 Nazi Germany and, 4
 news of, 150–51
 Speer on, 135, 136
 trauma of, 149
 war and, 18, 93–94, 105, 150, 164
George Washington (ocean liner), 68–69
German culture, antisemitism and, 106
German Democratic Republic (GDR or
  East Germany), 121–23
German Emergency Committee, 31
German Jewish refugees, 13
 states of denial, 115
German Psychoanalytic Society, 116–17
Germany
 addressing Nazi past, 6
 deaths and disability of soldiers, 62
 economic crisis of, 66
 escalating terror (1938), 81
 Fromm on collective dissociation in,
  under Hitler, 139–40
 Institute for Social Research, 3
 racially motivated riots in Chemnitz, 1
Gestapo, revoking Benjamin's
  passport, 107
Giddens, Anthony, 9
Gilligan, Carol, 71
Giordano, Ralph, 118–19
Globke, Hans, 119
Glueck, Peter, 76–77
Goethe, Johann Wolfgang von, 137
Gojman de Millan, Sonja, 15
Grass, Günter, 67
Great Depression, 62–63
Great Purge, Stalin, 81–82
Green movement, 125
Grieving Parents, The (Kollwitz), memorial
  to son Peter, 59
Groddeck, Georg, 68
Guilt and Responsibility (Adorno), 99–100

Gurland, Henny, 17–18
 death of, 150–51
 escape over the Pyrenees, 111
 Fromm's marriage to, 106
 letter to Adorno, 109
 marriage to Erich Fromm, 111–13
 photograph of, 112*f*, 114
 Spanish-Portuguese border with
  Joseph, 111
 tragedy in Portbou, 106, 109–11
Gurland, Joseph, 108
 escape over the Pyrenees, 111
 relationship with Fromm, 112–13
 Spanish-Portuguese border with
  Henny, 111
 travel with mother Henny and
  Benjamin, 109, 110–11
Gurland, Rafael, 108–9
Gustloff, Wilhelm, 67

Havel, Vaclav, 149–50
Heart of Man, The (Fromm), 126, 128–29
Herwig, Malte, 121
Himmler, Heinrich, 18, 118, 131
 aggression of, 129, 130–31
Hirschfeld, Charlotte (née Stein), 20–
  21, 24–25
historical trauma, Germany's memory
  culture, 51–52
Hitler, Adolf, 1–2, 5, 8
 election of, 95–96
 escalating terror (1938), 81
 implementing anti-Jewish
  legislation, 22–23
 Nazi Party and, 14, 16–17, 62–63, 70, 91
 Nazi Party election, 66–67
 Nazi regime and, 77
 rise to power, 16–17
 suicide of, 115
 symbiotic interaction of supporters
  and, 93
Hitler's Spa (Hitlerbad), Davos as, 67
Holocaust
 denialism, 4
 destructiveness of Nazism, 17–18
 Gay on own reluctance to engage
  with, 144–45
 German memory in aftermath of, 1

Holocaust (*cont.*)
   Germans denying knowledge of, 140
   history of Fromm's family, 4–5
   horrors of, 93–94
   humanity and atrocities of, 3
   impact on Fromm's life and work, 51
   letters in Fromm's family, 12–13
   Nazi Germany and, 14, 15–16
   as negative symbiosis, 137–38
   overwhelming grief in history of, 55–56
   perpetration of, 143
   term, 136
Holocaust (television miniseries), 136
Holocaust correspondence, 19–20
   beginnings of, 20–22
   downward spiral of, 22
   letters from Ostrow-Lubelski, 38
   letters of Gertrud Brandt, 25
   letters of Sophie Engländer, 42
hooks, bell, 156
Horkheimer, Max, 13, 21–22, 66
   antisemitism and, 98–100
   correspondence with Fromm, 82, 83–84, 85–86, 87–88
   Fromm and, 87–88, 103–4
   on Fromm's role at Institute, 103
   Institute for Social Research, 87–88
Horney, Karen
   Can You Take a Stand?, 92
   Fromm and, 68–69, 80, 82–83
Hornstein, Gail, 113
human compassion, 147
   toward theory of, 69
human destructiveness, 129
   Fromm study of, 134
   power and intensity of, 155
   problem of, 132
humanity, Holocaust atrocities, 3
Hunziker-Fromm, Gertrud, 20–21, 135

Imperial German Army, 95
Imperial Japan, invasion of China, 81–82
Inability to Mourn, The (Mitscherlich and Mitscherlich), 116
Indigenous peoples, 162–64
Inside the Third Reich (Speer), 134
instinctivism, 133

Institute for Social Research
   Adorno and, 115
   Benjamin and, 77–78, 107
   Favez as administrator, 30
   Fromm and, 3, 7, 9, 68, 76, 77–78, 107, 129
   Fromm and colleagues at, 13
   Fromm and Horkheimer, 87–88
   Fromm's changing position within, 90
   Fromm's departure from, 9
   Horkheimer and, 21–22, 66, 115
International Erich Fromm Society, 159–60
International Psychoanalytic Association, 9
Israel, West Germany agreement with, 117

Jacobs, Jack, 147
Jacobs, Lisa, Gertrud's correspondence with, 38–40
Jaspers, Karl, 21–22
Jewish Free Learning Center, 21, 153
Jewish Newsletter, 145
Jewish refugees, German, 13
Jewish World Congress, 34–35
Jews and Europe, The (Horkheimer), 98–99
Jim Crow legal system, 18, 126–27, 162–63
Judaism, 21, 24, 147
Junkers, 118

Kaplan, Marion, 50–51, 143
Kardiner, Abram, 80
Khoury, Gérard, 146
killing centers, 40, 41
King, Martin Luther, 156
Klarsfeld, Beate, 120
Kniefall (knee fall), 120–21
knowledge, loving relationships, 152–53
Kohl, Helmut, 121
Kollwitz, Käthe, 16–17, 56–58, 64–65
   critique of fascist ideals of motherhood, 71
   expressing totality of grief, 57
   funeral of Karl Liebknecht, 62, 63*f*
   Gestapo arrest of, 71
   grieving and suffering in art, 72
   loss of son Peter, 58, 59
   The Parents, 56*f*, 57, 58–59
   War series, seven woodcuts, 58

Kollwitz, Peter, 59
  death of, 58
  The Grieving Parents memorial to, 59
Korean War, 151
Kracauer, Siegfried, 21
Krakauer, Bernard, 42
Krakauer, Eva, 42
  letters from mother Sophie Engländer, 43–51
  Sophie Engländer writing to, 42
Krause, Johanna (née Weiner), 24–25, 47, 48, 76–77
Krause, Ludwig, 21
Krause, Martin, 24–25, 47, 48, 76–77
Kristallnacht, Night of Broken Glass, 85
  see also November Pogrom
Kristallnacht Memorial Lecture, 1–2

Landauer, Karl, 64
Lasswell, Harald, 68–69
Leschnitzer, Adolf, German Jewish refugee, 118
Lesser, Ruth, 157–58
letters. *See* Holocaust correspondence
Levenson, Edgar, 15
Levi, Primo, 138–39
  antisemitism, 143–44
Levy, Ernest, 37
Liebknecht, Karl, Kollwitz's woodcut depicting funeral of, 62, 63f
Lifton, Robert J., 134, 135
  on Speer, 135
Lindbergh, Charles, 100–1
Lohse, Alexandra, 141
Lorenz, Konrad, 133–34
love and concern, care, responsibility, respect, and knowledge, 152–53
Lowenthal, Leo, 99–100

McGovern, George, Fromm's letter to, 146
MacIntyre, Alistar, 52
malignant aggression, 129, 131–33
malignant narcissism, 127–28
Man's Impulse Structure and Its Relation to Culture (Fromm), 78–79
Marcuse, Herbert, 88, 99–100, 147
Marx, Karl, 10, 103, 137
Marxism, 5, 61, 82

masochism, sadism and, 93
matriarchy, patriarchy and, 70
matricentric cultures, 69–70
May Man Prevail (Fromm), 119
Mead, Margaret, 80
Menninger, Karl, 102–3
Mitscherlich, Alexander, 116, 135
Mitscherlich, Magarete, 116
Moreno, Vila, 110–11
Mother Right, The (Bachofen), 69
Munich Agreement, 84
Munich Beer Hall Putsch, 65
Mussolini, Italy, 70, 81–82
My German Question (Gay), 13

narcissism
  dangerous, 156
  Fromm on group, 130
  Fromm on racial, 126
  group, 127, 128, 129, 130
  nature of, 127–29
  racial, 6, 15, 105, 126, 127, 128–29, 134, 144
Nation, The (magazine), 102–3
nationalism, Fromm on, 59–60
National Socialism, 4, 5–6, 69, 75, 93–94, 121, 162
  antisemitism and, 98–99
  racial ideology and, 97–98
  rise in Germany, 75, 77
National Socialist German Workers' Party (Nationalsozialistische Deutsche Arbeiterpartei; NSDAP), 67, 97, 121
National Socialist Motor Corps (Nationalsozialistisches Kraftfahrkorps; NSKK), 52–53, 119–20
Nazi(s), unrepentant, 133
Nazi Brown Shirts, 66
Nazi Germany, 4
  connection of United States and, 127
  Fromm's family and, 4, 5
  history of, 161
  Holocaust and, 14, 15–16
  invasion of Poland, 44
  learning of horrors of, 52
  refugees escaping, 87

Nazi Germany (*cont.*)
  systematic murder of European Jews, 40–41
  as Third Reich, 7–8, 19, 96, 118–19, 128, 161
Nazi Party, 21–22
  duty of women as *Kinder, Küche, Kirche* (children, kitchen, church), 70
  election of, 66–67
  family history and memory, 52–53
  Frie's grandfather and, 95
  Hitler and, 14, 16–17, 91
  Lorenz in, 133
  rise of, 65, 91
  undesirables in worldview of, 22
Nazism, 151–52
  antisemitism as ideology, 98–100, 102, 103–4
  destructiveness of, 17–18
  Fromm's analysis of psychology of, 8–9
  psychology of, 75–76, 80–81, 88
  upsurge of, 1
necrophilia, 129, 132
Neumann, Franz, 99–100
New York Times (newspaper), 145
Night of the Long Knives, 103
Nobel, Nehemia Anton, 21
Nobel Prize for Medicine, Lorenz, 134
Not in My Family (Frie), 11
November Pogrom, 17, 19–20, 23, 24, 28, 52–53, 55
  see also Kristallnacht, Night of Broken Glass
NSKK. *See* National Socialist Motor Corps (Nationalsozialistisches Kraftfahrkorps; NSKK)
nuclear arms race, 151
nuclear disarmament, 3, 125
Nuremberg Laws, 22, 28, 119, 126–27
Nuremberg trials, 115–16

Oberlaender, Theodore, 119
On Aggression (Lorenz), 133
On the Feeling of Powerlessness (Fromm), 91
Orban, Viktor, 128–29
Origin of the Family, The (Engels), 69
Orthodox Judaism, Fromm and, 21

Ostrow-Lubelski
  on arrival of Posen's deportees to, 33
  letters from, 38
others, ethical obligation to, 160

Parents, The (Kollwitz), 56f, 57, 58–59
patriarchy
  Fromm's critique of, 71
  German women's duty as *Kinder, Küche, Kirche* (children, kitchen, church), 70
  matriarchy and, 70
patricentric principle, destructive nature of, 69–70
peace movement, 124
"Personal Responsibility Under Dictatorship" (Arendt), 140
Philosophical Review (journal), 103
Poland, Germany's invasion of, 22, 32–33, 84
Poliklinik, 65
Portbou tragedy, Gurland and Benjamin, 106
Prussian Academy of Art, 59, 71
Psychiatry (journal), 101, 102–3
psychoanalysis
  Fromm on profession of, 79
  practice of, 11–12
  as traumatized profession, 2
"Psychoanalysis and Sociology" (Fromm), 78
psychology, Nazism, 88

Rabinkov, Salmon Baruch, 21–22
racial narcissism, 127–29
  see also narcissism
racism, United States, 162–64
Reader's Digest (magazine), 100
Red Cross, 34–35, 48
Red Front Fights, 66
Reichmann, Frieda, 21–22, 68
  Fromm and, 64
  see also Fromm-Reichmann, Frieda
Remarks on the Relations Between Germans and Jews (Fromm), 137–38
respect, loving relationships, 152–53
responsibility, loving relationships, 152–53
restitution claim, Rosa Fromm, 117–18

restitution program,
    Wiedergutmachung, 117
Rickert, Heinz, 21–22
Rolland, Romain, 57
Rosenberg, Alfred, 70
Rosenzweig, Franz, 21
Rosinchen, Tante, 45, 46–47, 48, 49, 50
Runge, Irene, 121–22
Russell, Bertrand, 124

Sachs, Hanns, 64
sadism, masochism and, 93, 129, 131–32
Salzberger, Georg, 21
Sapir, Edward, 80
Schatzalp Sanatorium, 68, 85
Schechter, David E., 157
Schmitt-Maass, Hety, 138, 139
Scholem, Gershom, 21, 99, 147
Schreckliche Zeiten, terrible times and
    suffering, 52
Schwartz, Geraldine, 135–36
Search for a Third Way, The (Brandt), 125
Second World War. *See* World War II
Sender Freies Berlin (Amery), 132–33
Siemsen, Hans, 76–77
Snowden, Frank Jr., 8
social character
    concept of, 80–81
    Fromm on, 94
Social Democratic Party (SPD), 62–63, 108
*Social Determinants of Psychoanalytic
    Theory* (Fromm), 71–72
social psychoanalysis, Fromm and, 77
Social-Psychological Dimension
    (Fromm), 91
South American visa, 35–36
Southwest German Psychoanalytic
    Working Group, 64
Spandau Diaries (Speer), 136
Spanish Civil War, 108
Spanish flu (pandemic), 60
Speer, Albert, 18, 133, 134–37, 139
    admission of, 115
Spengler, Alexander, 67
Stalin, Great Purge, 81–82
Star of David, 47
Stein (née Krause), Martha, 24–25
Stein, Bernhard, 24–25

Stern, Fritz, 12–13, 162
Stolpersteine (stumbling stones), 55
Strauss, Franz Josef, 119–20
Streicher, Julius, 103
Studies on Authority and the Family
    (Institute for Social Research), 90, 91
Sudeten crisis, Fromm and, 84
Sudetenland
    German annexation of, 82
    German occupation of, 84
    Hitler and, 82
Sullivan, Harry Stack
    Fromm and, 79–81
    threat of antisemitism, 101–2
Survival in Auschwitz (Levi), 138
Sussman, Oswald, 61

Third Reich, 7–8, 128
    critical attitude toward, 118–19
    fears of descendants regarding, 96
    German Jewish families enduring, 19
    nostalgia toward, 161
    see also Nazi Germany
Thompson, Clara, Fromm and, 80
To Have or To Be (Fromm), 6, 125, 139–40
Treaty of Versailles, 25
Treaty of Warsaw (1970), 120–21
Tree of Life Synagogue, massacre in
    Pittsburgh, 1, 162–63
Trump, Donald, 128–29
tuberculosis, 17
    Fromm's convalescence in Davos, 67, 69
    Fromm's diagnosis of, 66–67, 82–83

United States
    antisemitism and, 100–1, 162–64
    civil rights movement, 126
    connection between Nazi Germany
        and, 127
    German Jewish refugees arriving in, 115
    immigration to, 29
    Jim Crow legal system in, 18, 126–27
    racism, 162–64
    Southern white supremacy in, 126–27
University of Frankfurt, 21–22
University of Heidelberg, 21–22
University of London, 8
Uruguay, 30–31

Versailles peace treaty, 62, 91, 130
"Victims of Fascism", 122–23
Vorwärts (newspaper), 108

Wallace, George, 126
Wannsee Conference, 23
Warsaw Ghetto Uprising, 120–21
Weber, Alfred, 21–22
Weber, Max, 21–22
Weimar Republic, 2–3, 5, 23, 62, 65, 88, 115, 162–63
Wertheim, Kurt, 45–46, 76–77
Western Europe, German Jews fleeing, 107
West German Metalworkers' Trade Union, 123
What Shall We Do With Germany? (Fromm), 94
Whitman, James, 127
Wiedergutmachung, program of restitution, 117
Wilkerson, Isabel, 128–29
William Alanson White Institute of Psychiatry, Psychoanalysis, and Psychology, 10
Wittenberg, Wilhelm, 64
Wöhler Gymnasium, 21, 60
Worker's Study
   Fromm's questionnaires to workers, 88–90
   history of, 90
Working Class in Weimar Germany, The (Fromm), 90
World War I, 16–17, 25, 61
   aftermath of, 95, 128–29, 155
   deaths of, 62
   Fromm's response to, 57–58
   outbreak of, 58–59
   feelings of Germans after, 130, 145
   veterans, 65
World War II, 16–17, 22
   deaths of, 62
   Holocaust and, 151
   Nazi Party membership, 95–96

Zehetner (née), Therese, 24–25
Zehetner, Bruno, 24–25
Zionism, 18
   Fromm critique of, 145–47